Friendly Relations'?

Feminist Perspectives on The Past and Present
Advisory Editorial Board

Lisa Adkins, *University of the West of England, UK*
Harriet Bradley, *UK*
Sara Delamont, *University of Wales College of Cardiff, UK*
Mary Evans, *University of Kent at Canterbury, UK*
Gabriele Griffin, *Nene College, UK*
Jalna Hanmer, *University of Bradford, UK*
Maggie Hunm, *University of East London, UK*
Sue Lees, *University of North London, UK*
Diana Leonard, *University of London, UK*
Terry Lovell, *University of Warwick, UK*
Maureen McNeil, *University of Birmingham, UK*
Ann Phoenix, *University of London, UK*
Caroline Ramazanoglu, *University of London, UK*
Sue Scott, *University of Manchester, UK*
Janet Siltanen, *University of Edinburgh, UK*
Dale Spender, *Australia*
Penny Summerfield, *University of Lancaster, UK*
Martha Vicinus, *University of Michigan, USA*
Claire Wallace, *University of Lancaster, UK*
Christine Zmroczek, *Roehampton Institute of WE, UK*

Friendly Relations?
Mothers and their Daughters-in-Law

Pamela Cotterill

© Copyright Pamela Cotterill, 1994

All rights reserved. No part of this publication may be reproduced, stored in a retrieval system, or transmitted, in any form or by any means, electronic, mechanical, photocopying, recording, or otherwise, without permission in writing from the Publisher.

First published 1994
By Taylor & Francis,
2 Park Square, Milton Park, Abingdon, Oxon, OX14 4RN

Transferred to Digital Printing 2004

A Catalogue Record for this book is available from the British Library

ISBN 0 7484 0150 4
ISBN 0 7484 0151 2 pbk

Library of Congress Cataloging-in-Publication Data are available on request

Typeset in 9.5/11pt Times
by Graphicraft Typesetters Ltd., Hong Kong

For Ursula and for Ruth.

Acknowledgements

This book has been made possible by the women whose family lives and relationships are presented here. My first and deepest debt of gratitude is to them for sharing so much with me with such generosity and good will.

Thanks are due to the Economic and Social Research Council which provided the funding for the original study on which the book is based. This was housed in the Department of Sociology at Staffordshire Polytechnic (now Staffordshire University) and I am especially grateful to my supervisors there, Ursula Dobraszczyc and Ruth Waterhouse. Their involvement with the original study was a constant source of support and encouragement, and their continued enthusiasm about this book has helped me through many a difficult patch during the writing. I owe special thanks to Gayle Letherby for her friendship and for our collaborative partnership, both of which have contributed so much to this book. I am indebted to Janet Finch for her interest in the original study and her personal generosity towards me. I would also like to acknowledge the students on the Women's Studies and Sociology courses I teach for their interest in women's lives and family relationships. Many of the ideas which appear in the book have been discussed with them.

Thanks are due to Jo Campling for helping me to get started and to Jacinta Evans and Comfort Jegede my editors at Taylor & Francis. I am also grateful to Kevin Rowe who helped me with a word processing crisis at the beginning and was able to solve such mysteries as 'incompatible discs'.

Thanks to my sister, Pat Bunn, who has helped me keep a sense of proportion about work and encouraged me to have some fun as well. Finally, my thanks, as always, to Sue Cannon and to Philip Cotterill who love and support me and who have lived with 'mothers-in-law and daughters-in-law' for a very long time with unfailing patience and good humour.

Contents

	Acknowledgements	vi
	Introduction	1
	Methodology	4
Chapter 1	Establishing the Relationship	11
Chapter 2	Keeping in Touch: Sentiment or Obligation?	33
Chapter 3	Emotional Investment: Empathy and Power	62
Chapter 4	Humour and Social Control	91
Chapter 5	Changes in Marital Patterns: Two Mothers-in-Law or None?	112
Chapter 6	Support Relationships between Women: Resistance to Care	137
Conclusion		170
Bibliography		184
Index		195

Introduction

There is very little positive imagery surrounding the role of the mother-in-law. In the past, music-hall jokes were made at her expense, and today the mother-in-law joke is still a stock-in-trade for many professional stand-up comedians. The verbal images portrayed in such jokes find pictorial form in caricatures of 'old women' in McGill-type seaside comic postcards. These caricatures inevitably depict a harridan in a hard hat, the belligerent female, interfering, jealous and possessive, for whom her daughter's husband could never be 'good enough'. Why do these cultural stereotypes persist and why do myths about 'interfering' mothers-in-law predominate? Why are mother-in-law relationships seen as fraught with conflict and not expected to go well? Why is it assumed that when conflict occurs it is between the husband and his mother-in-law and not between the wife and hers? What gives rise to these ideas, how are they maintained and how do they effect family life?

This book aims to answer these questions. It is about mothers-in-law and daughters-in-law and it focuses on women's experiences and perceptions of this relationship. Whilst a wealth of material exists on the family the significance of in-law relationships between women has been overlooked. References are largely confined to anthropological studies of kinship (Goody, 1976; Lévi-Strauss, 1971; Aberle, 1961; Radcliffe-Brown, 1950, 1952; Evans-Pritchard, 1951;) and to studies of women in Asian societies (Sharma, 1980; Jeffery, 1979). Other work concerned with in-law relationships includes Wolfram (1987) but does not specify those between women. They are a peripheral concern in the sociology of the family (Bott, 1964; Rosser and Harris, 1965; Young and Willmott, 1957) and later studies have also overlooked the place of mother-in-law and daughter-in-law relationships in the kin network (Holme, 1985; Cornwell, 1984; Leonard, 1980). Feminist interest in the family has concentrated on mothers and daughters (Nice, 1992; Apter, 1990; Eichenbaum and Orbach, 1985; Arcana, 1981; Chodorow, 1978) and on mothers and sons (Forcey, 1987; Rubin, 1983). None of these singles out relationships between mothers-in-law and daughters-in-law as a subject for examination.

Given that every woman who gives birth to a son has the potential to become a mother-in-law and every woman who marries has the potential to become a daughter-in-law, the fact that the relationship has received so little attention is surprising. Perhaps because notions of the family as a 'natural' and fundamental unit of society have informed much of the sociological literature, many aspects of

1

family life (and therefore women's lives) have been taken for granted. Even so, sociologists marry and have in-laws. Certainly, my motivation to write this book came from biographical experience which confirmed that this is an important but neglected area of women's lives (Cotterill and Letherby, 1993). I am a married woman and a daughter-in-law. I know that maternal relationships created by marriage between adult women can be difficult and ambiguous. However, I know too that they can have positive as well as negative aspects and that opportunities for affection also exist. This book, therefore, is not simply descriptive. It explores how people's relationships are structured by their positions in the family network and how those relationships are supported and maintained within the context of private and public notions of family life.

The first chapter in the book is concerned with how social relations are established in the new kin group and differences between women of different generations and between women and men in their perceptions and expectations of in-law relationships. It looks at the different meanings for those involved and the problems to be resolved prior to and during early marriage. These include terms of address in the absence of guidelines for naming parents-in-law, differences in domestic cultures and parental involvement in wedding preparations and the marriage ritual given that mothers-in-law have no formal role in either.

Chapter 2 looks at patterns of interaction between mothers and daughters-in-law: the frequency and types of interactions, forms of domestic and financial aid and the feelings of sentiment and/or obligation which underpin these activities. The focus is on rules which people refer to in order to regulate behaviour and minimize conflict between in-laws, and explores how such rules are involved in the negotiation of visiting patterns, domestic services and all forms of mutual aid.

Chapter 3 explores the way women sustain family relationships and their role as 'kin-keepers'. It looks at the potential for friendship between mothers-in-law and daughters-in-law and the sense of disappointment felt by both if this is not achieved. Attention is given to women's emotional work on behalf of others and their involvement as mediators. The chapter shows how daughters-in-law sustain relationships between mothers and sons and improve the quality of those relationships by interpreting and expressing the meanings attached to them by both parties. It also addresses the relatively powerful position of the daughter-in-law in being able to make choices not available to mothers-in-law. The figure of the 'interfering' mother-in-law is examined here as well as negative and potentially destructive emotions in in-law relationship, and the strategies employed by women to prevent conflict and hostility.

Chapter 4 is concerned with the social functions of humour and laughter in relation to mother-in-law jokes. Jokes are a way of relieving tension in potentially difficult relationships which may explain why mothers-in-law are a favourite subject. As jokes are almost always told by men about the wife's mother, this chapter look at ways in which jokes and joking behaviour are used as a control mechanism by men in relations with their mother-in-law. It also examines the implications of mother-in-law jokes and stereotypes and shows how these influence women's perceptions and behaviour.

Chapter 5 looks at the ways in which changes in marital patterns disturb and alter the focus of family relationships. Divorce, cohabitation and geographical mobility affect the structure of kinship networks and change the nature of in-law relationships. Increased incidence of divorce, cohabitation and remarriage also confuse traditional ideas about the family and can seriously disturb older women's understanding of marriage and family life. The chapter also considers post-parental life and both positive and negative responses to the 'empty-nest' period experienced when children marry and leave home.

Chapter 6 explores support relationships between mothers-in-law and daughters-in-law and considers short-term and long-term care. Pregnancy and childbirth are not necessarily problematic but are important occasions for fairly short-term care and support. The chapter considers the resources available to women at this time, the reasons why particular people in the family are expected to care and the circumstances when support from mothers-in-law is seen as appropriate. The next section focuses on widowhood and examines the impact of bereavement on women's relationships. It looks at the strength of affective bonds which can exist between mothers and daughters-in-law in times of intense loss and, paradoxically, shows how in-laws are sometimes excluded from family mourning and denied the 'right' to grieve. The final section is concerned with care of the elderly. It draws on interviews where women not yet involved as carers 'rehearse the future' and express their views about the perceived emotional and physical costs of caring. This chapter shows that fears about and resistance to care are not the prerogative of younger women; older women too have strong reservations about receiving support from female relatives. Interviews with both mothers-in-law and daughters-in-law reveal an overwhelming concern with personal autonomy and freedom of choice and a desire to avoid the 'structured dependency' of old people caused by a lack of viable alternatives to family care.

The concluding chapter draws together the main themes of the book. No hard and fast claims can be made about family life in contemporary Britain, for, although the family is presented as a privatized nuclear unit, extended relations with primary kin are still important. The meanings attached to in-law relationships by the women interviewed for this book are highly varied and interesting and show how opportunities for affection as well as conflict exist between mothers-in-law and daughters-in-law.

Methodology

Thirty-five women were interviewed for this book – ten mothers-in-law and twenty-five daughters-in-law. All the women were resident in North Staffordshire, living in or on the boundaries of Stoke-on-Trent, and twenty-three were middle-class. The women were white, aged between 19 and 72 years old, and only two were related to each other. Throughout the book I have used first names for the daughters-in-law and myself, reflecting the terms used during the interviews, whilst the mothers-in-law are referred to by their surnames. Again, this reflects interaction during the interviews, for although the women in the mother-in-law group addressed me by my first name they introduced themselves as 'Mrs....' and I used this style of address throughout our association.

Although the title of the book refers to 'mothers and their daughters-in-law' this is misleading. One of the methodological problems I encountered was the recruitment of women into the study, and this is why the research does not focus on pairs of mothers and daughters-in-law and also explains its unrepresentativeness in terms of class and ethnicity. There is no ready-made sampling frame of mothers-in-law and daughters-in-law, and no obvious place to sample family women of different generations. At the outset I planned to adopt the sampling procedure of 'snowballing' (Plant, 1975) by asking those I interviewed to put me in touch with others, but in practice this proved severely limiting for the research. Whilst tracing people through their social and family networks is possible for some research projects (Cornwell, 1984), it is not appropriate for others. The research for this book was concerned with a particular personal relationship within the family, one which often contains high levels of negative as well as positive feelings and which is not always expected to go well. Given the sensitive issues to be explored, it was essential that people felt able to trust me, and, because of this, 'snowballing' proved to be severely restricting. Only one woman was prepared to refer me to another who subsequently took part in the research; the rest were reluctant to do so. This reticence seems to be associated with the importance attached to protecting confidences within the family, for it soon became clear that whilst women would talk about their own relationships, the levels of confidence I sought would not have been reached if interviews with others in their social and family networks had occurred. Therefore, it was necessary to find a different way of constructing the study group. I did this by asking friends and relatives to put me in touch with people and by contacting women through their workplaces and through voluntary agencies.

A note on the location

The decision to locate the study in Stoke-on-Trent and its surrounding areas was affected by theoretical and practical considerations. First, the social and economic conditions unique to Stoke-on-Trent suggest that, as a place to study family relationships, it is particularly interesting. There is a high proportion of locally-born persons in the area and family life is characterized by close-knit networks which make relatives easy to trace. The limited economic base restricts geographical and social mobility, so that to find three or four generations of a family residing within a short distance of each other is not unusual. Historical evidence suggests that Stoke-on-Trent has an established tradition of close-knit relationships which were important sources of assistance for the young married, widowed and old (Dupree, 1981) and contemporary evidence supports this view. Close-knit family networks remain a dominant feature, strengthened and sustained by regular visiting patterns and exchanges of domestic and other services, particularly between women (Hunt, 1980). Secondly, from a mainly practical point of view, Stoke-on-Trent was an obvious choice because I am locally-born and have lived in the area all my life.

Stoke-on-Trent has a population of approximately 250,000, similar to many British cities but unusual in its distribution into a number of distinctive communities. Unification in 1910 of the six towns which make up the city did not lead to alliance into a typical city pattern. The towns – Tunstall, Burslem, Hanley, Stoke, Fenton and Longton – are still identifiable communities each having factories, housing estates, schools, shopping centres and parks and recreation facilities of their own. Public transport linking the towns and outlying areas is not good and travelling is also made difficult because 47.4 per cent of households do not have use of a car. This is a predominantly working-class area in which 68.8 per cent of the adult population work in skilled, semi-skilled and unskilled occupations. The city has manufacturing roots in heavy industry with a long tradition of coal mining and steel working. More importantly, the area, known as 'the Potteries', is renowned for producing fine bone china, earthenware and industrial ceramics. These industries provided the main sources of employment until the post-war decline of traditional forms of manufacturing led to an expansion of the distribution and service sectors and light industries. These provide the majority of jobs in the area today and 66.5 per cent of women in paid employment are concentrated in these industries.

Stoke-on-Trent has no established history of married women's employment and, in common with most other areas, the widespread employment of married women has taken place since the Second World War. In recent years the pottery industry has expanded opportunities for part-time employment and this has led to increased numbers of older women in the workforce. Today, well over half of all married women are in paid employment and the majority of these have at least one school-age child. However, the demands of paid employment and domestic commitments have not significantly reduced the importance of traditional family ties between women. In Stoke-on-Trent, women-centred kinship systems are an important feature of family life. Women occupy a pivotal role as helpers and mediators, supporting and sustaining family relationships and maintaining contact between generations.

The interviews

The interviews took place over a period of eighteen months during 1985–1986. Women were interviewed at least once, most three times and some four or five times at intervals of six to eight weeks. In all 106 interviews were recorded, each lasting up to two hours. Each person interviewed was invited to 'tell the story' of their in-law relationships. 'Telling the story' seemed most appropriate given the nature of the research. People tend to view their lives in stages and when they are asked to talk about them in a similar way, they are able to make sense of events and circumstances and relate personal experiences to social contexts. Life-histories were augmented by separate interview schedules consisting of semi-structured, open-ended questions which required individuals to reflect on specific themes and issues. In addition, a series of questions was constructed which invited informants' responses to hypothetical events likely to occur in in-law relationships. These were quite short, open-ended questions where informants were encouraged to reflect at length on a given set of circumstances, and were particularly useful for people who felt uneasy being interviewed or found the discussion of intimate relationships difficult. As Finch (1987b) points out, vignettes or hypothetical questions provide a means of obtaining information about commonly held norms, concepts and rules about what such relationships ought to be like. However, for this research, distancing questions from the informant's personal circumstances was also an unintrusive, non-directive method which had the advantage of allowing people to relate questions to their own experience if they chose to, and frequently this led to a more intimate discussion of the interviewee's own relationships.

The majority of interviews took place in the homes of interviewees although some people preferred to meet me elsewhere. Many of the women were in full- or part-time employment so interviews often took place in the evenings to fit in with respondents' paid work and domestic commitments. Oakley (1981) points out that by accommodating the researcher in their homes respondents are offering hospitality and that in doing so they are often defining the interviewer/interviewee relationship 'as something which exists beyond the limits of question-asking and answering' (p. 45). I too was conscious of the time, cooperation and hospitality respondents offered me, and welcomed the considerable degree of friendliness and rapport which was established between the women and myself. However, as the interviews progressed I also became aware of differences in the way other members of the family, and especially men, responded to the research and the interview. It is desirable that interviews are conducted, as far as possible, without interruption and without others being present, and I was struck by the efforts women made to ensure these conditions. Some arranged to meet me outside their homes, whilst others made appointments when they knew their husbands would be out and made sure that children were either occupied in another part of the house or in bed before I arrived. Sometimes, of course, husbands did not wish to go out in the evening and were in the house during the interview. Invariably this meant that instead of sitting in easy chairs in the sitting-room as usual, the woman and I talked in the kitchen or dining-room with the tape recorder placed on the table between us, whilst her husband occupied the most comfortable room in the house.

Unfortunately, the best-laid plans are sometimes unsuccessful and there were times when men disrupted interviews in deliberate or less obvious ways. There were numerous times when interviews were made difficult because women were distracted by the sound of a television programme coming from the next room, and on one occasion an enthusiastic member of a brass band chose the middle of an interview with his wife to engage in some cornet practice. Another whistled incessantly whilst wandering in and out of the kitchen where his wife and I sat, and spent some time rummaging in a cutlery drawer searching for a tin opener. This man was also unhelpful when his 5-year-old daughter, overtired but refusing to go to bed, had to be soothed by her mother whilst the woman talked to me. Although the father was present he was either unwilling or unable to comfort his daughter, and with a fractious child demanding her attention the respondent, not surprisingly, became increasingly less able to concentrate on the interview. During another interview, arranged because the woman's husband and sons were playing in a local football game, she and I were interrupted by an unexpected visit from her father. Somewhat put out to find the men of the household absent, he nevertheless sat down and, much to his daughter's dismay and my resignation, engaged in conversation with us for the rest of the evening.

Spender (1980) suggests that men fear single-sex talk between women because they have no control over the conversation or the topics women discuss. In a naturalistic setting men can devalue 'woman talk' by dismissing it as 'gossip' or 'bitching' but in a more formal or artificial setting such as the research interview, conversations between women are less susceptible to overt forms of masculine control. In Spender's view, knowing there are conversations beyond their control is threatening for men and, therefore, men's attempts to disrupt interviews may have been a way of seeking to influence an activity from which they were excluded. It should come as no surprise that some men responded negatively to the research and sometimes to the researcher. The family is founded upon ideas of domestic privacy which excludes outsiders and marriage, although associated with notions of love and loyalty, is also a power relationship which legitimates male authority over women and children. However, the family is also an area of vulnerability for men. Men have few opportunities for self-disclosure and expressiveness in the public sphere and therefore look for compensations at home which they are denied outside. The home is also an important symbol of their earning power, breadwinning role and self-worth. Therefore, men may have as much emotional investment in family life as women and may be equally susceptible to anxiety if it is invaded by outsiders. Consequently, the female researcher may not only be perceived as undermining traditional male authority in the home but, importantly, as someone who threatens to discover male vulnerability. She is regarded with suspicion both as a woman and as an intruder into what is an exclusively private sphere.

The research was particularly threatening for some men whose wives were in the daughters-in-law group, since it required in-depth discussions about the woman's relationship with the man's mother. I was always sensitive to the fact that entering a man's house in order to talk about his mother with his wife might cause him a considerable amount of resentment and anxiety and, consequently, was interested to know what these men thought about the research topic. Therefore, at the end of the interviews with married women, I asked them how their husband had reacted to the research.

> Andrew does ask what it's about. He says 'who on earth will want to read about mothers-in-law anyway'. (Deborah)

> I wouldn't say I've told him a lot. He thinks... nothing against you, but it's the same old story, why does she need to ask. Because I don't think men think you should explore relationships and how they're made up and what goes on between people. They shy away from that. And he thinks anything like that is encroaching on your... [Pam: Privacy?] Well, yes... But that was only his initial reaction. 'Why?' and 'it's prying'. (Dianne)

Only two respondents did not want their husbands to know the nature of the research. Mrs Williams had not told her husband because 'he wouldn't understand. He thinks you shouldn't talk about the family to other people. It's not their business', and Frances did not want her husband to know either.

> He'd feel a bit put out, you know, talking about his mum. I mean, he's very loyal and I think what he doesn't know won't hurt him. He knows you came the first time – I told him we were talking about childbirth. I think he'd be a bit hurt for his mother. (Frances)

The problems of ensuring the best conditions within which to interview women in their own homes have not, I believe, been satisfactorily addressed in standard methodology textbooks (Burgess, 1984; Cicourel, 1974) or in literature concerned with feminist research methods (Stanley and Wise, 1993; Oakley, 1981). Finch (1984b) suggests that 'the structural position of women and in particular their consignment to the privatised domestic sphere (Stacey, 1981) make it particularly likely that they will welcome the opportunity to talk to a sympathetic listener' (p. 74), but this requires some qualification. It seems to me that it is precisely their structural position in the family which prevents many women seeing the research interview as an opportunity to talk even if they wished for one. My experience of interviewing women in their own homes suggests that the priority of their domestic commitments over all others makes it uniquely difficult for women to allocate time and space for such an activity. In order to accommodate me and devote time to lengthy interviews, women first had to ensure that their primary responsibilities for the physical and emotional care of the family had, as far as possible, been met. Furthermore, although they are consigned to the domestic sphere, women have no absolute claim to their own space within it. The possible exceptions are those places socially designated female, and so it seemed appropriate, when sitting-rooms were occupied, that women talked to me in kitchens or across dining-room tables.

There were also difficulties to be overcome when I interviewed divorced and separated women, although these were of a somewhat different kind. Among the daughters-in-law I interviewed five women who headed single-parent families. These women offered me some of the warmest hospitality, were friendly and cooperative, and although occasionally they expressed doubts that they might not be 'saying the right things', seemed to enjoy the interviews and welcomed the opportunity to talk. Paradoxically, the conditions for these interviews were often difficult for the women and for myself. Of the five women in this group, two were in part-time, low-paid employment, another became unemployed during the time

Methodology

I interviewed her and two were claiming Supplementary Benefit. To say these women were disadvantaged is to understate their case: they were permanently short of money, some were in debt, and those claiming benefit were often waiting for an overdue cheque to enable them to buy food. I interviewed the women during the winter months and usually we wore outdoor clothes indoors because they could not afford heating. Sometimes we pooled what money we had, fed the meter and enjoyed the luxury of a gas fire. More often we drank endless pots of tea and warmed our hands on the mugs at the same time.

Interviewing in these circumstances was undeniably bleak. The women were often anxious and depressed, and some were unwell with interminable colds and chest infections. One had a child who was profoundly deaf. Another lived with her three children in one room, in a hostel for single parents. At the time of the interviews her baby daughter was severely burned on a faulty cooker in the hostel and was receiving prolonged hospital treatment. I worried a great deal about whether my visits were intrusive and sought reassurance, more than once, that they were not. I was, frankly, amazed that, given their many difficulties, these women were prepared to commit themselves, as far as they could, to a research project which seemed to offer them very little. Apart from the opportunity to talk to a sympathetic listener, there were few obvious rewards. Finch (1984b) suggests that for some women being interviewed is a welcome experience because 'it's great to have someone to talk to', and it seems to me that the opportunity to talk informally to another woman may also be therapeutic for some respondents, particularly if they are deprived of other forms of social contact. This is illustrated by variations on Tracey's comment, 'it's nice to have somebody to talk over your problems with', which I received at the end of interviews with many of the single mothers.

Three of the single parents had pre-school children and a problem I never fully resolved was how to interview whilst entertaining a 3-year-old. Small children have a short concentration span and are extremely difficult to keep occupied long enough to conduct an in-depth interview with their mothers. In desperation, I have stocked up with chocolate, colouring books and other goodies to use, unashamedly, as bribes, and I have interviewed women whilst nursing a child on my knee, sitting on the floor building Lego houses and painting pictures at the kitchen table. I have, in the space of an hour, been amused, frustrated and exhausted, emotions which came flooding back later during the transcription of tapes where the respondent's voice is inaudible, completely drowned by a vociferous child.

The events I have described are unpredictable at the planning stage of a research project and only emerge as it progresses. McRobbie (1982) says 'traditional social science cannot prepare feminists for many of the discomforts of research' (p. 55) and being female undoubtedly sensitizes the researcher to such things. It also questions how much control she exerts over her project and, ethically, what kind of choices she is able to make. For example, the occasions when interviews were disrupted by a toddler might merely be seen as an inconvenience which, on becoming unmanageable, I should have been able to deal with by curtailing the interview. Furthermore, in theory, I also had the choice to withdraw a woman from the research if conditions for interviews with her continued to deteriorate. Certainly, as far as the first point is concerned, there were several occasions when there was little alternative but to break off and hope for better things next time and, indeed, an interview comes vividly to mind which was brought to a sudden and abrupt end when a little boy hurled the entire contents of his toy-box down the stairs. However, I believe the option to withdraw before completing the interviews is too simplistic and ethically unsound. Women who elect to become involved as informants make a commitment to the research which, although individually it may be more or less than that of other interviewees, is always valid. Whilst it is an inescapable fact that some women's circumstances make them easier to interview than others it would be indefensible, in my view, to differentiate on the basis of what is a 'good' or 'bad' interview situation. As McRobbie (1982) points out, the majority of research projects are peculiarly dependent on those who provide the source material. Without them and their trust the research cannot proceed and therefore, I believe, it is up to the researcher to make what she can of the interview conditions. This means she has to adapt, as far as possible, to the differing situations and circumstances of all her interviewees.

The interviews were transcribed and analyzed according to theoretically developed themes. As themes emerged they were incorporated into subsequent interviews for further examination. The systematic generation of theory from data, or 'grounded theory' (Glaser and Strauss, 1967), meant the interviews changed and developed as the research progressed. The relationship between theory and data is reflected by drawing extensively on interview material throughout the book. The chapters are ordered to correspond with life-course events and also the process in which data was collected. In a study of in-law relationships the logical ordering of events begins with the period prior to marriage and therefore this appears in the first chapter whilst the chapter on ageing and dependency appears at the end. This is to illustrate the chronological connections between the life-course and developments in mother-in-law and daughter-in-law relationships and to integrate empirical and theoretical concerns.

Chapter 1

Establishing the Relationship

When two people marry it involves a change in their social and legal status and brings together two previously unrelated groups. Rosser and Harris (1965) refer to two basic terms in the English kinship system – the elementary family and the extended family – and suggest that the dynamics of the extended family arise from two sources: the two families involved in every marriage and the process of roles and relationships which develop and change through the family life-course. The marriage system linking previously unrelated groups is central to the English kinship system and has important implications for subsequent relationships. Troll (1971) points out that the task of forming close relationships with new kin whom you have had no part in selecting involves not only the young couple but in most cases two sets of middle-aged parents. Since there are no role models for in-law relationships between generations, people tend to pattern their behaviour on their perceptions of what is appropriate between parent and child. Consequently, the young couple must usually establish links with at least two new people which, superficially at least, mirror the parent-child bond and the parents, using the same criteria, must respond in a similar way. Fitting into a new kin group also depends on a number of factors relating to individual perceptions of what the family is. Much of the individual's understanding will come from patterns of behaviour and interaction in the family of origin, some of which may conflict with those acceptable in the new kin group. Differences of this kind have to be acknowledged and resolved if they are not to be a source of tension both in the marriage and between in-laws.

Berger and Kellner (1980) write that marriage is both a dramatic act which unites and redefines two strangers, and a traditional rite of passage meaningful to almost all members of society. The strangeness refers to the fact that, unlike in the past, couples who choose to marry do not typically come from the same social circles. According to Berger and Kellner 'they do not have a shared past, although their pasts have a similar structure' (p. 306). They have, however, 'chosen each other', although their choice will have been circumscribed by a variety of social and economic factors. But there is little in the way of choice when it comes to in-laws, although parents may seek to exert some influence if they believe their child's choice is mistaken. Generally, though, the parents-in-law and children-in-law one gets are something of a social risk, given by the act of marriage and over which one has very little control. As Firth *et al.* (1970) point out,

11

'one takes over the social debts as well as the social assets of the marriage partner – and his or her parents may represent a pretty solid social liability' (p. 414).

According to Berger and Kellner (1980) candidates for marriage (and their parents?) are often handicapped by the grave misapprehension that marriage changes nothing. That is, the individual's world, relationships and perception of self remain the same but are now shared with a new person. Clearly this is a naive view, since marriage creates a new reality within which all relationships are experienced in a different way. However, this is not immediately evident to those involved, so that problems which arise from the marriage (of which 'in-law problems' are typical) may initially be perceived as external to it. Most people do not consider in-law relationships before marriage except for vague hopes that 'one will get along with them'. Consequently, when difficulties occur they are often attributed to individual incompatibilities, ignoring the structural context of marriage where in-law relationships are both ambiguous and a major source of conflict and tension.

If marriage is a dramatic act in which the couple hold centre stage surrounded by a supporting cast of relatives and friends, it cannot be overemphasized that the drama has different meanings and consequences for the man and for the woman (Delphy and Leonard, 1992; Leonard, 1980; Delphy, 1976). Leonard (1980) suggests that before marriage, the couples' preoccupation with love, romance, choice and attainment obscures the inevitability of entry into what is essentially a labour contract. This derives from Delphy's view (1976) that in marriage a woman pledges her labour, sexuality and reproductive capacity in return for upkeep, 'protection' and certain rights to children. Marriage for women can seem to be essential since most do not earn enough to achieve a comparable standard of living to that provided by marriage to a man from the same background as themselves. Paradoxically, a wife is an economic asset who supplies domestic and sexual services which would otherwise have to be paid for, in return for access to some of the resources bought by her husband's income. Marriage, then, is a contract of exchange and a labour relationship undertaken when a man chooses a wife who agrees to 'work' for him. But because, subjectively, his choice is usually based on less fundamental considerations and reflects his own status, the woman must also embody all the physical and emotional attributes which fulfil his expectations of a 'good' wife (Delphy and Leonard, 1992).

Although the function of marriage is essentially economic, young people about to marry are unlikely to concern themselves with such a basic and unromantic tenet. People marry for 'love' not money and even the most cynical would be hard pressed to admit to choosing a partner with the sole intention of forming a labour contract. In contemporary society the individual understanding of marriage is associated with companionship, security, sexual fulfilment and emotional support, notions which are encompassed and expressed in the word 'love'. This, together with the social pressure on young adults to marry and have children, makes marriage seem 'natural', highly desirable, and almost inevitable. People who choose not to marry may be seen as failing to marry (Leonard-Barker, 1978, p. 240) and have doubts cast upon their sexual orientation, physical attractiveness and maturity. Parents and married friends who urge marriage merely reflect the wider view that cohabitation is both a poor substitute and a temporary state, to be legalized eventually and certainly before the birth of any children.

Marriage, then, has different meanings for those involved. Young people marry because they love each other and via marriage achieve adult status, emotional independence and freedom from parental control. Parents are concerned with more fundamental compatibilities and some, perhaps with the benefit of hindsight, look upon marrying for love with a jaundiced eye. They want to see their children 'settled' but this refers as much to economic security as to ideas about romance. However, few express their doubts too overtly, since a dissenting voice risks alienating the child. Most are pleased their children are 'in love' and understand marriage as both founded on, and an expression of, the couple's love for each other.

First impressions

Before marrying, most people embark on a courtship period which allows time for prospective in-laws to establish their relationship. This is an important period involving adjustments on both sides, for if those concerned fail to get on the marriage will be beset by conflicts and divided loyalties. Much depends on personality factors and also on the type of relationship between parents and child and what sort of person is regarded by both as a suitable partner. For example, daughters-in-law referred to the existence of social expectations against which they were judged by their partner's mother, and often spoke of 'feeling not good enough'. Certainly the first meeting between mother-in-law and daughter-in-law can be a daunting experience, and sometimes results in misunderstandings and negative impressions which may never be resolved. On the other hand, it can have a positive outcome establishing the basis for warm and friendly relations between the two women.

The first meeting usually takes place in the mother-in-law's home and is an event which seems to remain vividly in the memory. Only one woman could not remember meeting her mother-in-law for the first time; the rest gave very detailed accounts. This is perhaps not surprising as often the first meeting set the tone for how the relationship subsequently developed. Here then, are some recollections of the event:

> I didn't really know what to make of her. She was something completely different to what I'd been used to. My daughter was very quiet and I thought my son was very quiet. But when I met her I really and truly thought 'whatever have you got?'. She'd got a green streak in her hair and she was as flashy as they make them, all made up. She was the sort of girl ... I felt I'd got to open the walls to let her come in. I just didn't know ... I'd never met anything like her and I just didn't know what it was. (Mrs Brown)

> I just thought Patrick's mother was totally devoted to her family ... a very hardworking lady and I liked her. I did like her a lot. (Dianne)

> When I met her she was ever so, ever so pleased that her son had brought a girl home because I was about the first girlfriend. She was very pleased, very careful about what she said and tried hard to make me feel welcome. In a strange way. She'd say, 'would you like this?' and 'do you

> like that?', and asked me about my family and where I came from, that sort of thing. (Ruth)

> I think I'd been seeing him about three months when I met his parents. I thought straight away they didn't like me. They'd got their own image of what they wanted their daughter-in-law to be. They wanted better things, but it never put me off. I wasn't good enough for them, but we **got** on all right, I suppose, because we had **to**. (Rosemary)

The question of 'feeling not good enough' is worth exploring, since some women referred to the expectations against which marriage partners are judged. Opinions of disapproval were expressed about class or religious background and whilst these did not deter people from marrying, they do reflect the view that in the English kinship system, marriage is ideally between equals. Indeed, although marriage is a matter of individual choice, opportunities to meet people of higher status than oneself are comparatively rare and, consequently, like tends to marry like. Choice is circumscribed and limited by social and economic factors and to some extent by parental influence. For example, people can only marry who they meet so unless they are geographically and socially mobile their choice will be limited to people living in the same area and with a similar social background as themselves. In addition to geographical limitations, a variety of other factors also determine choice including sexual attraction, similar educational levels and commonly-held values, attitudes and beliefs. Unions between people of radically different social backgrounds not founded on mutual experiences and attitudes might be expected to suffer more than usual marital disharmony. Equally, relations between the families on both sides, which are often nothing more than an uneasy truce, may be rendered even more difficult if one group is markedly different from the other.

Differences in social class were sometimes referred to as a cause for tension between prospective in-laws, that is until, as usually happened, first impressions were found to be mistaken. In other instances, feeling 'not good enough' or even 'too good' was associated with expressed attitudes and individual perceptions, rather than conscious awareness of inferior or superior status. For example, some women simply believed they were thought of as rivals for the man's affection and felt disliked or resented as a result.

> The eldest boy, that was a bit traumatic. With it being the first one and the eldest one. It was a bit... I think we were both very wary of one another. I was trying to do more than what I should have done instead of... I mean, I learned from my mistakes then. I mean, you try and put a show on, but I think everybody does, I don't care who they are. Whether that's had some bearing on what's happened since, I don't know. Because she came from a middle-class family, shall we say. As we thought. We thought they were a bit higher than us, although we since learned that this just wasn't the case. (Mrs Jones)

> She was very welcoming but she was very down-to-earth. And she actually used those words... 'Well, take us as you find us'. And I think she was expecting something a bit different, actually, and she was apprehen-

Establishing the Relationship

sive. She knew I was living in London on my own and she thought I was middle-class. But as soon as we sorted out that I came from a working-class background... because with this idea that I was middle-class, she thought she wouldn't be able to get on with me. (Pauline)

I still feel a lot of the time that I'm not the one she wanted for him. Now, I don't know whether that's my insecurity or whether there is actually something there anyway. I've always had this impression that the main thing she had against me was that I wasn't from Yorkshire so I wasn't going to take him back up there... (Laura)

I think James must have talked to Stella about us and I can only assume he gave her a sort of picture of us on a pedestal, and whether she felt she couldn't live up to that, I don't know. (Mrs Swann)

One of the difficulties in fitting into a new kin group is that often one is treading where others have gone before. If a man has had a previous girlfriend of whom his mother had become fond and whom he was expected to marry, it can be distressing for her if the young woman is replaced by another. Given this, it is understandable that some mothers-in-law are initially reluctant to form close attachments in case the relationship ends. However, this does not augur well for the prospective daughter-in-law, who might be forgiven for interpreting this attitude as dislike. Daughters-in-law were often anxious about their mother-in-law's affection for a predecessor, fearing they were compared unfavourably, and sometimes their fears were compounded by a seemingly insensitive attitude on the part of the older woman.

Before he went out with me he had a girlfriend... well, they were practically engaged, and it happened to be the daughter of her best friend. She was over the moon about this relationship, but anyway to cut a long story short, it broke up. And she was very, very annoyed because she liked the girl and she liked the family... She never lost an opportunity to refer to this girl whenever I visited and I think a lot of the reason why she resented me was because Roy had chosen me on his own. (Joyce)

His mother took twelve months to get my name right. He used to go with this girl called Pauline and when I came on the scene... not deliberately, I don't think, she used to call me Pauline. I used to think 'if she calls me Pauline again...'. So I used to think she didn't take any notice of who I was because of that. (Jenny)

He had two girlfriends before and they used to come and stay here many a time. I liked them both really. He didn't have them both at the same time, of course, but one after the other. They were both very nice girls, actually. Very nice. And I think I was quite disappointed that one of them didn't work out. One girl in particular, she was very nice and I think she would have suited him. Mind you, you don't know that really.

Friendly Relations?

> You think that from your point of view, but you never know. (Mrs Harris)

And some more thoughts on this from Mrs Harris:

> As a matter of fact, what I find about girlfriends is that they bring people home and I always make them welcome, you know, try to make them feel like one of the family. But the girlfriend comes and when she comes you see them several times and you get on well with them, and the next thing is they've changed their girlfriend. And so then you have to start again adapting to another person. I think that's the worst of it. And you don't want to be too friendly in the way of making them fully part of the family because the next thing they've gone.

Whilst mothers may worry that their prospective daughter-in-law is not 'good enough' for their son, or compare her unfavourably with a predecessor, there is a limit to the amount of influence they can exert once his choice is made. Although a mother may try to express her concerns if she feels the choice is mistaken, pressure of this kind involves risks and might provoke estrangement between parent and child. Indeed, it seems she has few options but to suppress any misgivings and learn to get along with her daughter-in-law if only to maintain contact with her son. Thus, in most cases, largely by a process of acceptance and adjustment, women established good relationships with their prospective daughters-in-law. Initial misgivings were either overcome or forgotten by the time the couple became engaged and, consequently, very few people married against their parents' wishes.

What do you call your mother-in-law?

One of the problems to be resolved between in-laws is the problem of naming. In any kinship system it is necessary to understand the terminology by which relatives are referred to or addressed, yet in Western society there is a marked absence of guidelines for addressing close relatives acquired by marriage. Although anthropological studies of kinship terminology abound (Lienhardt, 1966; Radcliffe-Brown, 1950), they have generally been confined to the study of terms of reference rather than terms of address. In the English system, terms of address for commonly recognized kin are the same as for reference – father, mother, son and so on. Other kin are less easily identified because a single term for two or more types of relatives is employed, so that uncle, aunt, grandfather etc., refer to certain categories of kin found on the mother's or father's side of the family. This general use of kinship terminology for some relatives indicates that distinctions between the mother's and father's relatives are unimportant and because terms of reference and address coincide, naming is unproblematic.[1] However, we have only terms of reference for close relatives acquired through marriage and there are no clearly defined rules for naming parents-in-law. As Firth *et al.* (1970) point out, the English use of nuclear family terms on which terms of reference for in-laws are based on stress conflicting principles. Close affines are seen as close blood relatives like father and mother, but the relationships are formally established by the legal act of marriage. In short, they are formally achieved but take their role models from those informally ascribed. Given this ambivalence, it is unsurprising that in-law relations are often strained, a condition reflected in the difficulties associated with naming. Consequently, acceptable ways of addressing parents-in-law often pose quite serious problems for those planning to marry and at best have to be negotiated, or at worst left to chance.

In the absence of prescribed rules to provide guidelines, Firth *et al.* have identified six options from which a mode of address may be drawn. These represent three status groupings: parental or grandparental terms denoting kin status; first names or nicknames denoting equal status; surnames or the avoidance of any name associated with formality and social distance. People in this study usually selected one of the six terms although its relation to its status group was not always so clearly defined. For example, the terms 'Mum' or 'Gran' did not necessarily mean the mother-in-law was perceived as close kin, whilst using surnames was more a mark of respect than an indication of coolness in the relationship. As for avoiding names altogether, this is often the result of embarrassment rather than of any intention of being distant or hostile and reflects the dilemmas experienced by most people in their social relations with in-laws.

> To start with I called her nothing at all. I managed to avoid it. After a time ... after quite a good time, actually, because you don't use names that often, she actually said 'Oh, you can call me Mum if you like or Rose'. So I said I would call her Rose if she didn't mind. It was a bit of an awkward spot. I didn't want to call her Mum, because that's what my mum's called. So I call her Rose, and she's quite happy with that. (Ruth)

> I would love to have a mother-in-law whom I could call on first-name terms. I honestly can't remember a time when I've called her anything. Not even Mrs ... (Rachel)

The problem of 'what to call your mother-in-law' is, for many women, associated with the ambivalence of a relationship which mirrors that of mother and daughter but is, in fact, nothing like it. As Goody (1976, p. 52) so aptly states, 'the role of mother or father, whether socially or biologically defined, is usually regarded as irreplaceable'. Consequently, many women find it difficult, if not impossible, to address someone else by the name they reserve for their mother. Sometimes the problem is resolved by resorting to grandparenting terms. Variations on 'Grandma' are one removed from parental terms but still have connotations of warm and close relations. Of course, it is usual to produce grandchildren before the term is acceptable, although in one instance a daughter-in-law was so relieved to find a solution to her dilemma, she grasped the opportunity when she and her husband acquired a dog!

Some women found it easier to confront the problem of naming than to leave it to chance. Occasionally daughters-in-law elected to do this but more often mothers-in-law, perhaps reflecting on their own experiences as daughters-in-law, took the initiative and suggested a name the younger woman could use. Such a move was almost always welcomed by the daughter-in-law, and only in a very few cases was it rejected. However, one mother-in-law did express doubts since she felt the younger woman might feel pressured into adopting a term she did not like.

> I called her by her Christian name. She asked me to do that. Actually, I think probably my husband said to me 'call her by her Christian name' originally, but I do remember when we were getting engaged, she did make a point of saying... because she'd always called her in-laws Mr and Mrs and she didn't think it was right, you should be closer. And my parents introduced themselves to my husband by their Christian names when they first met him. (Deborah)

> I've called her Mum from the day I got married. I've got three brothers two of whom are married and the eldest one, his wife always got on well with my mum I'm not saying she didn't, but she couldn't call her Mum. And I used to feel that she tried not to mention it at all, which I think a lot of people do through embarrassment. Now, the other daughter-in-law used to call my mother Mum and I know she always noticed that the eldest one didn't. So I decided that when I got married I would call their parents Mum and Dad straight away, because I think if you leave it a while it's harder. So the day we got married I just turned round and said 'Hello Mum'. (Jenny)

> She didn't call me anything when I first me her and she still doesn't now. She talks to me fine but she doesn't address me as a person... as a mother, no. Maybe I should suggest she calls me Mam or something, but I'm not so sure about suggesting because if you tell them to call you a name... I feel it is really up to the person when they are ready to call you Mother. I think suggesting to the girl that she *must* call you that... I don't know, I think it's up to her. (Mrs Harris)

The problem of 'what to call one's mother-in-law' is a difficult one to resolve. Most people cope by adopting a particular term, although some avoid using names of any kind. Equally, some people manage to negotiate appropriate names at some stage in the relationship, whilst others leave it to chance.

Domestic cultures and formal meals

Clearly, fitting into a new family and establishing good relations with in-laws is a difficult process for all concerned. This is not surprising given that the family is an institution familiar to us all, yet each individual family unit is essentially private and exclusive. Consequently a person's understanding of family life comes from the patterns of behaviour which are acceptable in their family of origin, and inevitably comparisons are made between these and what is considered appropriate in the new family. Perhaps the most significant for women are the differences perceived in domestic cultures. These range from evidence of material possessions which indicate the comparative wealth or poverty of the household, to observations of housekeeping standards and, most importantly, the social arrangements associated with the preparation and serving of food.

Studies of domestic labour confirm that responsibility for household tasks is primarily assigned to women (Edgell, 1980; Oakley, 1974), and that those who report symmetrical marital relationships are, at the very least, optimistic (Young and Willmott, 1973). Women are socialized from childhood to fill the roles of wife and mother, and at the heart of these lie their responsibilities to ensure the family is well fed and cared for. Much of women's self-esteem is bound up in their domestic roles, for competence in domestic matters not only marks out their housekeeping skills but sets the standards by which women are judged by other women. Consequently, most daughters-in-law commented on differences in domestic cultures between the two families and on standards of housekeeping observed by their mothers-in-law.

> It was a very different household from my household. She was quite houseproud. She kept a nice house and she had a front room that was for guests. My own mother's house was more ... she'd probably shout at you if you did trudge through the lounge with boots on but only after she'd cleaned after you half a dozen times. I mean, she keeps a clean house but it wasn't quite so precisely tidy as my mother-in-law's. So I felt I had to be careful putting glasses down on wood or things like that. It wasn't overtly so. Probably more me thinking I mustn't do anything wrong. (Ruth)

Daughters-in-law were also conscious of differences in attitudes towards housework and how much importance the older woman attached to it.

> She can't cook but her cooker is as clean as the day she bought it. She keeps it clean but she never uses it, it's like an ornament. Everything has to be very clean. She does tend to judge people on how clean they are. If she was coming today I'd have to make an effort to make sure everything was clean and tidy. I suppose that's because I must, in some ways, still want her to like me even now, you know. (Joyce)

> She was an extreme example of the work ethic. Everything had to be hard work. If it was hard work it was worth it, if it was labour-saving it couldn't be any good. I used to think 'Oh God, how can she do it?' I mean, sweeping the carpets out. She had this very old-fashioned hoover which would have been useful but she didn't like using it. It was a hard stiff brush down on your hands and knees. That sort of thing. (Pauline)

> She'd got a rigid routine of cleaning in the morning and shopping in the afternoon. She'd get up, breakfast, then she'd wash the dishes, go and clean the fronts. And then she'd clean upstairs and clean downstairs. She had a rigid routine and she didn't like anybody upsetting it. Coffee at eleven. Lunch was always at twelve on the table. Everything was always neat and tidy. I've never, never seen it untidy. It didn't look like home. Nothing was out of place. (Janet)

Whilst standards of cleaning may vary, much more significance is attached to the preparation of meals. Writers have referred to the importance of cooking in family life and the symbolic meanings attached to the preparation and serving of food (Graham, 1984; Murcott, 1983). They suggest cooking is a mark of a woman's skills as a cook and a housekeeper (Graham, 1984), whilst the family's consumption of a 'proper meal', lovingly prepared by the mother, reinforces women's roles as nourishers and sustainers of others (Blaxter and Paterson, 1983).

Food is deeply significant in all societies, yet the way it is prepared and served is far from uniform. Both cooking itself and perceptions of what makes a good cook are highly individual, but generally based on the ability to transform basic ingredients into a meal which is both appetizing and attractive. For most people 'home cooking' produced by their mothers meets these criteria simply because what is cooked and how it is presented is familiar. Given this, it is not surprising that unaccustomed food or food cooked and served in unfamiliar ways is sometimes difficult to accept.

> The way she put different foods together was different from what I was used to. You know, we'd have bacon for the main part of a meal and I was used to bacon in the morning. I've since learned that bacon is used very much as a staple meal in Stoke, so there's a difference. And they had things like sterilized milk which I'd never come across and I hate it. (Pauline)

> She puts bicarbonate of soda in her peas, she says it keeps them green, and it took me a long time to be able to say, 'you're destroying all the goodness', but she doesn't do it now. And she doesn't cook with salt because they always put on lashings of salt afterwards. They always have Yorkshire pudding as a starter, but now when we visit we just have a small portion like this and then have the rest with our dinner, because she knows Simon prefers it that way. (Laura)

Graham (1984) suggests that the provision and consumption of meals outlines the division of responsibility and resources in the organization of family life and has important links with the exercise of control. Food may allow women some control over the family budget and is also a highly effective means of controlling adults and children, although the question of who controls whom is not always clear. Food is also an important form of communication between women whether as the hostess or guest. Women understand the preparations required for a formal meal with guests, and how these differ from everyday family meals. Food also plays a significant part in family relationships since coming together to eat may be the only activity the family shares. Meal times mark out roles within the family but these are not clearly defined for in-laws. Consequently, a new or prospective family member is likely to be treated initially, at least, as a guest.

> Sunday was the significant day because we had Sunday lunch. I was so used to my mum's Sunday dinners I suppose. And she did try to put it out in a way that I knew wasn't normal for them. She made a special effort. Because I know since that they'd just have ate off an ordinary tablecloth or even had it off their knees watching television. But they were all sitting up to the table with a white cloth you know. It was a nice

meal but it was a bit strained. You see, my mother-in-law is not used to having a formal meal and when people come to visit she feels very insecure about what she's cooking. (Pauline)

Clearly, the meanings attached to food in our culture are both complex and significant. For example, Douglas (1975) suggests that social categories can be identified by what is offered to particular individuals. She states:

> Drinks are for strangers, acquaintances, workmen and family. Meals are for family, close friends, honoured guests. The grand operator of the system is the line between intimacy and distance. Those we know at meals we also know at drinks. The meal expresses close friendship. Those we know at drinks we know less intimately. So long as this boundary matters to us (and there is no reason to suppose it will always matter) the boundary between drinks and meals has meaning. (p. 256)

Meals, then, are ranked in relation to importance and there is a difference between being offered tea and biscuits and an invitation to Sunday lunch. Thus, the structuring of meals from the smallest to the grandest mark the levels of intimacy in personal relationships. Presumably, therefore, the girlfriend who is invited to share the most important meal of the week can take this as a sign of welcome and acceptance by her future mother-in-law. Nevertheless, there are tensions and anxieties for both women. The older woman may be worried about cooking and serving the meal to a comparative stranger, whilst the prospective daughter-in-law may experience similar anxieties about consuming food with people she has only just met. Formal meals, then, can be something of an ordeal and for some women associated with a feeling of being tested or auditioned throughout.

Although it was usual to invite a prospective daughter-in-law to a family meal, at first she was unwelcome in the older woman's kitchen and certainly not allowed to prepare food. Initially, at least, any offer of help on her part met with refusal from the mothers-in-law. Women in both groups commented on the difficulties involved when two females attempt to work in one kitchen and the danger of overstepping boundaries when it is someone else's domain. This is probably inevitable in circumstances where one woman hopes to impress another with her culinary skills, but is obviously more acute when the women are strangers. There are also clear divisions in the importance attached to various domestic tasks, for whilst cooking is undertaken by the older woman thus corresponding with her status, she may delegate lesser tasks, such as washing dishes, to the prospective daughter-in-law.

> When they first came for meals they asked to help but I wouldn't let them. Say they came for dinner, I'd prepare dinner, get the dinner and put it on the table. It's not that I wouldn't allow them to help get meals. It's just I didn't think it was right. That was my job. (Mrs Jones)

> I was very conscious that her kitchen was her domain. Setting the table was OK, but I didn't actually give her any help with preparing the meal and she was very hesitant about letting me help with the dishes. I think

Friendly Relations?

> I dried at first and she did the washing up. She liked to clear up and get rid of the dishes and the untidiness. (Pauline)

Clearly, food is highly significant and not just as a means of sustaining life. The preparation, serving and consumption of food is also an expression of social relationships (Graham, 1984). Food is to do with the business of caring; women use it to express their concern for the welfare of others and, significantly, for adult children when more overt expressions of affection are no longer appropriate.

> She gets very upset if we won't eat a cooked breakfast, when we stay there. But we don't eat cooked breakfasts. But it's just her being very traditional and motherly ... And Simon's favourite chocolates, she always gets those. And she'll always cook special things for him and buy special things. But she gets pleasure from doing that. (Laura)

Good food and home cooking are inextricably linked with family life, so that when the mother invites her prospective daughter-in-law to a family meal it is usually in the spirit of hospitality and welcome. Although both women may be apprehensive about the event, honouring a prospective family member with a meal has a sense of ceremonial for the mother. Just as fathers 'give away' their daughters formally in the marriage ceremony, mothers begin the process of 'giving away' their sons through the medium of food and hospitality. Thus food contains coded messages affirming the mother's favour and approval of the young woman. It is also an indication of her relative power at the beginning of the relationship. However, power is constantly shifting between family members and usually changes in the daughter-in-law's favour as her relationships with her husband and his mother develop.

When two mothers meet

The second stage in the relationship occurs when plans for the engagement and marriage of the young couple are first mooted. Whether or not there is a formal engagement, an equally important event which takes place about this time is when the two sets of parents first meet.

Anthropological studies of kinship have stressed that the importance of marriage lies not just in the union of two people but in the alliance of two families (Evans-Pritchard, 1951; Radcliffe-Brown, 1950), and sociologists have commented that marriage connects two previously related groups if only through the expectation of grandchildren (Fagin and Little, 1984; Rosser and Harris, 1965). However, Rosser and Harris also point out the infinite varieties in the relationship between the respective parents of a married couple, ranging from almost no contact to deep friendship, and suggest there are no guidelines for socially expected behaviour towards relatives who are not defined as 'close'. There is no reason to suppose that because two people choose to marry, their respective parents will have anything in common other than an interest in the marriage and its forthcoming offspring. Therefore, the nature of the relationship between the four parents is ambiguous, yet comparable in one sense with that between parent and child-in-law in that there is little element of choice. Their relationship has been created by the act of their children but, unlike that between close in-laws, is not formalized by marriage. Given this, the quality of relations and the amount of informal contact between the parents varies in accordance with individual preference and compatibilities.

Relationships between parents can range from close friendship to tolerance and indifference and even active dislike. Nevertheless, whilst there are no expectations that parents will get on, or that their failure to do so will adversely affect the marriage, most people believe it is easier for all concerned if they do. This is understandable, given the idealism which surrounds family life in our society and the high levels of sentiment and obligation which are expressed about family relationships. However, this idealism is also a source of anxiety because it diverges from the reality of most people's lives. In other words, the ideal is that parents will get on well, thereby reflecting the cohesion of the family, but often they do not. Moreover, in reality the behaviour of their parents towards each other makes very little difference to the couple's relationship or the success of their marriage.

Although several women reported good relations between the two sets of parents, contact between them was not particularly frequent and in some cases no more than between those who felt little attachment to each other. As might be expected, people rarely met other than at family celebrations such as anniversaries, weddings and christenings, or during the Christmas and Easter festivals. However, some parents did become close, forming lasting friendships which were not wholly dependent on their children.

> They get on very well. They're all very friendly. They go to each other's homes and have a lot in common. Both men are retired and the mothers sit and chat about grandchildren and things. They're the same age group, you see. They were both in the WRAFs and they can reminisce over little things like that. They're both basically home people, so yes, they got on quite well. (Susan)

> We got on with her parents right from the beginning, no bother at all. Of course, my husband enjoys another man's company, obviously, and the men go out together now and then. (Mrs Tagg)

Most parents met at least once before the wedding, although some were not introduced to each other until the wedding day itself. Relations were usually amicable but there was little effort to maintain contact and many people did not meet again until the christening of the first grandchild.

> We met all the parents before the wedding day. Because some people never meet before the wedding do they, and I think that's awful. We're great ones for having a party on any special occasion. We had one for our Silver Wedding and all the boys had twenty-firsts. So they'd be invited to those. And all the boys had engagement parties. Oh yes, we'd all met well before the weddings and we all got on very well. (Mrs Richardson)

> Our parents met a week before the wedding. Because of the circumstances, because I had to get married. But after the wedding they never

met on more than, I suppose, half a dozen occasions, really – christenings, that sort of event. (Jenny)

We didn't meet Sally's family until just before they got married ... we didn't meet her dad until they did get married, on the wedding day. And Sid's wife, I met her brother and I met her mother once. That's one thing ... we don't, er, the in-laws never get together. I think in all cases we tolerate one another. We're very friendly when we have to meet, but we don't make the effort to meet. That's how it's gone all the way through. (Mrs Jones)

The initial meeting between respective parents was either instigated by their children, or at the invitation of one set of parents with the young couple's approval. As it is more often women who issue and respond to invitations, a great deal depends on whether the two mothers like each other, for this often determines the amount of contact between them in the future. Evidence suggests that women sustain family relationships (Eichenbaum and Orbach, 1985; Hareven, 1982) but since a child's parents-in-law are not always perceived as 'family', only tenuous links may be maintained if the relationship seems unrewarding. First impressions are important and if the initial meeting is acrimonious, further contact is usually avoided.

I couldn't make her mother out either. Her mother was the same type. She was a little blonde – you knew very well it wasn't proper blonde – but it was blonde hair cut short. Very flashy, red trouser suits and short dresses ... You see, I hadn't come across it before. We'd led rather a staid life, you know. (Mrs Brown)

My parents met his before we got married because I invited them up to meet them. They didn't get on – my mother didn't like her from the kick-off. (Marian)

They got on terribly. I mean, when they met it was terrible. My mother is a gossip, she just thought they were going to sit down and have a good chat, but my mother-in-law just drove her into the ground. She was very rude. I don't know if she felt inferior because my mother is an intelligent woman, she's a headmistress. But she did tell Andrew that she thought my parents were very stuck-up because they were two teachers, and 'just because I work in an office doesn't mean I'm not as good as them', whereas my mum's just not interested in that. She was more concerned that they were a happily married couple and I was marrying into a happy family. But my mother-in-law was very rude. She wouldn't make conversation, she just retorted to everything that was said to her. And they never meet now. I mean, Andrew and I decided that it would be better for everybody to keep the two families apart. (Deborah)

Generally speaking, unless the mothers are compatible they will not form a close friendship. This is perhaps not surprising, given that each woman will be primarily concerned with her child's welfare and if this is all the two have in common, conflict between them might be expected. One way of managing a potentially difficult relationship is by limiting contact so that differences are minimized and conflict avoided, and in most cases this is what people do. Consequently, most people agreed that on the few occasions respective parents are required to meet they usually manage to get along together tolerably well.

Arranging the wedding

The formal engagement of the young couple informs all interested parties of their intention to marry. The engagement, unlike contracting a marriage, involves no legal procedures, and a formal announcement accompanied by the purchase of an engagement ring is a matter of personal choice. Indeed, some couples, particularly if they have lived together before deciding to marry, may prefer to dispense with a seemingly old-fashioned and unnecessary convention. However, most women in the study did become engaged although the manner and duration of their engagements varied considerably. For example, some were engaged for just the few months it took to arrange the wedding; others waited a couple of years before they married and one woman waited patiently for ten years for her husband to break free from his mother. The formalities surrounding the engagements also differed. Some couples let their intentions be known well in advance and celebrated the occasion with families and friends. Others were more secretive and announced their engagement without warning, thus presenting their somewhat disconcerted parents with a *fait accompli*.

> They got engaged. Paul brought the ring in but they didn't have a party or anything then. When they said they were getting married I was a bit taken aback because I didn't think they would get married then... Paul was only 21. So it was a bit of a shock. We didn't object to them getting married. Dad was all for it, he was more for it than me. (Mrs Brown)

The announcement of a forthcoming marriage has different meanings for those involved but is, in every case, a disruption and rearrangement of the family structure. New relationships are formed between husband and wife and their respective parents and existing relationships between parents and child are inevitably changed. Mothers, particularly, anticipate these changes and whilst they may not welcome them, they accept that their children will marry and leave home eventually. Consequently, the period between the engagement and marriage is a time of adjustment which helps them prepare for their child's imminent departure. However, some are unable to make the necessary adjustments and instead adopt a negative attitude towards the marriage in an attempt to delay it indefinitely. This behaviour seems only to occur when the marriage plans are under way and suggests that the mother's primary concern is to maintain the status quo. She does not object to the relationship per se, providing it does not bring about a change in her own situation. That is, a girlfriend may share her son's affections but she does not threaten the mother's position in the same way as a wife who succeeds her. Therefore, the engagement can herald a stressful period for this mother, and her anxieties are often manifested in an overtly hostile attitude towards her son's partner.

Friendly Relations?

> I think the trouble started... we'd got engaged and that was all right... when we actually decided to go and look at property. She was very different. When she found we were going to buy a house there was a distinct change. When I went in and said 'Hello', she would ignore me. The only explanation I could give was that she expected us to live with her... I think she just assumed that we would get married and live with her. (Annette)

> We got on quite well until she really realized it was serious and we were talking about getting engaged. I think it was with Jeff being the youngest and the last one at home. I think she wanted to hang on to him a bit longer. But anyway, we'd been courting about four years and we decided to get married. We told her and then... I don't know, it was little things. You know, like she'd say 'don't be dragged into it' and 'if you don't want to get married yet, don't let her rush you into it. You're only young'. Because I'm nearly two years older than Jeff. (Frances)

> My husband was one of four sons and he was the last one at home although he wasn't the youngest. So he was actually left with his mother. There was the son and the mother together and I was the girlfriend. While I was the girlfriend the relationship was OK, but I think she wouldn't have liked any girl he married because she had married her son. (Joyce)

The circumstances of these women were similar in two respects: the men they married were sons of widows (one woman was widowed only three months before her son married) and each was the last child to leave home. Townsend (1957) suggests that the bond between widow and unmarried child is particularly close if the father died when the child was in his teens or twenties, and that a son may make a conscious effort to take on the father's roles and responsibilities. In this study some widows were very dependent on their sons for practical services but, more importantly, an adult child at home allowed them to prolong the mothering role and thus alleviated some of the loneliness associated with widowhood. Consequently, the men concerned found themselves torn between a sense of duty and attachment to their mothers and a desire to marry and have children of their own.

> The engagement lasted ten years. After ten years... I decided I would tell him that if we couldn't be married by the following March, it was off. Anyway, he realized that we couldn't go on forever, but I mean, he was torn between two women... But a couple of days later he turned up and said he'd rented a flat and we actually got married in March... I suppose I was surprised at how quickly he acted but of course I was pleased. Looking back on it, perhaps he had to do it quickly because he was living at home. I think he was aware that his mother would do what she could to prevent it and if he was living there she'd have more chance to... wear him down, I suppose. (Joyce)

Although a hostile attitude on the part of her mother-in-law was distressing for the younger woman, she usually understood the reasons and tried to make allowances for them. However, when the strain of organizing the wedding was taking its toll it was sometimes difficult to be patient.

> I just put it down to maybe she was thinking what it would be like for her when Stuart left. I mean, it is awful when you're losing your youngest son. He was definitely the baby of the family. And I could see all this. I could see her point of view, she was losing the last of her children. Her life was going to be changed... (Annette)

And:

> I don't suppose I did ever sit down and say 'are you worried about being on your own?' Because I don't think at the time... well, I did care about it because she was making life very hard for me... And I'd always considered her and suddenly she turned against me. And to be quite honest I thought, 'well, I've got enough to cope with, with getting married, doing the house and going out to work'. So no, we never sat and had a chat. And she'd never had that kind of chat with Stuart. Even now they don't have that kind of chat. (Annette)

> She said she wouldn't come to the wedding. She started making scenes. She went to where his father was buried and cried over his grave until the priest found her and took her away. She came up to the shop where I worked and made a scene in front of the girls there. You know, 'this woman's taking my son'. But I think it was just the fact that some woman, any woman, was taking her son from her. (Joyce)

This somewhat extreme behaviour indicates the severe distress some women experience when their sons are about to marry. Indeed, some experience feelings associated with bereavement but the 'loss' of a child to marriage does not allow for legitimate expression of such emotions. From Joyce's point of view, whilst she was undoubtedly embarrassed and upset by her mother-in-law's behaviour, she also recognized some personal advantage in what had occurred.

> You see in a way these little difficulties, like her coming to where I worked and making a scene, it sort of helped my case. I mean, I'd told my friends that I couldn't get married because she was so difficult and so the things she did fitted this pattern. I mean, coming back from lunch and the girls at work saying 'Guess what, your mother-in-law's been here and she's been crying', well, it sort of showed them what it was like. (Joyce)

Because marriage is seen as 'normal' and desirable, to delay for a long period defies social expectations and invites the negative evaluations of others. Clearly, Joyce was concerned about this and her mother-in-law's conduct at least provided an explanation for her own 'abnormal' situation.

Strained relations between the mother-in-law and daughter-in-law did not prevent people marrying, but obviously cast a shadow over their plans and preparations for the wedding. For example, when, for whatever reason, the mother-in-law was opposed to the wedding, she usually made her feelings clear by refusing to express any interest in it. Ill-feeling was then compounded by the daughter-in-law who, sensing the older woman's disapproval, made little effort to involve her in the arrangements.

> She wasn't really interested in the wedding, not at all. I talked to her about the reception but she thought that was a load of nonsense. When she got married they got all the guests in one car, so she couldn't understand why you'd waste money on a wedding. (Rachel)

And so:

> I didn't really involve her at all. When we'd actually done everything I didn't write and tell her. I don't think she knew what was happening ... she came and that was it. I mean, she wasn't really interested anyway. To her it was just a total waste of money. (Rachel)

Clearly, when people plan to marry, relations between themselves and their prospective in-laws are highly significant if the event is to be anticipated with pleasure. Equally important in this respect is the quality of relations established between the two mothers. In Western culture the marriage ceremony provides an important role for the father who 'gives away' his daughter, but mothers and mothers-in-law have no formal roles in the ritual. However, because the woman's family are traditionally responsible for all but a few of the wedding expenses (although in reality costs are often shared between the two families) the bride's mother usually has a central role in the wedding preparations. This expectation is not overlooked by the numerous magazine articles and other advice literature on weddings, which attach almost as much importance to the 'mother of the bride' as to the bride herself. For example, a brief glance at the specialist magazines which focus on weddings finds a fashion spread headed with the words, 'Mother of the Bride: how to dress on *your* big day' (my emphasis) and articles with titles such as 'Mother and Father of the Bride: for the bride's parents a daughter's wedding is a moving occasion'. There is no mention here of the groom's mother, and in etiquette books she fares no better. In a somewhat dated advice manual (Norman, 1958) twenty-five pages are devoted to 'getting married', in which the groom's parents are scarcely mentioned. However, under the subheading 'Responsibilities of the Parents of the Bride', Norman says:

> These, as has already been mentioned, are considerable and, except perhaps in a financial sense, bear far more heavily on the bride's mother than on the father. Broadly speaking, the mother is likely to find herself responsible for practically everything connected with the preparations for the actual ceremony and for the reception afterwards. (p. 130)

He goes on to provide an exhaustive (and exhausting) list of twelve 'problems with which she must grapple', from announcing the engagement to ordering the wedding cars. On the other hand, Bracken's *Instant Etiquette Book* (1963) manages to dispense with 'getting married' in five pages. She takes a less formal approach than Norman and, perhaps reflecting social trends, ends her section on weddings with the words, 'that's enough about weddings. Now about divorces' (p. 178). However, both manuals scarcely mention the groom's parents and his mother is assigned no important tasks, or indeed any tasks at all, in the wedding preparations. Indeed, in most advice literature she is conspicuous only by her absence.

The role of the mother-in-law is, therefore, ambiguous in that she has no formal right to be consulted about preparations for her son's wedding, and any involvement is at the specific request of the bride and her mother. Consequently, people interviewed revealed a variety of expectations and experiences which ranged from consultation at every stage in the wedding arrangements to almost none at all.

> The nice thing about Lynne when the wedding was being planned, because I hadn't got a daughter they were ever so nice about including me in everything. You know, because I would never have had the fun of that. So I was consulted and we all went shopping together and the two mothers went to get their outfits and that was really nice. And the same thing happened with Mandy, because I made all the bridesmaids' dresses for Mandy and for Sharon. So I've always been included. (Mrs Richardson)

> My mum helped me arrange the wedding... I talked to Patrick's mother about it, about the arrangements we'd made. But obviously you don't have the same contact do you, when you're living at home. Obviously, it's your mother who's most involved. But yes, she was interested... nice about it. (Dianne)

> She was very good, I mean, she tried to help with the wedding, financially more than anything else. But my mum refused because she said it was her daughter's wedding and she wanted to do it. (Rosemary)

Whilst it was generally considered courteous to at least keep them informed, some mothers-in-law made it clear that they expected to be consulted and have their preferences taken into account. Furthermore, if these conflicted with the wishes of the bride's family there was resentment on all sides.

> We originally arranged to have the wedding at this hotel, and we ordered it. Me and Jeff went on holiday and while we were on holiday his mother altered it. She cancelled the hotel we'd chosen and made arrangements to go to another she preferred. We rang her in the middle of the week and she said she'd done all this... When we got back she's made arrangements for us all to go to Sunday lunch to look at the place, my mum and dad had got to come too. Well, that was when my mum got a bit annoyed about it because, I mean, my father was paying for it. (Frances)

Arranging a wedding, then, is an activity which does not always bring out the best in people. Nevertheless, most couples undertake to go through some form of ceremonial since a 'proper wedding', or a variation of this, marks the traditional rite of passage which inevitably transforms the lives of the central actors. Consequently, the sort of wedding one has is either the end result of a series of compromises, or else, by largely disregarding the views of others, exactly what one wants.

> My mother-in-law said, 'Look, you normally only get married once, so make it a good day'. It felt a bit silly in this long white dress. I mean, I've never been one for charades and that's what it felt like. It seemed totally unnecessary to me and I think my husband felt the same. We would have liked to do it our way, but his mother and my mother wanted all the fuss. (Nancy)

> She didn't like these things being dropped on her... she didn't like being presented with a *fait accompli*. She always liked to know what was going on, to be a party to what was going on. And the fact that we had decided to get married... maybe it wasn't the right way of doing it, but we made the arrangements and just came home and told them. (Pauline)

Whilst there were several accounts from daughters-in-law about opposition to the wedding, those from mothers-in-law were much more positive. The majority of mothers-in-law welcomed their son's marriage, expressed warm sentiments about their daughter-in-law and were glad to see the couple settled. Initial misgivings were disposed of by the time the wedding took place, and any lingering doubts were more concerned with practical considerations than personality factors.

> I had no qualms about him getting married, none at all, not at the time. Once I got to know Caroline I realized she was definitely good for him. I couldn't see how he could find anybody better. The only thing I worried about was that he wasn't getting the money... They hadn't got the money and they had to be very careful what they spent. (Mrs Brown)

Although the period before the wedding could be a stressful time for the bride and the two mothers with strained relations between all three, on the day itself the women usually managed to bury their differences if only for the sake of appearances. Despite the traumas, most daughters-in-law said their wedding day was a joyful occasion which, celebrated with family and friends, had fulfilled all their hopes and expectations. Indeed, in some cases this happy outcome was due in no small part to the mother-in-law who, by a word or gesture, had surprised and delighted the bride.

> She did a very nice thing, actually, on the wedding day... Some of her family came from Scotland originally, and secretly she had sent off for little sprays of white heather. So when we met at the registry office she produced this box and we all had a spray. And I thought that was so nice... that meant more to me than a bouquet or anything. It was such a lovely touch. (Pauline)

> My mother-in-law did come up to me at the reception and she said, 'We think you're lovely and we couldn't think of anyone we would have

wanted Andrew to marry more than you'. And that was the most important thing she'd ever said to me and I'll never forget it because it was just the right thing to say. (Deborah)

Whilst it would be unrealistic to suggest that one generous act by the mother-in-law meant the relationship progressed harmoniously from then on, it was nevertheless highly valued by the daughter-in-law as a mark of the older woman's approval and acceptance. Therefore, in the heightened emotional atmosphere which surrounds weddings, gestures like these were extremely moving. This is clearly reflected in comments from women who hoped for such a gesture but were disappointed.

I was very very disappointed that after we were married I didn't get 'you're one of the family now, this is what you must call us. You're one of the family and we're happy'. I expected that and I didn't get it. (Laura)

She ignored me all day. She never spoke to me once. I had a very small wedding, only a couple of dozen people but it was all very nice. We all gathered together to have a drink, and then me and Roy and my sister and his brother went to the registrars. Everybody else stayed and had a drink and within twenty minutes we were back again... actually married. So everybody said 'Congratulations' and there was champagne, and she totally ignored me. But then you could say 'why didn't you approach her', you know, why didn't I make some effort? But I didn't. I just thought it was my day. I thought 'this is my wedding day and if she isn't going to embrace me...' (Joyce)

Although these comments show that some women feel they are judged unfavourably, in this study mothers who regretted their son's marriage are in the minority. Most women expressed very positive views about their daughters-in-law; they approved of their son's choice and were not disappointed.

Conclusion

This chapter has concentrated on the the courtship period prior to marriage when relationships between prospective in-laws are established. It has focused on the development of affinal relationships between women by examining their perceptions and expectations of the mother-in-law and daughter-in-law relationship. By tracing the relationship from its inception it has been possible to examine women's perceptions and expectations of the mother-in-law and daughter-in-law relationship and to see whether these are borne out in reality. The relationship has both positive and negative possibilities, and the quality of relations established before the wedding helps determine subsequent levels of physical and emotional interaction between the women involved. Marriage is, in every case, a disruption of existing family relationships and a creation of new ones. The period between engagement and marriage is a time of adjustment for parents and children alike and whilst most mothers are well prepared for their son's departure, others are distressed by the prospect. Some mothers experience a sense of loss so acute they

Friendly Relations?

demonstrate a hostile attitude towards the daughter-in-law, and in these cases contact is infrequent and stressful. Whilst frequency of interaction between mothers-in-law and daughters-in-law depends to some extent on residential proximity, job considerations and notions of duty and obligation, much more important is the quality of individual relationships. In the next chapter these factors will be examined in further detail.

Note

1 For example, in traditional Chinese society men were greatly concerned with kin. There was at all levels a vast difference in the number of people recognized as kin from either side of the family. Men acknowledged a great many relatives as close kin and for each relationship there was a specific kinship term. On the maternal side of the family very few people were recognized as kin, and relationships were generally traced no further than the mother's brother (Baker, 1979).

Chapter 2

Keeping in Touch: Sentiment or Obligation?

When people marry they must decide where their marital home will be. Much depends upon this for, according to Young and Willmott (1957), their choice of residence helps determine both which of their relatives they will see most and which family of origin they most closely ally themselves with. However, for many young couples personal choice is constrained by practical and emotional considerations. In Stoke-on-Trent, for example, patterns of residence are determined to some extent by social characteristics unique to the area and the unusual distribution of the population into distinctive communities. These are known as the Six Towns but are more accurately described as six urban villages each with a metropolitan identity. Each community is discrete both physically and socially and, therefore, most local people have a deep sense of place and a loyalty to a particular area. Much of this attachment is rooted in the past and occupational patterns in the pottery, mining and steel industries which restricted mobility and determined that people lived and worked in one place. This established in the area a pattern of family life characterized by close-knit networks which is still significant today, with the result that young couples are often bound by an obligation to live near their parents. Therefore, most locally-born people in the study groups expressed a preference for an independent household but one located within reasonable travelling distance of both families. Even so, perceptions of what is 'reasonable' varied considerably and sometimes people referred to geographical distance if their family resided in the next town. Decisions were also influenced by the geographical development of Stoke-on-Trent and the fact that some locations are considered better than others. Consequently, local people not only have a sense of place but also acknowledge a hierarchy of place and for many couples (and their parents) being able to set up home in one of the more desirable residential areas assures 'a good start' to married life. Clearly, then, both material and social factors constrain personal choice and determine who will be able to live where and this is reflected in the varied experiences of the people in this study. For example, residence was not always associated with a desire to be near parents or because daughters especially wanted to be close to their mothers as in Swansea and Bethnal Green (Leonard, 1980; Rosser and Harris, 1965; Young and Willmott, 1957). The most often stated reason for residing in a particular area was job considerations and the convenience of being close to workplaces. In effect this referred to the man's workplace and if, as in the majority of cases, he had lived with his parents before marriage, it followed that the couple found a home closer to the husband's family than the wife's.

Visiting

Living close to one another facilitated interaction between mothers-in-law and daughters-in-law but did not guarantee it or determine the quality of their relations. Some women had only minimum contact and rarely visited each other but these were the exception. In the majority of cases regular visiting patterns and other forms of interaction were well-established, underpinned by varying levels of affection and obligation. More significant then, than the amount of contact between women was the strength of feeling on both sides. In this respect 'contact' is a dubious measure of anything since it tells us nothing about the feelings involved. It is easy to assume, for example, that frequent contact indicates liking and estrangement means dislike but, since family relationships are framed by both negative and positive feelings, this is a simplistic view. It is not always possible to separate the feelings which motivate interaction between kin. For example, Allan (1979) has commented that whilst maintaining contact between parents and married children may be enjoyable and undertaken voluntarily there is a strong element of obligation involved, and for most people it is this combination of affection and obligation which reinforces family relationships.

If, however, an attempt is made to separate feelings of obligation and affection, it seems, as far as daughters-in-law are concerned, that the former is the primary motivation for interaction with in-laws. Daughters-in-law tended not to visit unless accompanied by their husbands, although there were exceptions, particularly amongst those receiving childcare services when 'visiting' was merely delivering and collecting children from their mother-in-law's home. Similarly, few daughters-in-law initiated telephone contact with their mothers-in-law, although in many cases the wife reminded her husband to telephone his mother.

> We visit about once a week, maybe once a fortnight. But we talk on the phone a lot. We visit as a family, all four of us, although sometimes, not very often, Patrick will visit alone. (Dianne)

> I don't visit much alone although I might pop in from time to time if I've got the children. But I wouldn't ever stay and have a meal or anything. I wouldn't visit in that sense. (Wendy)

> I don't go and visit her... No I don't visit her, I've never actually visited her on my own. Never. Even if I'm going past... I wouldn't call in. (Joyce)

> We have to phone them usually once a week. Which I find very, very aggravating because it's a very expensive phone call to them and really nothing of any consequence is said. Simon's mother doesn't cope very well with the phone, she always says she doesn't know what to say... But it is expected that we phone. Simon usually phones. In fact until we

invited them here at Easter I hadn't spoken to them since Christmas. But I remind him. It's usually on Sunday but around Thursday I'll say, 'Have you phoned?' and he'll say, 'Oh, I'll get round to it at the weekend'. (Laura)

It has been argued that women sustain family relationships by operating as 'kin-keepers', in the centre of family communication and occupying a pivotal role as mediator between its members (Delphy and Leonard, 1992; Hareven, 1982; Yanagisako, 1977). Thus, while some daughters-in-law had infrequent contact with their mothers-in-law, most of them practiced kin-keeping on their mother-in-law's behalf by actively encouraging their husbands and children to visit and keep in touch. Sometimes, of course, encouragement was unnecessary because the husband, motivated by his own sense of obligation and affection, wanted to see her. In other instances, communication between men and their mothers existed at only the most superficial level and their relationship depended to a great extent on the daughter-in-law's intervention.

He sees his mum every day and I think he likes to see his mum every day. Now, if he's not down for a couple of days she rings or he rings. (Frances)

We always used to visit as a family. Tom, in fact, until very recently would never go to his parents without me. I don't think that was because he didn't want to go without me, but because he felt embarrassed to say 'Wendy hasn't come'. He does go more often now on his own and takes the boys. It doesn't bother me that he goes but I couldn't cope with the fact that he needed me to go as much as they needed to see each other. (Wendy)

The thing is, he never uses the phone to her. Very, very rare. In fact, once in about six weeks I think, 'Come on, you phone, you talk to your flippin' mother'. And she rambles on and he listens dutifully but not through any pleasure. (Ruth)

We'd still go down and do her gardening. Although after a while with a young baby I found it was too much. When I stopped going, he stopped going. So it got to the stage where Stuart wouldn't go unless I went with him and his visits just got less and less. (Annette)

These comments show that women understand what kin-keeping involves and that women, as wives, kin-keep on behalf of mothers and sons and mothers and sons-in-law. Consequently, despite the prevailing myth, relations between mother and son-in-law are generally unproblematic because the wife takes responsibility for smoothing the way between them. Conflicts are more likely to arise between mothers and daughters-in-law because there is no-one to undertake the mediating role on their behalf. Men rarely kin-keep, so mothers and daughters-in-law are left to themselves and must establish and sustain their own relationship as best they can.

Rosser and Harris (1965) suggest that in every marriage

> the relationship between the families on either side not uncommonly reminds one of a tug-o'-war, with the wife's mother giving the main tug on one end of the rope and the husband's mother at the other end, with various family members joining in from time to time. The husband and wife, in this image, are of course the two white handkerchiefs tied to the rope. Neither side is pulling to win, rather to hold their own. (p. 236)

This is a useful analogy which can also be applied to relationships between mothers-in-law and daughters-in-law if it is modified to represent a tug-o'-war between the two women with the husband in the middle (although we must be beware of the dangers of oversimplified imagery in assuming the man with the white handkerchief is the innocent party between two determined females). Nevertheless, the attitudes of daughters-in-law towards interaction between mother and married son were influenced by their perceptions of the balance between insufficient contact and what seemed excessive. If the mother continued to have high expectations of her married son, his efforts to please her might prove unacceptable to his wife. Some daughters-in-law did resent their husbands' apparent neglect of their feelings and yet showed a marked reluctance to discuss the problem openly.

> She became quite upset if we didn't visit her and I think we dealt with that by keeping the lid on it, by placating her as much as we could. It probably caused most friction when the Saturday morning visiting started, which was probably a reaction to the fact that we couldn't be there as much as she wanted us to in the week. So she came to us. We used to be visited by her every Saturday morning. I can remember the Saturday mornings quite vividly. I didn't actually do anything, I just felt resentful. (Wendy)

And:

> I don't know what stopped me from being direct with Tom about it. I suppose I was a lot younger then and a lot less able to deal with anyone like I am now. But, you see, quite honestly I thought it was my problem. I could feel these hostile feelings within myself but at the same time thinking, 'What is the matter with you? What has she done to you?' and it was nothing really. Except that I think I thought she was invading my space. (Wendy)

> My husband visits her regularly at least twice a week, but his brother does a lot more. If he's not around my husband steps in ... takes her to the pub you know, or wherever she wants to go. Makes sure she can get out, you know. (Gaynor)

And:

> I've come to accept it now. I did resent it when I was a lot younger, you know. We have talked about it in the past ... you know, had words about it. But I've never sort of stopped him going or said 'You're not to go', or caused too much of a fuss ... I think he sees it as his duty but

then I think she's instilled this into them, you know, that they have this duty anyway. You know, 'I'm your mother, you must do this for me...' and they've accepted that. (Gaynor)

I mean, my husband's been away for a month on business and he came back on Friday. He got in at half past four and went to his mother's at half past seven. That was Friday. Saturday night we went out for a meal at six o'clock because he had to be at his mother's for half past eight. Sunday she wanted the lawn mowing because he'd been away, so he went and did that... I think, 'God, I'm seeing less of him than when he was away, he keeps going to his mother's', you know. His excuse is she hasn't seen him for a month but I'm all right because I've got the kids. (Joyce)

It should be pointed out that Gaynor and Joyce are sisters-in-law who share the same mother-in-law, and that the brothers they sometimes refer to are their respective husbands. There seems to be little love lost between the women and their mother-in-law and both expressed mainly negative feelings about the relationship. For example Joyce provides a vivid illustration of what seems excessive contact between a married man and his mother, and also reveals the unhappiness and powerlessness which this behaviour can engender in his wife.

He takes her to the pub every Saturday and Sunday night. She meets all her friends there. They all sit together, all the old dears... He sort of sits with the men, you know. I do feel resentful sometimes when my husband takes her for a drink and I'm sitting here... I don't really want to go, I just wish he wouldn't. I would be so thrilled... I'd just feel it was a show of love really... I mean you might think I'm in control. But you must remember I don't really... I don't win this battle. (Joyce)

Joyce's experience when compared with other women in the study is, to say the least, extreme. Most people had informally negotiated and established visiting patterns which, if not entirely satisfactory, at least allowed them to preserve a sense of freedom and autonomy. For some this meant a regular day and time for visiting their in-laws, whilst others, who feared the danger of getting into 'routines', had more flexible arrangements. Indeed the emphasis on voluntarism in interaction between generations was highly significant for married children and applied equally to parents and parents-in-law.

We go down every Saturday to see her. That doesn't bother me. I mean, we go to my mum's most Sundays as well. (Frances)

I didn't feel obliged. I looked forward to going. And it was basically the most convenient time to go, every Sunday. I didn't feel obliged to go, I enjoyed going. And the same with Patrick's mum, I think. (Dianne)

We see them quite often, you know, they pop round. But when we were first married I think it was a situation where if one had allowed it, it could have got into a routine going over there once a week. Which I wouldn't want and Douglas wouldn't want either so we didn't start that. (Susan)

For the majority of mothers-in-law, visiting and other forms of interaction were frequent and enjoyable and notions of obligation and duty, whilst acknowledged, were not characteristic of their relationships. Contacts were maintained via visits and telephone calls and were generally less formal than those referred to by daughters-in-law. Mothers-in-law welcomed unexpected visits by married sons either alone or accompanied by their wives and children, and only one woman said she preferred visits which did not include her daughter-in-law.

Oh, it's lovely if he comes on his own. James is still as close as he's always been when he's here on his own. Our boy has always been very affectionate... Even now when he comes, he loves us both and hugs and kisses us. So I don't feel he's grown apart from us, but I don't think she encourages it at all. (Mrs Swann)

We don't overdo it and we don't take offence if something happens that they can't keep that date, you know? There's no sulking. They mostly come on Tuesdays. But sometimes my son will say that he's got something else to do on Tuesday and I say 'all right, we'll leave it until the weekend', and then I don't see them all week. You just accept that. But we do see them most weekends either Saturday or Sunday. (Mrs Williams)

I don't think a week would go by without we'd see one or the other of them. But, as I say, we've never made a formal, big thing about visiting. Everyone, I think, just calls on a Saturday or a Sunday when the kids aren't at school. Or they'll call and say 'Can the kids stop while we go shopping...' They're very flexible and always have been. And that's the way I like it. (Mrs Richardson)

An important difference in perceptions of appropriate visiting behaviour between mothers-in-law and daughters-in-law is reflected in their attitudes towards informal visits, for whilst mothers-in-law welcomed them, daughters-in-law tended to discourage this type of informality. Visits to the parental home were often perceived by parents and married children alike as 'going home' and, therefore, prior arrangements were usually unnecessary. However, those in the opposite direction were quite a different matter. They tended to be less frequent and more formal with the daughter-in-law preferring to issue invitations well in advance thus allowing herself time to prepare. Such diverse behaviour also reflects the view that married children are entitled to a degree of privacy and freedom from parental 'interference'. Most mothers-in-law were acutely aware of this and had sanctioned their own behaviour.

When you're first married you only want to be with each other don't you? You've got eyes for nobody else. And you certainly don't want people just popping in when you're not expecting them. It's a big occasion when you have your in-laws for a meal and I wouldn't have liked mine just dropping in without any announcement. (Mrs Richardson)

I've never gone unless they've asked me. I've never been one of these as drops in unexpected. If I've wanted to go I've got on the phone and said 'do you mind if I come over?' But I've never, ever gone ... any of them. I've always been that way. I don't like folks dropping in on me. They say, 'Well, we come'. I say, 'Well, that's different. This is your home'. (Mrs Jones)

We don't drop in. I don't think it's fair to just drop in. You know, I usually phone and say 'is it all right if we come over on Thursday night?' And they say, 'Of course, what are you phoning for?' But we do. (Mrs Tagg)

Given that differences in domestic cultures are a potential source of tension in relationships between affinal women, it is not surprising that unexpected visits were discouraged by daughters-in-law. Women often fear the real or imagined judgments of other women and because of this may develop an obsessive approach to housework (Comer, 1974; Oakley, 1974), and certainly the majority of daughters-in-law, at least in the early years of their married life, were anxious to gain the good opinion of their mothers-in-law. For many women this prevented a relaxed attitude towards informal visits since they increased the risk of being discovered in a home which might be less than immaculate.

Sometimes my mother-in-law would arrive unexpectedly. She'd decide to come and she'd just turn up. I didn't like that very much. She'd come sometimes when my husband was at work. He used to work on Sunday mornings then, and I used to think, 'Oh gosh, I've only just got up ...' you know. I wasn't organized. I felt perhaps she was criticizing, you know. I mean, she was up with the lark, all her housework done and she was much older than I was. (Gaynor)

Nobody likes to be a failure do they, for a start. I'd hate for anyone to think, 'Oh, she's a hopeless wife, she can't do this and she can't do that'. So perhaps I did try too hard to show her, perhaps I still do. I mean, when she comes here she's a guest, she has to sit down and I get her a chair ... I keep her in the lounge so she doesn't see all the mess in the kitchen. (Jenny)

It does appear that it is easier to cope with visits from parents-in-law if, initially at least, they are received formally as guests. This is not to say they are unwelcome; most daughters-in-law responded positively to issuing invitations if only to please their husbands and whilst they might feel nervous about preparing a meal for his mother they did try to make a special effort on her behalf.

If she's coming for a meal ... he was going to go down on Friday night anyway, and he said 'Is it all right if Mum comes for tea tomorrow?', because she hasn't been since before Easter and that's about six or seven weeks ago, you know. So I said, 'yes', but if I'd have said 'no', he wouldn't have taken offence, although I would try and have a good reason why I didn't want to invite her. But I said 'yes'. Whenever he asks I always

> try and say 'yes'. I don't say, 'well...' because I think if you hesitate that's as good as saying 'I don't want her to come'. So I always say 'Oh yes', straightaway. (Jenny)

> When she was here, on the day she came up, I did try very hard. I didn't think, 'well, you can take pot luck', and do baked beans or something. I did try to do something special. (Annette)

Skilful housekeeping, then, was a sign to both women that the daughter-in-law had succeeded the mother-in-law in the primary responsibility for the care and welfare of the man who connects them. Consequently, young wives were extremely sensitive to any perceived criticism of their role or their ability, in the words of one woman, to 'look after her little boy'.

Given that so many young women feared their mother-in-law's critical eye, it was interesting to discover that, in the main, these fears were unfounded. Most of the older women interviewed felt very positively towards their daughters-in-law and, whilst they were aware of such anxieties, having experienced them themselves when newly-married, ordinarily very few women actually made a point of scrutinizing domestic arrangements. Bearing in mind the widespread ethos that married children should be allowed to lead their own lives, the behaviour of most mothers-in-law was marked by self-imposed restraint. They were acutely aware that criticism on their part would be an infringement of the social rules which define relationships between in-laws. Most of them had a relaxed attitude towards domestic life anyway and felt that, whilst polished housekeeping skills were commendable, the healthy state of their son's marriage was much more important. Indeed some women were amused to discover that their daughter-in-law's standards were far higher than their own.

> I know that when we go to their houses for a meal, I know they're trying to impress me. And I don't overdo it but I make sure that I do praise them. I get very angry with my sons if they torment them about it because they don't realize how important it is to the girls. They think, 'Oh, what's all this fuss about, it's only my mum', but I know that they want it all nice and I appreciate it. (Mrs Richardson)

> Oh yes, she's very different from the way I would do things. But I would never dream of saying anything. It's their life and I wouldn't interfere at all. Mind you, I'm not particular about my house but she's even less particular than I am. She's too easy-going. Mind you, she has two children and she's very, very good... they're lovely children. And that's more important than the house. (Mrs Harris)

> She's looking after him and obviously making a good job of it so it doesn't bother me at all. Same as my mother-in-law, she never interfered... You see, just acknowledge when they have got better points. Same as my daughter-in-law, she irons much better than I do. She's very intricate and does things beautifully. But I let her get on with it. I've got my own house to run and I think 'let them do it their way'. (Mrs York)

> Oh, her cooking. She can cook the most beautiful, complicated things. She really is excellent. Much, much better than I am. (Mrs Colclough)

Generally, then, women were quick to praise their daughters-in-law, particularly their success in delegating some of the household tasks to their husbands. Conversely, others, accustomed to more traditional gender roles, were concerned that their son's contribution to routine chores was excessive. However, since the unequal nature of the marriage relationship is well documented and nowhere more evident than in studies of domestic labour (Cromer, 1974; Oakley, 1974), it is difficult to assess how far these observations reflect reality.

> He doesn't cook, but he washes up and he didn't wash a dish at home. But there again, I think girls are sensible now, they say 'Come on, share the jobs'. I mean, my son grumbles about it, but she says 'get on with it', and I think she's very sensible. (Mrs York)

> I've always said to him, 'James, anyone you marry you take your share of the duties, you do things in the home and help and don't leave it all to your wife'. And I rue every word I said because he does everything in the house. He cooks and cleans. She leaves everything to him, she's bone idle. (Mrs Swann)

It seems clear, then, that contact is maintained between parents and married children from a sense of obligation and also sociability although this is not an end in itself. Sociability is the prime motivation in relations with friends, attitudes towards whom are mainly positive, but kin relations are more ambivalent and have both positive and negative possibilities. In kin relations it is difficult to separate notions of duty and affection although choice seems to be a key factor. For example, whilst interaction between mothers-in-law and daughters-in-law is largely framed by a sense of obligation, between mothers and daughters this is often blurred by a strong positive affective bond and the intrinsic enjoyment both derive from their contacts with each other. Consequently, many daughters-in-law said that, given the choice, they preferred to share outings, shopping trips and other activities with their mothers. Even where interaction was no more frequent than with their mothers-in-law there was a marked difference in the feelings involved. This was acknowledged by both mothers and daughters-in-law and reflected the widely-held view that mother/daughter relationships are 'natural' and, therefore, more important than those between in-laws.

> Unless I know Jeff's mum is ill, I won't ring her. Because I know Jeff sees her every day more or less. I ring my mum... I just ring her. It's wanting to you see, not having to. (Frances)

> Her mother, ever since Cheryl left work, she goes over there Wednesdays and Fridays. Because she only lives at Chesterton and it isn't too far away from them. Cheryl has got a very close relationship with her mother, much closer than I am with either of my boys. I suppose it's different with daughters. (Mrs Tagg)

> I don't especially do anything with my mother-in-law apart from visiting each other. I used to do a lot with my own mother before the baby came and I think I would tend to more so ... I think it's loyalty. I think when you've got your own mother and you're close and not that far away ... I mean, if my mother-in-law asked me if I'd like to go out, I'd go. But really, I wish I was nearer Mum sometimes. It would be nice to meet her for coffee or something. I miss her more now I'm at home because you're by yourself more with a child. (Susan)

This is not to say, however, that mothers-in-law and daughters-in-law did not share joint activities or derive pleasure from each other's company. Indeed, compared with interaction between mothers and daughters, much of their contact was prescribed by similar exchanges of domestic services underpinned by an element of enjoyment. Again, the quality of feeling is the significant, if elusive, factor for whilst many relationships between family women have a degree of ambivalence it is, perhaps, more evident in those between mothers-in-law and daughters-in-law.

> Well, one of them visits a lot on her own. And the other one, I see her because we went to cake decorating classes together when I finished work. (Mrs Colclough)

> We used to go to the Women's Institute together and we used to sing in a choir together. So we did a lot together, really. (Sonia)

> I never visit her on my own although when she comes here, of course, we're often on our own. And we sort of have a neutrality treaty. Well no, it's hard to say really, because sometimes it's wonderful. We go shopping together ... or we'll garden together or you know, we'll clean up together. But she's so moody, you never know how she's going to be. Sometimes it's OK, other times oh, I have to clench my teeth and go out and dig the garden for half an hour. (Elaine)

Although most people regard interaction with kin as largely a voluntary matter, there are a number of occasions in the year when family obligations take precedence. These are the Christmas and Easter festivals and, to a lesser extent, family birthday celebrations and annual summer vacations. Perhaps the most important of these is Christmas both for its association with the values of family life and for the family gatherings which traditionally take place. There is, as Firth *et al.* (1970) point out, an overwhelming obligation to celebrate Christmas and, furthermore, to share the celebrations with 'obligatory guests' (p. 263). Obligatory guests are mainly relatives and, as the name suggests, their inclusion may have little to do with voluntary choice on the part of the hosts.

Christmas's unique association with the idealism attached to family life does not alter the fact that for many families it is a stressful and tension-ridden event. Much of this stems from obligations to blood relatives and those acquired by marriage with the conflicting demands from both sides. Furthermore, because women occupy a pivotal role in family communication, they undertake most of the negotiating and pacifying and, consequently, suffer most stress. Aspects of hospitality are crucial and ridden with anxiety about 'who goes where and when', for even with careful forethought and due attention to 'balance' and 'fairness', there is always the risk of offending one side or the other.

> We've always gone one year one parent, one year the other parent. But the first Christmas Toby was born we had Christmas here and my mum and dad came and stopped with us because it's local for them. So last Christmas I said, 'Right, we'd better go to your mum's now'. So I told my mum and she was most disappointed, she said, 'I thought you might come to me this year, you haven't been to our new house'. So I said, 'I've got to be fair. We saw you last year. All right, you came to us but we did see you and I've got to go to Kevin's this year'. So that's what we did. (Vicky)

> We have to sort of negotiate. We have to share it out amongst everyone. We spend Christmas morning at home just the three of us, and Christmas dinner tends to be 'Oh, where were we last year, whose turn is it this year?' The ideal situation would be for us to be at everybody else's house, you know. (Deborah)

A great deal of variety exists in Christmas arrangements depending on stages in the family life-course. In the early years of married life young people tend to divide their time between both sets of parents but later, when children arrive, they prefer to stay at home. This practice does not avoid decision-making for now they must invite either one or both sets of parents to come to them. Competing claims between grandparents can complicate the situation still further but, unless there is to be a continuous round of visiting, people have to make the best arrangements they can. If both sets of parents get along it may be feasible to invite them all on Christmas Day, although this creates extra pressure in having to cater for and entertain several people at once. Most daughters-in-law preferred to avoid this if they could, and found the simplest solution was to see one set of parents on Christmas Day and the other on Boxing Day.

Helping one another

Studies of kinship confirm that the family is the preferred source of assistance both in times of crisis and in long-term reciprocal exchanges and that obligations apply to primary kin rather than secondary kin and especially between parents and children (Finch, 1989; Firth *et al.*, 1970; Young and Willmott, 1957). Duties and responsibilities towards kin are unlike those defined in a contractual relationship where certain obligations are fulfilled and the contract terminated. Obligations in kin relationships are incidental and normally continue throughout life. However, obligations are not fixed. They are flexible according to need and, as such, the focus tends to shift from children to parents during the family life-course. Furthermore, to function successfully and with minimum resentment, they must contain a sense of being voluntary and mutual with no obvious imbalance between givers and receivers unless parents are elderly and dependent.

Concepts of obligation and responsibility which underpin patterns of assistance cannot be fully understood without reference to the warmth and affection commonly associated with close kin relationships. This is a significant factor in blood relationships, say between mothers and daughters, but is more ambivalent between affinal women. Nevertheless, the quality of relationships seems to have little bearing upon whether short-term obligations are honoured or not. Mothers and daughters-in-law, regardless of individual feelings, felt morally obliged to help each other and exchanged a variety of domestic and other services. Other than in exceptional circumstances when the mother-in-law was very dependent, services tended to be mutual and short-term. In this respect, the age range of the women interviewed is significant. For example, the majority of daughters-in-law had 'young' mothers-in-law and women in the mother-in-law group were also 'young' if one accepts their view that the onset of old age occurs at some point past the mid-seventies. Consequently, for the majority of women, a long-term, one-way flow of practical assistance was not, as yet, a feature of their relationships.

Informal assistance was generally welcomed by those who received it, particularly women in paid employment who appreciated help with domestic chores. However, because of their primary association with the domestic sphere, women were extremely sensitive to another's intervention. Conflicting opinions on acceptable behaviour meant that if assistance was not carefully negotiated it could easily be resented.

> She used to come into the house and wash up and tidy up and she'd do the washing... She'd take washing and at times that really aggravated me because, you know, I'd come home and I'd know somebody had been in. And a couple of occasions when we went away on holiday she took the curtains down and washed them you see, and defrosted the freezer and things like that. Well, it's all very helpful but it's an imposition really, when you're not agreed upon it. (Pauline)

Older women understandably wished to retain their independence for as long as possible, and were only prepared to accept assistance insofar as they could reciprocate. Even the widows, one of whom said she 'couldn't even change a plug' when her husband died, were determined not to make demands on their married children. Mrs Jones, for example, was greatly encouraged by her daughters-in-law to maintain an independent outlook, whilst Mrs Brown, who had more reason than most to require assistance, preferred to pay for the services she needed.

> She always wants to but I won't let her because I think she's got enough to do. But she would, she'd come and clean my house and she doesn't like cleaning, she hates it. But she'd do it if I asked her. But I never ask her. I'd rather pay somebody else to do it because I know she doesn't like it. (Mrs Brown)

It is worth saying some more about Mrs Brown's circumstances because she provides an excellent example of the need for independence which many women referred to. Mrs Brown was in her mid-sixties and had been a widow for six years. She suffered from a crippling form of arthritis which meant she was obliged to use a walking frame indoors and a motorized wheelchair when she ventured out.

She was further handicapped by impaired vision, the result of an inherited condition which also severely affected her son. Nevertheless, she lived alone and was fiercely independent. After a shaky start she and her daughter-in-law had developed a close relationship but despite this Mrs Brown was determined to cope, as far as possible, without Caroline's help.

> Caroline will do anything I ask her, I've only got to phone her no matter when and she'd be here. And if I said I'd got to go somewhere she'd take me, no trouble. She's very, very good. But, then, I'm very independent. Because I think she's got enough to do looking after them two lads and Paul. (Mrs Brown)

Whilst most people responded positively to the short-term practical needs of their in-laws, it also seems that a sense of responsibility has some clearly defined limitations. This has been well documented by Firth *et al.* (1970) who point to a number of factors restricting action, including personal like or dislike and shortage of time and energy. Although daughters-in-law and sons-in-law did not normally restrict their actions, they often faced a dilemma as to how much practical support parents might reasonably expect. When demands seemed unnecessarily high people did feel some resentment although actual behaviour was not significantly affected.

Attitudes towards obligations were also related to the conduct of donor and recipient. There were strongly held views that people should not exploit their relatives by making excessive demands or insisting on an immediate response to non-urgent situations. The concept of reciprocity was also significant in that it took a number of different forms. Motives for helping kin were not calculative in the sense of obtaining some fairly immediate return. For example, whilst kin relations allow – but may not contain – varying degrees of sentiment, they are not expected to have an economic dimension and, consequently, women rejected the notion of performing services for financial gain as totally unacceptable kin behaviour. On the other hand, the fulfilment of obligations was not incompatible with a sense of grievance if other, emotional, satisfactions were not met.

> It's this taken-for-granted attitude that really gets me in the end. This thing of ringing Tom up and saying, 'will you . . .', not in a week, *now*. And it's the taken-for-granted aspect at the end of the day. Not the fact that you do help your parents because, obviously, parents do sometimes need help. It's the demands that are put on, the taken-for-granted that he can be there. Because he usually is, of course. (Wendy)

> She'd knit for us but she used to charge. You know, you'd get a little bill with so much an ounce and so much for knitting it. I thought it was awful, that she'd actually charge for knitting for her own family. (Janet)

> I took her shopping and did her sewing for her. But she never, ever said thank you. She was like that with a lot of people. Her daughter might say, 'Well, don't I get a thank you for doing that?', but I didn't feel I was in a position to say that. (Annette)

Friendly Relations?

Clearly, a sense of duty and obligation underpinned interaction with mothers-in-law although some daughters-in-law were motivated by genuine affection. Furthermore, in most cases, whether the daughter-in-law felt positively or not towards her mother-in-law, the amount of contact between them was about the same. Conversely, mothers-in-law evaluated their relationships more highly and reported mainly positive feelings. Whatever the levels of satisfaction, except in extreme cases, mothers-in-law did not disengage from their daughters-in-law for fear of losing contact with both sons and grandchildren.

Childcare services

The arrival of grandchildren is, in any event, an important stage in the family life-course and has positive meanings for both women, providing an absorbing focus of attention and a shared interest and concern. Grandchildren also change patterns of interaction in families and affect the balance of exchange in domestic services between women. Putting aside the intrinsic enjoyment grandmothers derive from contact with their grandchildren, it is fairly obvious that provision of childcare services involves a one-way exchange in which the daughter-in-law is the main beneficiary. It was important to discover, therefore, how donors and recipients perceived childcare services. Two separate, although not mutually exclusive, forms of provision required examination. First was short-term, ad hoc services, such as babysitting or having grandchildren to stay for short periods; and the second, long-term, permanent childcare support for working mothers.

With regard to short-term provision, the first thing to say is that the type of services given and received were as many and varied as the attitudes expressed towards them. However, paternal grandmothers seemed to fall roughly into two categories: those who would provide informal and fairly regular support and those who would not.

> I babysit if ever they want to go out. Sometimes we have the children to stay the night . . . I mean, if they're going to be late it's better to have the children here so they can go to bed at their normal time. (Mrs Richardson)

> I go there and they put the children to bed before they go out. It's not a lot really . . . they haven't got a lot of money, you see, so they can't go out very much. (Mrs Harris)

> I will babysit when they ask but I don't make a habit of it . . . But any special occasion or during the day if they wanted to go shopping, they'd bring them and I'd look after them. That way. (Mrs Jones)

Although there were strongly-held views among women in both groups that parents should assume responsibility for their own children, very few respondents objected to occasional requests for childminding. Generally, those who were reluctant to help did not want to become involved in another bout of childrearing, albeit informally. Even so, no-one in the mother-in-law group refused childcare provision under any circumstances, although, for some, these were quite clearly defined. For example, an emergency such as illness was a legitimate request for assistance; a social occasion was definitely not.

> She never once said, 'If you want to go out I'll babysit for you'... She sort of said, 'I've had my children, you must look after your own'. (Janet)

> I never believed in babysitting. I've had them here once for a weekend, but I think that was when they were going to a hairdressing conference. It's always been for work that I've had them, I don't believe in having them while their parents are out enjoying themselves. (Mrs Brown)

> Now that's not to say she hasn't helped me out, she has. When I was working full-time the youngest one was quite poorly... So I rang her and said, 'can you come over?' and she caught the bus and came over and stayed with him all day. (Jenny)

These comments seem to confirm the anticipated behaviour of prospective grandparents interviewed by Cunningham-Burley (1985) in her study of grandparenthood. She found that grandparents anticipated being involved in babysitting but that this was constrained by the view that parents should not leave their children too often. As in this study, formal social events and business trips were mentioned as occasions when grandparents would babysit, but frequent requests from parents who leave their children because 'they were just going down to the pub at nights' (1985, p. 431) would probably be refused.

Most women considered grandmothers the best source of childcare although wherever possible, daughters-in-law preferred help from their own mothers. Strong affective bonds between mothers and daughters meant that the maternal grandmother either shared her daughter's views on childcare, or at least could be trusted to carry out her instructions. Therefore, mothers were seen as more reliable than mothers-in-law and this, together with the element of formality in in-law relationships, meant that paternal grandmothers did not routinely provide childcare services unless the maternal grandmother was absent or unable to help. Mothers-in-law usually understood and accepted this, although grandmother-care did have the potential to cause conflict if one of the grandmothers felt excluded.

> We see a lot of my parents because they look after the children while I work and that's OK. But my mother-in-law, that's a bit different. You see, I never feel I could leave the baby with her because I always worry that when I come back he'll be crying in his cot. I know that if he wakes up she'll leave him in his cot crying because 'he has to learn'. I don't bring children up that way, if he cries I pick him up and I don't care if I spoil him. (Elaine)

> I think a girl's mum... she's naturally more for her mum. I mean, I was with my mum. So the grandchildren get to know those grandparents more. (Mrs Richardson)

> Oh no, I never minded when Caroline's mother had the children. I was glad she wanted to look after them, because I'm not that fond of them.

I'm not that fond of little boys at all, because they can be little devils. (Mrs Brown)

In the school holidays ... normally, she'd have them a couple of days a week and my parents would have them another couple of days, trying to spread it a bit. This is because having kids is tiring but it also minimized the conflict and jealousy that one tends to have against the other over the children. (Wendy)

Turning now to long-term, permanent support systems required by working mothers with young children, it is necessary to consider the circumstances of the women in both study groups. The first observation in respect of the mothers-in-law is that, at the time of being interviewed, no-one was providing full-time childcare services for her daughter-in-law. Consequently, theirs are expressed views and may be contrary to actual behaviour. Land and Rose have commented that 'altruistic practices are structured into women's lives' (1985, p. 93) and this underpins assumptions that family women will undertake caring roles in support of each other should the need arise. The term 'compulsory altruism' has been used to describe other-regarding behaviour which does not involve free choice, and Land and Rose argue that the taken-for-granted 'naturalness' of female caring masks what is often involuntary action in the absence of viable alternatives. Thus, it is possible that some mothers-in-law who expressed negative views about providing childcare services would do so in certain circumstances and, indeed, there was some agreement that if real financial hardship in the parental family forced the mother into paid employment, the mother-in-law would feel obliged to look after the children in her absence.

Conversely, three women in the daughter-in-law group depended on their mother-in-law for childcare services: two women were in full-time employment, a third was pursuing a university course. Their respective children were all of school age but under the age of 10 and so required care and supervision outside school hours and during the holidays. There were others in the daughter-in-law group with dependent children (under 14 years of age) who worked outside the home but their jobs were part-time and fitted in and around school hours. Furthermore, those who were economically inactive either because of family commitments or lack of suitable employment opportunities expressed their intention of entering the labour market as soon as circumstances would allow. It is fair to say, therefore, that daughters-in-law were employment-oriented in theory if not in practice. Paid work was regarded as important and not just for the benefits derived from an additional income. The motivation to work was also related to career development and self-fulfilment and, not least, the companionship derived from being with others after a relatively isolated period spent at home with small children.

The rapid growth of employment rates for mothers since the Second World War has precipitated debates at two levels. Within the household, contributors to the analysis of domestic labour have argued that women's responsibility for housework is imposed on them via the roles of wife and mother (Barrett and McIntosh, 1982; Delphy, 1977; Coulson et al., 1975) and that despite optimistic suggestions (Young and Willmott, 1973), the sharing of household tasks between women and men has not become noticeably 'symmetrical'. However, it has also been noted that feminist debates have been relatively muted with regard to childcare, and that concerns with women's 'double burden' of domestic and paid labour have paid little attention to the lack of public policy to support working mothers (David, 1991; Borchorst, 1990). In the public arena, the debate has centred on the welfare of young children and has led to a reassessment of the respective obligations of state and family towards the provision of childcare (Leira, 1987). Much of the rhetoric has also concerned fathers' employment patterns and innovations such as job sharing and paternity leave. However, the government response to these debates has been one of non-intervention. During the last decade the present government has promoted the 'traditional family' where mothers stay at home with their young children, and whilst objections to mothers working are now less explicit, dual-earner families are largely dependent on private childcare arrangements. There is no universal provision of parental support for those with children under 5 and little in the way of public facilities for the care of children outside school hours and during holidays. Lack of social policy in this area means that childcare is the responsibility of parents, arranged privately either through informal support networks or by paying for childcare services.

The rhetoric of 'shared parenting' and 'parental responsibility' does not obscure the fact that it is mothers who are the primary caretakers of dependent children. When the mother works and some of the childcare is delegated to others, it is she who must plan, organize and coordinate those resources and if she is let down she must have readily available alternatives. Consequently, grandmother-care has a number of advantages for working mothers. It is relatively cheap, if not free, and is often more convenient than a nursery in that grandmothers do not usually close down their services at six o'clock. It also allows the mother the peace of mind she might not get from other support systems, since grandmothers are familiar and reassuring figures in children's lives and have their best interests at heart.

> She goes to granny's every day because I go to work. My mother-in-law said right from the start that she would have her... (Deborah)

> It is nice and I do appreciate having somebody to depend on and I feel safe when the children are with her... (Wendy)

Paternal grandmothers provided a variety of services for daughters-in-law with regard to their children. Not only did they deliver and collect children from school, caring for them in the interim periods until their parents returned, they were also a valuable resource in the school holidays and when illness struck. A co-residing grandmother who could provide childcare in the family home was also a valuable asset. She was able to perform a number of tasks which allowed her to feel useful and supported her daughter-in-law. Co-residence was not typical among the women interviewed, but the one daughter-in-law who shared her home with her mother-in-law found this to be mutually advantageous. She benefited from knowing that her children were well cared for in her absence, whilst her mother-in-law, by undertaking childcare and other tasks, had a useful and supportive role within the family.

> Now, of course, she lives with us and the children are older anyway. But she's here if I can't be when they come home from school and if they're

ill or anything like that, I always know they'll be all right with her.
(Sylvia)

However, grandmother-care is not unproblematic and if tensions between the mother-in-law and daughter-in-law already exist they are likely to increase if there are differences about the grandchildren. A source of information about grandmotherhood comes from American literature which refers to the less benign features of grandparenting and suggests that grandmothers can have a negative influence on family life (Robertson, 1977; Kahana and Kahana, 1971). Grandmothers have been accused of stimulating conflict by usurping the mother's role, overindulging grandchildren or seeking to control their behaviour. Whilst not wishing to go too far down this road without examining the positive aspects of grandparenting, it is important to note that conflict does occur and may be exacerbated if the grandmother has a major role in the care of her grandchild. It is almost inevitable, when day-to-day care is concentrated in the hands of the grandmother, that the mother's role will be diminished. Nevertheless, she will have her own ideas about bringing up children and will expect her mother-in-law to abide by them. Conflict is most likely to occur if there are marked differences in their methods and if the mother-in-law consistently overrides the wishes of her daughter-in-law.

I've always known she could be relied on and she's been there but there have been times when we haven't got on, when I would have liked not to have been relying on her. And because you rely on someone I think you have to compromise on values and habits and on what you'd allow. And I've had to come to terms with that and it wasn't always easy.
(Pauline)

Normally, however, grandmothers are expected to exercise some restraint in relations with their grandchildren. There are well-defined guidelines for appropriate grandparenting contained within the general rule that the upbringing and discipline of children is the responsibility of the parents. (Cunningham-Burley, 1985; Crawford, 1981). Therefore, most grandmothers condition their behaviour and involvement with grandchildren so as not to overstep these boundaries or appear interfering. This is not to say, however, that mothers-in-law always approved of their daughter-in-law's childrearing methods. Some felt their grandchildren lacked discipline and good manners, aspects of upbringing which were important when their own children were young. These differences were seen as those which occur across generations and, set against historical time, the impact of social change on parent/child relations. Therefore, mothers-in-law were reluctant to comment on the behaviour of their daughters-in-law and, indeed, most women took the view that the exercise of grandparental authority was almost always inappropriate.

Although a few women were receiving long-term childcare support from their mothers-in-law, overall mothers-in-law were not the first source of assistance and nor did they want to be. A recurrent theme referred to by women in this group was that of freedom from parental responsibilities and the opportunities available in middle age to pursue long-deferred interests and activities. Some were in part-time employment and others simply felt they were 'too old' to take on permanent childcare. There were also strongly expressed beliefs in the traditional mothering role and the daughter-in-law's responsibility to be at home with her child at least in the pre-school years. This view was upheld by all the women in the mother-in-law group, none of whom in normal circumstances were prepared to undertake long-term care of grandchildren.

> One thing I've always said, even with my own daughters who live locally, I would never look after grandchildren on the same basis during the day while they go to work. I don't agree with that. I've brought up my own family and I don't want to be tied down every day looking after grandchildren. It's never really cropped up, but they know my feelings on this so they've never asked me. I know it has to be done and people do it, but I don't feel as if I could be tied down every day looking after children and nothing else. (Mrs Orchard)

> Well, I don't like to see granny-reared children as I call them. But there again, in this economic situation it's very unfortunate but some mothers have got to go to work. But if they do go to work I don't think they should pass the responsibility on too much. (Mrs York)

> Well, I wouldn't say 'yes' straightaway because I think it's a thing you've got to think about. I think a full-time job while your children are still young enough to need you is selfish really. If it's that necessary, if times are that bad, fair enough. But if it's just a matter of getting out away from the children, I think it's unfair on the children really. If it's illness or something like that, I'd have to, I would. Because I know I could. But I don't think I'd do it from choice, you know, just to suit them. Because I like my freedom as well. (Mrs Richardson)

> I wouldn't do it. Only if they really, really needed the money. I was a teacher and I retired before I had to. But for freedom, you see, not to be a babyminder. And I told them that from the very start. But she does work part-time and she has a childminder locally, and I said if the child is ill or she's ill, then I would in those circumstances but not every day. (Mrs Colclough)

> Oh no, that's something I said I'd never do. I have had them, you know, for weekends like grannies do, or the odd night here and there but I'd never look after them while they went to work. (Mrs Jones)

The fact that mothers-in-laws do not hesitate to make their views known and, therefore, pre-empt requests for long-term assistance, was also referred to by women in the daughter-in-law group.

> When the eldest one was about six weeks old... I can always remember... she said, 'don't ever expect me to finish work to look after your children'. And I hadn't asked her, it came right out of the blue. I was a bit upset about that. I mean, I would have asked my own mother before

> her, really. So I was always aware that I must never ask her anyway. (Jenny)

Although there has been a rapid increase in numbers of married women in the labour market, successive post-war governments have consistently cut back on nursery provision for the under-5s and studies suggest that relatives, especially grandmothers, are an important source of childcare support for working mothers (Moss, 1982; Ginsberg, 1976; Yudkin and Holme, 1963). What seems to be lacking is any analysis of how grandmothers actually feel about providing this sort of assistance, but it appears that paternal grandmothers, at least, are unwilling to undertake full-time childcare and are prepared to do so only with reluctance if there is real hardship in the parental family. It would seem, therefore, that social policy which cuts back on state provision for the under-5s, in the belief that all family women are 'naturally' altruistic and prepared to subordinate their own interests in support of each other, is based on a false premise.

Financial aid

Sociological studies of economic support in families have concentrated on the middle class (Firth *et al.*, 1970; Bell, 1968, 1970) for in Bell's view the middle-class extended family can provide forms of aid that the working-class extended family cannot. Two observations made by Bell are particularly significant for this study. Firstly, he suggests that the large amounts of financial aid exchanged in middle-class families cannot be equalled by working-class ones, not because of differences in sentiment but because working-class parents very rarely have access to this type of resource; secondly, that financial aid among members of middle-class families demonstrates an important structural relationship between men. Taking the second point first, in Bell's view it is predominantly men who operate the mechanisms by which economic support is transferred between members of the middle-class extended family. He states: 'It is by means of the male link that the elder middle-class generation channels financial aid to the next generation' (1970, p. 223), and suggests that this represents an important dimension of kinship frequently overlooked in sociological studies because of a tendency to concentrate on mother/daughter relationships. However, contrary to Bell's findings, women interviewed for this study revealed that negotiations relating to extended family aid are not always or necessarily between men. They also occur between women and between other family members including parents-in-law and children-in-law and, to a lesser extent, between siblings.

> Martin's mother does all the financial things in their house anyway. So it's always been me. Martin's mother is quick to pick up on things like that. I'm not saying she pays all the bills or anything like that but if something has been worrying me, then if I approach Martin's mum she tries. But it's always been me and Martin's mother. Perhaps Martin and I have talked it over first but it's always been me that's spoken to her. (Helen)

> He always goes and asks his mum. I have nothing to do with it. But I would if it was my mum. Then I'd go and ask. (Jenny)

I'd discuss it with Gareth and then I'd negotiate with his dad. His dad said, 'do you need some help?', and I said, 'well, yes'. But any financial matters were his father and me and then I'd relate it... I mean, Gareth could be in the same room but his father would address me. (Ruth)

We're always having offers from Simon's sister. She has lots of money and... she's always said, 'Look, I've got the money, you can have it interest free. In fact, you can have the damn money if it gets you what you want'. And we're grateful for knowing, you know, that the offer is there. (Laura)

The second observation of Bell's concerns the disadvantaged position of working-class extended families in relation to financial aid. According to Bell, working-class parents are rarely in a position to provide economic support in similar proportions to middle-class parents because they have limited amounts of disposable income. However, in this study many working-class parents gave continuing financial aid to their married children in comparable proportions to those found in middle-class extended families. This raises a number of questions about complex problems of gender and social class and also how money is controlled, managed and distributed within households and kinship groups.

Most writers on social stratification have adopted a labour market approach, either defining social class in terms of the individual's occupational status or the household and patterns of consumption derived from the income of the main (typically male) breadwinner (Goldthorpe, 1980; Parkin, 1971). Both definitions have been criticized because women are generally excluded or categorized in accordance with the occupation of their husband or father (Abbott, 1987; Dale et al., 1985). For example, Abbott points out that when the household is taken as the basic unit of class analysis it ignores the work experience of individual members whilst assuming that each has equal access to household resources. On the other hand, stratification on the basis of occupation excludes economically inactive maried women other than to locate them by reference to their husband's class position. This has led Delphy (1981) to argue that gender should be separate from class analysis and that all women should be regarded as comprising a distinct social class. Delphy's point is that married women working within the home belong to a patriarchal mode of production defined by inequality and to classify a wife according to her husband's occupational status obscures her dependent position in the marital relationship.

However, it is not particularly helpful to define women as a separate class in order to avoid categorization based solely on the husband's occupation. Another way is to make a clear distinction between occupational class where the woman has a direct relationship with the labour market and the class position of the household unit for women who are not employed outside the home (Dale et al., 1985). But again, the difficulty with using the household or family unit for class analysis is that it assumes the married woman's equal access to resources and conceals the dimensions of power and control which exist within families (Abbott, 1987; Hartmann, 1987; Delphy, 1981).

Although these writers provide a useful framework within which to examine gender and social class, stratification studies generally tell us little about patterns of consumption and support in the extended family. Indeed, there is scant literature on material resources in working-class families, perhaps because sociologists have tended to concentrate on domestic services transacted between women, thereby underestimating financial exchanges and the amounts involved. The fact that little is known about the way money is organized within households is not surprising given that this is usually considered a private matter, and what information exists seems to refer only to the domestic economy and not the economy of the wider kinship group (Pahl, 1983; Hunt, 1980). Notions of privacy also have implications for this study, for whilst people were invited to discuss the giving and receiving of financial aid, direct inquiries about how large sums became available for the purpose were considered inappropriate. It must be emphasized, therefore, that the following discussion necessarily involves a degree of speculation.

Money enters the household in various forms but for most families the main income is derived from the earnings of the breadwinner. It is assumed that this is utilized to pay household expenses and any surplus is also for collective family consumption. However, Pahl (1983) suggests that money is controlled by individuals at the point where it enters the household and typically the amount brought in by respective partners influences their role in decision-making. Thus, if a wife has no earned income of her own she may have less say on major financial decisions and unequal access to personal resources. In other words, the wife's control over money in relation to her husband's is highest when she herself is economically active. It has also been suggested that where the husband is unemployed and the wife is the breadwinner she has most financial control (Stamp, 1985), although many studies show that in working-class families ultimate power is always retained by the man (Hunt, 1980; Rubin, 1976; Komarovsky, 1967).

It does appear that married women in paid work have more control over the flow of money in the household and an active role in decision-making. Hunt (1980) found that the women in her study were determined to control the money they earned and although much of it was earmarked for family consumption, the decision on how it would be spent was theirs. It is plausible, therefore, that evidence of working-class extended family aid from this study bears some relation to the mother's earning power. For example, there has been a post-war expansion of employment opportunities for married women in Stoke-on-Trent, and this, together with relatively stable employment generally, low property prices and a tendency among the adult population towards late marriage, has enabled the majority of working-class families to maintain reasonable living standards. Morever, it seems likely that the wife's financial contribution provided an opportunity for married couples to accumulate some savings during their working lives, and it is these reserves which are utilized to assist subsequent generations.

Another means of accumulating financial resources is to save from the housekeeping allowance. The wife who does not earn may have no personal money of her own but, by stringent economies, may manage to claw back small amounts which over the years accrue into a sizeable sum. In some cases this is achieved without her husband's knowledge and reflects the difference between money reserved for regular basic expenditure and any surplus. Pahl (1983), for example, has shown how men often regard their basic wage as being for family needs, whereas bonus or overtime pay is reserved for their personal use. Thus, there is often an element of secrecy in the way individuals regard the money they control. The wife who receives only housekeeping money may never know the real contents of her husband's wage packet and, similarly, he may be unaware of the fact that she manages to save. However, this is not to suggest that all, or even most, couples operate segregated financial management. Pahl has pointed to the infinite variety of allocative systems in households including shared management where both partners have equal access to money in the common pool. Hunt (1980) too, states that

> both men and women see the family-unit as the site for the fulfilment of life-projects and consumption aspirations. The individual worker's involvement at the place of paid employment tends to be seen as a means through which finance can be secured which will enable the individuals to live a satisfactory life in the privacy of their families. (p. 183)

and therefore, whilst people are sometimes possessive about 'their' money, others favour an integrated system in which the family unit has priority over individuals. This view is supported by evidence from the study groups, for whilst there was occasionally an element of secrecy in the way money was channelled between generations, in most cases those not directly involved in the transactions were, nevertheless, aware of them.

Finally, insurance and endowment policies, often the only form of savings adopted by working-class families, tend to mature in middle or later life and can be used to benefit children and grandchildren. This has particular significance for widows who may find their financial circumstances improved by their husband's death as a result of provision made during his lifetime. Large sums obtained from death insurance are likely to increase the guilt feelings widows commonly experience when their partners die and some may be reluctant to use the money for more than their basic needs. However, opportunities to direct it towards married children may be particularly welcomed as a means of maintaining a useful role within the extended family and as a link between the deceased and the next generation.

These, then, are some factors which make working-class extended family aid possible. They demonstrate how money may be reserved and accumulated by the elder generation to assist the next and, importantly, the decisive roles women are able to play in this process. The women in this study revealed not only the large amounts involved but also the varied circumstances in which aid is given and received. Parents responded to a variety of needs from paying an overdue bill to help with purchasing a house, and supported their children in various ways with cash inputs and tangible goods.

> She's helped us in lots of ways we've not been able to pay back, particularly financially. Whenever we're really stuck ... you know, bills mainly, that sort of thing. There's no way we could ever pay back the amount of money she's given us. (Pauline)

> Patrick's parents lent us some money when we bought the car. Patrick went to his dad and asked ... it was £600. And my mum and dad are very good to us. They don't loan us money, they give it generously. But I don't ask. I'd rather do without than ask. But my mum offers and my dad is very good. When we moved from the last house they paid the

> mortgage off. I think we owed about £2,000 and they didn't want paying back. (Dianne)

> She paid a deposit on a house for us which was about £300 then. And as a surprise wedding present she gave us a weekend in Blackpool at a four-star hotel... (Rosemary)

> We gave them some financial help when Paul opened the business. He said he was going to the bank for a loan and we thought that was a waste of money, you know, paying interest. I said, 'See that you pay your dad back'. When he paid his dad back I said, 'Are you sure you can do without this money' and he said yes, he was all right. So Dad said, 'All right, give him half of it', so we gave him half of it back and we gave my daughter the other half. (Mrs Brown)

> My mother's just lent us £600 to buy a car. It's a loan. It'll definitely be paid back, but it's paid back interest-free. But my mother, and my father when he was alive, have also given us sums of money and they were actually given to us. But if we've asked for money we've always said, 'You'll definitely get this money back'. (Gaynor)

The above comments indicate the extent of aid in working-class families, since in all cases the people giving aid (that is, the parents) were, to paraphrase Bell, 'working-class by any of the definitions customarily used by sociologists'.[1] They demonstrate that working-class family aid operates in similar ways to that in middle-class families, although the consumption aspirations and life-styles of individuals in both groups may be very different. It is unwise, therefore, to underestimate financial ability or the flow of money between generations within working-class kinship groups.

There were several ways of channelling economic support in both working-class and middle-class extended families and very often overt negotiations were unnecessary because parents (usually mothers) 'sensed' a particularly urgent or pressing need. Sometimes, therefore, money was not asked for but was offered as a gift; sometimes it was negotiated as a loan but, with a low expectation of repayment on both sides, was eventually reinterpreted as a gift. There was, in any case, no time limit imposed upon repayment and even if loans were not forgotten they were almost always interest-free.

Referring to 'loans' rather than 'gifts', although in reality the reverse might be true, is one of the mechanisms by which financial assistance flows from parents to adult children but still allows the young couple to maintain an appearance of independence. Certainly status is in giving not receiving and, as the wish of married children is to be independent, gifts of money from parents must be given with discretion. A subtle way of doing this is for the parents to provide a loan, part of which is repaid and the balance written off.

> We had a loan when we were buying a house, but it was done on the same basis as the building society, it was with interest and we paid that off as well. Now when my father-in-law died she stopped that debt... I think it was for about £500. (Ruth)

Parental aid was usually based on sentiments held by parents towards their children and mothers were often concerned about fairness. Most of them agreed that unless there was an urgent need all their children should be treated equally.

> I try to be completely fair. I bought my daughter a Hostess Trolley, that was £150. I didn't give it to Paul straightaway, I waited until there was something he wanted. He needed some help with his central heating so I gave him £200, and so of course I owed my daughter £50. She'd broken her glasses so I gave her the money for some new ones. That made it exactly right. (Mrs Brown)

> I think you've got to be as fair as possible. Well, I think you've got to try to do that. As I say, they can have £60 or so, that's all right. Now my son he's asked us for some money to go on holiday with his friends. So I said to my husband, 'That's all right, he can have the money but he must pay it back when he starts to work'. Because that is a luxury, you see, and it wouldn't be fair to give him that and not the other three. (Mrs Harris)

Sometimes parents were scrupulously fair towards their children, but were less so towards their children-in-law. Conflict occurred when the mother-in-law discriminated between her son and his wife to the point where the daughter-in-law was excluded from all direct financial assistance. When quasi-secrecy operated between mothers and sons, daughters-in-law were placed in an intolerable position even if, as in most cases, the money received was for a joint expenditure and mutually beneficial for both husband and wife.

> Obviously, they know I know we've borrowed money for the car. I did say to his mum 'we will start paying you that money back', and she was a little bit snappy, she said, 'Oh, that's between Patrick and his dad' and I've never mentioned it again. I wanted her to know I was concerned that we hadn't paid the money back and that's why I said it, and she was saying more or less, 'it's nothing to do with you'. (Dianne)

> She helps us out a lot financially, usually unasked. But then again, she doesn't include me. She gives it to Terry. She knows whatever he has he'll share it with me once she's gone home but she wouldn't give it to us both. She gives it to Terry and then Terry will tell me. And I'll say, 'I'll write and thank her', and he'll say, 'No, don't mention it'. (Rachel)

> She has given him money but it's for my husband. I mean, like last Christmas she gave him a present of £100. Perhaps with her getting older now, she wants to give her money away but she didn't say it was for us. That was for him. He went and bought himself a coat he'd always wanted. But I didn't object. (Gaynor)

Each of the three women contrasted her mother-in-law's behaviour with that of her mother and, perhaps not surprisingly, their mothers were perceived as more sensitive in their dealings with the married couple and more openly generous to both daughter and son-in-law. They did not, for example, create conflict between husband and wife by treating their child's spouse unfavourably.

> My mum would never do that with any of us. That's what she says... 'I'd never dream of giving you money behind Terry's back, or any of the others'. In fact she gave us some money when we got married for the wedding but she gave it to Terry. In front of me, you know, but... Completely the opposite. (Rachel)

> I think perhaps she should say it's for all of us, really. My mum has given me small sums, just for me, come to think of it but she's also given all of us a lot as well. But I don't think my mother-in-law would be all that happy if she gave him so much money for him and then he went back and said, 'I've bought Gaynor something with it', or for the children. It's for him. I mean, that's what she wants, for him to have it. (Gaynor)

> It's usually my mum's instigation. She offers it to both of us. She thinks of Patrick as her son, really... (Dianne)

Clearly, financial aid divides families as well as unites them, and conflict over money can cut deep into kin relations. This is reflected in the many conditions which affect the giving and receiving of parental aid. They apply to both parents and parents-in-law and depend to a great extent on the quality of their relations with the married child. A crucial factor concerns the expectations of both parties and their mutual understanding of the basis for financial assistance.

> I wouldn't have anything from my dad as a loan unless I knew I could pay it back. My relationship with him is pretty dire and I wouldn't want to be obligated to him. I hate having to ask him. He's probably the last resort, my dad. (Pauline)

> But if his mum did give you anything it was, 'I've given you this', and 'I've given you that'. She once let Colin's sister borrow some money off her for a deposit on a house and I said I'd never, ever borrow money off her because she told us about it, which I thought was terrible. She kept going on about it, which isn't nice not when it's your family. It should be confidential shouldn't it? So I avoided that... ever borrowing money off her. (Janet)

Economic support may be underpinned by subtle power relationships which affect generational perceptions of parental authority. For example, many women were reluctant to approach their parents or parents-in-law, because the conditions imposed on receiving aid increased their personal anxiety and had a negative effect on the parental relationship. Others, who perceived the mother-in-law as an interfering person, felt that large subsidies were potentially damaging to their independence by strengthening parental involvement in matters of personal choice.

I've never had money off my parents because I know my mother would remind me of it for the rest of her life. Because she's the sort... she always reminds you of what she's given up and what it's cost her. (Laura)

She's always willing to help but I always feel there would be strings. I mean, if I asked her for £1,000 I think there would be strings there. There might not be, but I think ... say, she wouldn't lend us £1,000 for another motorbike but she would for a car because that fits in with her ideas. Which is fine. But we wouldn't ask her because we wouldn't want to be restricted to her ideas. (Ruth)

Bell (1968) suggests that the flow of financial aid from parents to children is greatest during the first two phases of marriage when couples are home-making and childrearing and evidence from this study supports this view, although some people continued to receive support after these cycles. Others who had needed help for lengthy periods despaired of ever being independent of their parents and worried about repaying long-overdue loans. Attitudes towards financial aid also varied: some felt subsidies from parents were perfectly acceptable and contributed to family stability; others believed they were damaging in their ability to increase dependence and reduce adult children to a childlike state.

Patterns of financial aid between generations can tolerate long periods when one party is the recipient but this usually changes over the life-course (Argyle and Henderson, 1985; Troll, 1971; Burchiveil and Sussman, 1962). Financial aid to parents is the other side of the help pattern and as married children grow older the flow of aid may be reversed. However, very few mothers-in-law had reached the stage where they required economic support and those in the mother-in-law group expressed the hope that they never would. They were united in their desire to prolong their independence well into old age, whilst continuing to help their married children in various ways as long as they were able. In return, subtle forms of help such as goods and services were preferred as these were easier to accept as gifts or exchange. Financial aid to parents was not, then, a significant factor and in the few cases where children did provide assistance the amounts involved were quite small. There was only one instance of major expenditure which was met by a daughter-in-law and her husband.

They've never been in a position to help us because they've always been as poor as crows. But we've had to help her in the past when his father was alive. ... There was never enough money and the house fell into a terrible state of disrepair. So we had to have things like pointing done and new windows put in. ... They were both at home and pensioners, and we did it because they just did not have enough money. (Nancy)

Indirect assistance is another means of channelling economic support in the extended family. This can be achieved by giving expensive presents or cash gifts on socially approved occasions such as birthdays or at Christmas and is considerably different from other financial contributions. It is more acceptable by parents and children alike and can be received without loss of independence. Indirect aid is also more discreet than negotiating assistance, yet has the same effect of benefiting the family by releasing some of its income for other expenditures.

Friendly Relations?

Expensive gifts begin at the wedding and continue at annual celebrations and in due course extend to grandchildren. Transmitting financial assistance via grandchildren is especially effective since it is perceived as an expression of grandparental affection and does not threaten the financial autonomy of the parents.

Both instrumental and affective elements are involved in exchange between parents and children and it does appear that gift giving and the values involved are quite significant in mother-in-law and daughter-in-law relationships. Nearly all expensive presents are limited to close family (Argyle and Henderson, 1985) and whilst most women said the gifts they exchanged were costly, carefully selected and given with pleasure, others revealed contrary attitudes and behaviour. For example, more than one woman commented on her mother-in-law's frugality, particularly in relation to grandchildren, whilst conversely, another said her mother-in-law's generosity precluded the ability to reciprocate.

> She's very very thrifty ... she knows where every penny goes. I wouldn't say she's mean, but sometimes she's too careful. Especially over the children. They've always had a birthday present and they've always had a Christmas present, but never anything in between. I'm not saying she isn't generous but she's never been overgenerous with the grandchildren. I don't know why it is. Perhaps she thinks they have enough. (Jenny)

> I don't think I would mind going at Christmas if she didn't go overboard on presents. I mean, we just don't have the money and I find it embarrassing. I mean, she starts buying presents in September ... (Laura)

It is also clear that gift giving can be a somewhat less than subtle means of showing disapproval. When mother-in-law and daughter-in-law dislike each other, they may hesitate to express their feelings overtly since this might provoke discord not just between the women but with the man who connects them. However, there are various ways of expressing disapproval, one of which is negative discrimination at Christmas and on birthdays.

> She always gives him more. She buys him, like a good present and then she gives me, perhaps a pair of tights. It doesn't bother me that much, although I don't think she should, really. (Gaynor)

> I know she's got plenty of money and when she comes at Christmas I get her a lovely present. I get her this nice present and she says to my daughter, 'Go to the corner shop and get your mother a pair of tights'. Forty-two pence! And I have to be appreciative ... (Joyce)

> You see, I do things now that I know are bound to annoy her. You see, we bought some lovely cut glass crystal glasses that I wanted to buy for James for Christmas. I certainly didn't want to buy them for her but I wanted James to have them in his home ... But I don't buy things for her now, I buy them for James. And I'm sure she must know. (Mrs Swann)

Generally, however, gift giving between affinal women was associated with the same sense of fairness evident in other forms of interaction and exchange. This reflects the importance which women attach to 'fairness' and 'balance' in their relations with in-laws. The concern with 'fairness' and 'balance' in gift-giving and other transactions stems from women's pivitol role as 'kin-keepers' which allocates them the responsibility to sustain family relationships both physically and emotionally — a point which will be further examined in the following chapter.

Conclusion

Three broad areas have been examined in this chapter. Firstly, it seems clear that notions of obligation and duty underpin the interaction of daughters-in-law with mothers-in-law although some are motivated by genuine affection and that, conversely, mothers-in-law evaluate their relationships more highly and express mainly positive feelings about their son's wife. Secondly, the exchange of services between affinal women was mutual unless the mother-in-law was elderly and dependent, with no clear givers and receivers. Thirdly, contrary to generally held views, financial aid between parents and children involving large sums and high values occurred in both working-class and middle-class extended families. Finally, all forms of exchange were part of a pattern of interaction which was social as well as instrumental and sustained generational relationships within the kin network.

Note

1   In his study, Bell used the Registrar-General's Socio-Economic Groups to classify husbands' occupations. This is also applied here in that the parents referred to had occupations classified by the Registrar-General's Groups IIIM, IV, V.

Chapter 3

Emotional Investment: Empathy and Power

It is well documented in studies of kinship that women are the 'kin-keepers', in the centre of family communication and occupying a pivotal role as helpers and mediators (Argyle and Henderson, 1985; Hareven, 1982; Yanagisako, 1977). Less well documented but equally important is women's role as peace-keepers, pacifying family members and maintaining peace by non-confrontation and avoidance of conflict (Forcey, 1987). This chapter, then, focuses both on kin-keeping and peace-keeping and is concerned with the emotional interaction between daughters-in-law and mothers-in-law, mothers and sons and husbands and wives, which underpin these activities. Consequently, kin-keeping and peace-keeping refer not only to the contacts women maintain between family members but also to the emotional energy invested in relationships and the feelings of expectation, fulfilment and disappointment involved.

Before proceeding, two points need to be made about the composition of the study groups and the data. Firstly, as previously mentioned, more daughters-in-law than mothers-in-law were interviewed and the women were not related to each other. Importantly, therefore, women were talking about their relationships with other women who were themselves not interviewed. Secondly, there is some discrepancy between the views expressed by mothers-in-law and by daughters-in-law. The majority of mothers-in-laws held positive views about their daughters-in-law and looked upon the younger women as friends or 'like a daughter'. However, comments made by the daughters-in-law interviewed reflected a broader range of views, both positive and negative, about their relationships. In short, many of the attitudes expressed by daughters-in-law seem to contradict those held by mothers-in-law and the meanings attached to them will be explored in what follows. However, the validity of all the views expressed cannot be over-emphasized. They reflect the realities of individual relationships as perceived and experienced by one half of the dyad and the complex nature of mother/daughter-in-law relationships in general.

Kin-keeping between mothers and sons

Simplistic explanations as to why women are assigned responsibility for the emotional realms of family life are found in psychological analysis which suggests that women's 'affectiveness' is biologically determined and deeply entwined in marriage, motherhood and the family. However, others, writing from a psychoanalytic stance, suggest that the roles of wife and mother are socially constructed and determined by the reinforcement of gender differences in the way women reproduce children (Eichenbaum and Orbach, 1984; Chodorow, 1978). Taking women's pivotal role in the rearing of children as their starting point, they suggest that because mothers differ in gender from their sons they experience boy children as different from themselves, separate and as 'others'. They have a clear sense of the boundaries between themselves and their sons but less so with their daughters. Here the boundaries are blurred. When a woman bears a son she knows his life will be very different from her own but she identifies with her daughter as someone who will lead a similar life, one spent nurturing and caring for others.

According to Chodorow, mothers teach their girl children nurturing skills so that as women they are able to 'mother' in various ways whether or not they choose to have children of their own. Nurturing, therefore, is not 'natural' or 'given' simply because one is female but it does constitute the feminine which is why it is not solely confined to domestic and kin relationships. However, it is closely associated with what it is to be a wife and mother and because these roles are socially constructed and are determined by an early training, many writers have likened them to having a job (Eichenbaum and Orbach, 1985; Miller, 1978). Although the work is not valued, the training is woven into a woman's life from childhood and comes to be accepted by herself and others as 'natural'. For example, Eichenbaum and Orbach state:

> Being a wife and mother is like having a job, but the training for this job is not overt, nor is the job itself valued. Because the preparation for this job is woven throughout a girl's life it can actually come to feel natural. The way she has come to know herself as a person in the world is as a girl and then a woman. Part of being a girl and a woman, as we now know it, means having the skills necessary for being a wife and mother. (1985, p. 6)

Thus, women are provided with the skills to be wives and mothers and prepared for their responsibilities as carers who support the emotional structure of family life. Other people's emotions and needs are their concern. As wives and mothers they keep contacts with and maintain links between their own and their husbands' extended families. They care for others, help them express their emotional needs and then nurture and satisfy those needs. This in itself may not be as problematic as it seems. Many women achieve a considerable sense of self-worth from their support of others and by reacting to, and processing, their needs and indeed some have argued that women's unique moral strength is derived from their concern with nurturant relationships (Gilligan, 1982; Miller, 1978). According to Miller, the problem comes when women are expected to take on these responsibilities and when their own needs are unrecognized and unmet. She states:

> Women do have a much greater and more refined ability to encompass others' needs and to do this with ease. By this I mean that women are better geared than men first to recognize others' needs and then to believe

> strongly that others' needs can be served – that they can respond to others' needs without feeling this as a detraction from their sense of identity. The trouble comes only when women are forced to serve others' needs or when they are expected to do so because it is the 'only thing women are good for'. (1978, p. 65)

That this is a common feature of women's lives stems from the fact that they are expected to meet the emotional needs of others but men are not. Consequently, in the emotional realm of family life there exists an imbalance where women give far more than they receive and in the process their own needs are subordinated and largely ignored.

Much of women's emotional work in the family is not recognized by those on whose behalf it is carried out. One of their activities is mediation between family members who are unable or unwilling to communicate effectively with each other. Writers suggest that in the socialization process, boys are encouraged to diminish emotional ties with the mother and identify with the masculinity represented by the father (Flax, 1981; Chodorow, 1978; Tolson, 1977). In order to do this, men learn to suppress within themselves those feelings which they recognize as feminine and so find it difficult to be nurturant adults. However, in repressing their attachment to the mother, men need to seek out another female who will help them understand and express the feelings they have denied. According to Chodorow,

> Men defend themselves against the threat posed by love, but needs for love do not disappear through repression. Their training for masculinity and repression of affective relational needs, and their primary nonemotional and impersonal relationships in the public world make deep primary relationships with other men hard to come by. Given this, it is not surprising that men tend to find themselves in heterosexual relationships. (1978, p. 196)

In other words, men need to form a relationship with someone having the same relational abilities as their mother. To this end the majority of men succeed in obtaining a wife who takes responsibility for the emotional functions of the marriage relationship and relations between her husband and his family.

Boys, and later men, know what they will always have a 'mother' and are secure in the knowledge that a woman will provide for their emotional and physical needs. Women do not have this security because, paradoxically, although men's emotional needs are recognized and met consistently by women, men themselves have learned to deny their needs and therefore find it difficult to understand and respond to those expressed by others. This has led many writers to conclude that marriage is an unequal relationship which benefits men far more than women (Barrett and McIntosh, 1982; Bernard, 1975; Oakley, 1974). Others have criticized Berger and Kellner's (1980) assertion that marriage is a 'play area' in which the individual is given 'plenty of leeway to "discover himself"' (p. 317). Burgoyne and Clark (1984), for example, have pointed to the use of masculine terms in Berger and Kellner's work and how it persistently ignores the different meanings and consequences of marriage for both sexes.

Sociological investigations into marital relationships have placed considerable emphasis on the way roles have been redefined in terms of companionship and shared affection and activities (Young and Willmott, 1973; Bott, 1964). However, if men are taught to be inexpressive and deny relations whilst women are preoccupied with them, it seems likely that men will be unable to fulfil this role, thus making marital relationships extremely difficult (Rubin, 1976; Balswick and Peek, 1971). For whilst men confide intimate feelings to their wives and for many this is their only outlet (Phillips, 1986; McKee and O'Brien, 1983), they do not consistently provide the same service in return. According to Miller (1978), men do service others but how and when they do so is a matter of choice not available to women. Furthermore, men control their availability in a physical sense and, because their physical boundaries are recognized and respected by their wives, they are able to withdraw from the relationship and maintain a sense of autonomy outside it (Eichenbaum and Orbach, 1984).

On the other hand, Balswick and Peek (1971) suggest that the marriage relationship may be the one area where men have learned to be more expressive while remaining inexpressive in other situations. They say that this behaviour stems from 'a double emotional standard, where men learn to be expressive toward their fiancée or wife but remain inexpressive toward women in general' (p. 366). Balswick and Peek do not reveal how men 'learn' to be expressive to their fiancées or wives, but it is fair to assume that the women themselves are involved in the learning process with all the emotional work this implies. Nevertheless, if mothers are included in the category 'women in general', it may explain why communication between adult men and their mothers often exists at only the most superficial level. In addition, mothers, recognizing the boundaries between themselves and their sons, tend to limit conversation to 'acceptable' topics which avoid self-disclosure. Consequently, whilst women may define their relationship as 'close', too often much of the intimacy associated with closeness is missing. Sometimes open displays of physical affection or mutual expressions of concern are confused with intimacy but in fact few aspects of their personal lives are talked about and shared.

> They haven't grown away from me because they come home and they put their arms around me. Same as yesterday, all of them phoned to see if I was all right because of the snow. The phone was going all the time. You know, 'are you all right Mum, do you want anything?' (Mrs Jones)

But:

> I'd like a daughter. I think you can confide more in a daughter, they understand more as regards how a woman feels. I think if I'd got a daughter I'd talk to her more about how I truly feel... (Mrs Jones)

Other women said their relationships with their sons were not really 'close' because of difficulties in communicating.

> I haven't really got a close relationship with him. He's a loner, or at least he was. He never told us anything at all. I don't know why... It's just one of those things. (Mrs Tagg)

> I've not got a close relationship with my son. I never have had... He can't show his feelings. He never talks. I mean, my husband would be working nights, you know, and on the very rare nights Glyn would stop in we could sit a whole night and not say a thing. I wanted to talk to him but he isn't the type you could talk to. I could speak to him, approach a subject and he'd say, 'yes', 'no', and that would be it. (Mrs Williams)

Daughters-in-law, too, were aware of the superficial level of relations between some mothers and sons. Many women commented that their husband and mother-in-law 'do not really know each other' and, reflecting the way men control their physical and emotional availability, often blamed their husband for not 'giving her what she wants'.

> They don't exactly communicate. They don't exactly talk. He wouldn't confide in his mother, he doesn't seem to have that sort of relationship. He's not close to his family in any way, shape or form. (Valerie)

> I quite like it if they hug, I think they should have something special. I just feel I wish it were more meaningful. It obviously must have some meaning but perhaps because it's all unspoken... I mean, it seems to me that it's 'Hello', 'Goodbye' and a goodnight kiss. They don't talk... They're close, but they're not close and I don't think it's much of a relationship. I often feel she doesn't know him. They may be close but she doesn't know him. (Laura)

> When I see them together I sometimes feel very annoyed because he doesn't pay his mother any attention. She's very, very fussy, she wants to give him things and do things for him and she wants some attention off him too. But he doesn't... he just shuts up. He doesn't particularly get on with his mum and he doesn't give her what she wants because he doesn't think he has to. He gives her what he wants and really that isn't much. (Ruth)

It seems that communication difficulties between women and their married sons is part of the mother/son experience. The gender-identification process means that both boy and girl children must be socialized into gender-roles by learning appropriate forms of behaviour and because fathers are inconstant figures it is the mother who introduces her child to her or his gender identity. In short, the mother/daughter relationship consists of preparing the child for an inferior status; the mother/son relationship affirms and confirms masculine prestige (Seiter, 1986; Eichenbaum and Orbach, 1985; Tolson, 1977). However much they may wish for expressive sons, the mother's priority is to help them take their place in the dominant culture. This is confirmed outside the family where boys learn a masculine language which prescribes and avoids certain topics (Tolson, 1977) and inside the family where mothers speak to their sons 'in a different voice' (Gilligan, 1982), treading cautiously for fear that overt emotions are burdensome for men to bear (Forcey, 1987). For as Rich points out, women 'fear alienating a male child from "his" culture', because a son might 'accuse us of making them into misfits and outsiders' (1977, p. 205). But not only sons, women, too, judge mothers and sometimes find them guilty of failing to produce 'real' men.

> It's a funny kind of love and she doesn't really know him very well. I get the impression she doesn't really see Simon as grown-up... He's her only son and in many ways they are very similar. There's a lot of traits she's encouraged in Simon that, without this sounding very sexist, I would find more acceptable in a woman than a man. He is very soft, very, very caring and loving which is lovely in a husband but he hasn't got a lot of aggression. So when he's competing in a man's world I feel she's let him down a little bit. I think if she'd encouraged him to be a bit more independent I think he would have been a bit more outward-going. (Laura)

This suggests that some women see assertiveness in men as a positive trait which signifies masculinity. This is because wives relate to their husbands as adult men whilst mothers relate to their sons as both men and children – a point to which we shall return.

Whilst some women were highly critical of the childrearing abilities of their mothers-in-law, those daughters-in-law who were themselves rearing sons commented on the differences between boy and girl children, generally agreeing that boys are somehow more affectionate, less confident and in greater need of the mother's protection. Yet paradoxically, whilst she protects him she must encourage his separation from her and it is, therefore, not surprising that women often spoke of sons 'growing away' whilst daughters 'stay close'. Relations with sons diminish as they reach adulthood and the mother's role is relinquished to the wife when a son marries. Much more than with daughters, therefore, the mothering of a son is seen as a temporary state and perhaps more highly valued because of it.

Thus, there are contradictions experienced by women in the mothering of sons. It is precarious because whilst a son is perceived as separate by the mother, as her child he is an extension of herself. A daughter is also an extension of the mother but because she is the same gender, the mother's identification with her child is less complex. Motherhood and being a mother is different, then, depending on the gender of the child. Moreover, because mothers are not required to separate from their daughters, adult women can remain 'children' in the mother/adult-child relationship. Men cannot because in order that sons achieve masculinity, mothers are required to treat them as opposites and therefore the relational basis between them is inhibited.

As we have seen, communication difficulties are a common feature of relations between women and their adult sons and reflecting this, some daughters-in-law said that their husband had little to say to his mother and that it was up to them to keep the conversation going. They often resented being assigned this responsibility, either because they had little in common with the older woman or because they were convinced she would prefer to converse with her son. Indeed, given that women's talk is socially devalued in relation to men's, it is hardly surprising that daughters-in-law attached more importance to conversations between mothers and sons than to those between the women themselves.

> I do get cross about it and there have been times when I've said, 'I'm not going unless you promise that you'll talk when we're up there'....

Friendly Relations?

Because really she doesn't want to hear me talking, she wants to hear him talking. (Laura)

I do mediate when we go there ... I wander out into the kitchen and we have a natter. We always talk about dieting and whether I've lost any weight and what she's done ... Sort of general interest but there's a lot of politeness in there as well. And then we trundle back into the lounge and it's normally conversation between her and me, until she asks him a direct question and then he will start talking. (Ruth)

Terry's mother talks so much ... I mean, she really does go on and on and it does get you down after a while. It's really hard work and after a few days it really gets you down. And he knows that, he knows very well but he sits there and he doesn't do anything about it. He won't intervene and take the attention off me for a while. And that really annoys me. I think he should intervene more because, after all, it is his mother ... (Rachel)

It is worth mentioning that young women do not necessarily identify with older women on the basis of shared gender. Age divides women, and often the experiences and concerns of one age group seem uninteresting and irrelevant to the other. Moreover, because women are influenced by cultural definitions of femininity they tend to judge each other by those standards. Consequently, in common with most men, many younger women perceive older women as sexually unattractive and obsolete.

Nevertheless, women in this study were prepared to undertake a great deal of relational work for each other regardless of whether they perceived themselves as having much in common. Consider, for example, Ruth's reference to 'womanly chats' which nevertheless contain 'a lot of politeness' and Rachel's comment that conversation with her mother-in-law is 'really hard work'. These comments illustrate how women invest in a relationship which may offer limited personal satisfaction, in order to sustain links between others. It is perhaps not surprising, therefore, that they experience this as 'work'.

Much of this evidence seems to contradict Spender's (1980) view that men talk more than women and in mixed-sex conversations tend to interrupt females and rarely listen silently when they speak. Spender says that men deny women equal status in conversation because they resent discussion of topics which do not cater to their interests or which divert women's attention from them. However, within the family it seems the opposite occurs. Men contribute little to family conversations and, indeed, mixed-sex discussions are not an obvious feature of family interaction. Rather, talk and topics are sex-specific with male and female areas of interest, so that women and men converse separately from each other. Apparently individual men do not converse more with their own family than that of their wife; participation depends on the appeal of certain topics and personality traits which make some men more talkative than others. Furthermore, men often do 'listen silently' to women because they are not prepared to contribute to the conversation and, indeed, may avoid being brought into it by various withdrawal tactics. Men do this because they often see women's talk as inferior and trivial but, on the other hand, when mothers and wives talk the husband/son usually is the topic of conversation and, consequently, all their attention is focused on him whether or not he chooses to participate himself.

It has been suggested that power is an important factor in interaction (Spender, 1980; Goffman, 1967) and it is clear that power differences between men and women make it possible for men to opt out of conversation if they choose. Because women can never take for granted when men will or will not talk they do what Spender has called 'the support work' (1980, p. 49) in mixed-sex conversation and thereby, in this instance, sustain relationships between mothers and sons.

When communication between women and adult sons exists at the most superficial level, if they are to have any understanding of each other's feelings these must be mediated and expressed through a third party – usually the wife. Many women practise self-imposed restraint when interacting with adult sons, believing that certain topics or expressions of intimacy are inappropriate. They may worry about embarrassing their son or alienating him by excessive demands for his attention. But just as women expect less from their sons so they turn to daughters-in-law for reassurance that the sons care. Consequently, daughters-in-law are centrally involved as mediators, sustaining relationships between mothers and sons and seeking to improve the quality of those relationships by interpreting and expressing the meanings attached to them by both parties.

> I know what she feels about Gareth and I hope she realizes that he actually does like her and care about her. There have been occasions when she's said, 'Oh, sometimes I just don't think he cares'. And I say, 'Of course he cares, he just doesn't show it', you know. (Ruth)

> I saw a lot of her separately and I began to be a mediator between Alec and his mother. He didn't see a lot of his mother and I used to pass on information and news and so on. And she was beginning to ask me how he was and what he was doing and what he was eating, you know. I did sometimes resent that and I wasn't as understanding as I could have been in that I realized she was very anxious about his well-being. (Pauline)

It appears that these are two important dimensions to mother/daughter-in-law relationships: the perception of the mother-in-law as a mother and the perception of her as a friend. The above comments are illustrative of the first dimension. As a mother, the woman's significant relationship is with her son and one way (for some, the only way) of retaining a degree of intimacy with him is via his wife. Therefore, within the concept of kin-keeping there exists a subtle power relationship between wives and mothers. In other words, kin-keeping between mothers and sons is a matter of negotiation between mothers and daughters-in-law in which the younger woman has the power to decide how much relational work she will undertake on the older woman's behalf. However, whilst women in the daughter-in-law group acknowledged their mediating role, it would be misleading to suggest that they experienced it in terms of power. Rather, they saw it as an obligation to act which was underpinned by varying degrees of anger and frustration. Some were concerned that the mother-in-law used them in an attempt to influence her son and persuade him to act in her favour, whilst others just felt disappointed that they were required to channel important personal information which their mother-in-law could not tell him herself.

> A few years ago she said, 'Come into the kitchen we can have a talk' and she'd never done that before. And she just told me everything that had happened about her divorce and Gareth's father losing his job and how she'd gone back to try her first marriage again and the very messy divorce and everything ... And she said, 'I just want to tell you so you can tell Gareth if he wants to know'. Now that absolutely amazed me, that she'd bottled it up for so long and never thought she could tell him and then that she should approach me to tell him ... (Ruth)

The last comment is illustrative of the second dimension in the relationship: the mother-in-law as a friend. Whilst it is possible that Ruth's mother-in-law felt unable to discuss personal matters with her son because of communication difficulties between them, it may be that she was seeking intimacy with Ruth for its own sake and on the basis of friendship. Mothers-in-law often present intimacy as mediation, which daughters-in-law may then interpret as manipulation because, unlike intimacy, it is easier to reject. The point is, the mother-in-law may see herself as her daughter-in-law's friend but the daughter-in-law might not and nor might others outside the relationship: hence the continual reinforcement of negative stereotypes of the mother-in-law as someone who is 'manipulative' and 'interfering'.

Much of the work involved in mediating is an extension of what Finch (1983) has called 'the "helpmeet" model' (p. 86), where women meet the needs of others at the interpersonal level. The problem for daughters-in-law is that by supporting mother/son relationships they also collude in maintaining the status quo, and several women in the daughter-in-law group expressed considerable ambivalence about their mediating role. They felt strongly that they should not have to mediate but, fearing further erosion of the relationship, were usually resigned to doing so.

> I got to the point where I thought, 'No, I'm not going to do this'. I resented having to be the one to mediate and also I resented having these little heart-to-hearts with Lily about various things. If she had a worry or maybe she was concerned about Alec or something ... And she'd say, 'don't tell Alec'. And I thought, 'I'm just in the middle and I'm not having it'. (Pauline)

> I do mind mediating between them, very much so. But I feel ... maybe I don't give it a chance but I feel that all that would be happening would be that his mother would keep getting upset and Gareth wouldn't do any more. In fact he'd become worse, because if you push him to do something he'll push harder not to do it and there's no reasoning behind it at all. (Ruth)

This discussion of communication and mediation in in-law relationships has endeavoured to expand the meaning of kin-keeping. It involves much more than physical interaction associated with visiting and other forms of contact, for even women who have poor relationships with their mother-in-law can feel obliged to facilitate communication between mothers and sons and help them express their feelings for each other. This activity is rooted in normative expectations of female 'affectiveness' but in fact is socially constructed and determined by the socialization of girl children into their specific gender identity. Mothers, as the primary caretakers, are responsible for teaching children appropriate forms of gender-related behaviour and via this process become distanced from their adult sons. Eventually, when sons marry, mothers turn to daughters-in-law who, as 'naturally' caring women like themselves, relieve their own nurturing responsibilities and support the mother/son relationship. Furthermore, although daughters-in-law often resent the assignment, normative prescriptions for 'what women do' influence and reinforce their obligation to carry it out. This confirms Yanagisako's (1977) assertion that psychological explanations for what females do 'naturally', although misleading, 'carry powerful normative sanctions for there is little more condemning than to fail to do what is "natural" to one's sex' (p. 221). However, there is also a negotiated element in kin-keeping which should not be overlooked. Whilst all women are kin-keepers as a consequence of their gender and socialization, there are some aspects of kin-keeping which women are not prepared to undertake. In other words, the generalized expectation that women will accept all the responsibility for sustaining family relationships is rejected by individual women, so that kin-keeping is particularized and open to negotiation.

Kin-keeping between mothers and daughters-in-law

Kin-keeping is an important aspect of relationships between mothers-in-law and daughters-in-law. Like all social relationships, these are based on rules which enable those involved to construct meanings and provide accounts of their actions. Normative rules and common-sense knowledge are resources which people draw on to make sense of relationships and determine behaviour within them (Argyle and Henderson, 1985; Cunningham-Burley, 1985; Voysey, 1975). Relationships differ in terms of expectations and rewards but in close family relationships expectations are high, as are the levels of disappointment if they are unmet. Furthermore, the emotional energy invested in such relationships creates a corresponding increase in the potential for conflict and, therefore, the rules are complex and profuse. Argyle and Henderson (1985) suggest that rules have two major functions: firstly, to regulate behaviour and minimize conflict; secondly, to provide for an exchange of rewards which make the relationship worthwhile. Both sets of rules provide guidelines for action. Regulating or proscriptive rules suggest non-action, for example, the dictum not to interfere in the lives of married children, whilst rewarding or prescriptive rules suggest commissive action such as interest and support, which allow for relationship growth.

Rules are highly significant in relationships between mothers and daughters-in-law. Some, reflecting the varying degree of formality involved, refer to social distance, but others provide guidelines for affective behaviour and what might be expected in terms of warmth, friendliness and cooperation. Lack of role models for in-law relationships leads many women to pattern their behaviour on their perception of what is appropriate between parent and child, but if this is unrecognized or unacknowledged by the other party a sense of disappointment prevails. Caplan (1981) suggests this is because all of us find it disconcerting to encounter a woman who, for whatever reason, is not nurturant, and women seeking understanding from other women are likely to feel particularly hurt if they are let down. Moreover, if the woman is a mother or daughter (or a woman who should be like a mother or daughter) the disappointment is even more acute. It is, therefore, not surprising that women referred to the emotional investment in their relationship and their unhappiness when after they had 'obeyed all the rules' it remained empty and unfulfilling.

I always felt it was her and Ron and I was the outsider. (Marian)

I would have liked to have been close to her really but I don't think she would ever have let me. She just didn't seem to want it. (Janet)

I can't get near to her or anything. I don't know why... Do you think some people are like that, they're distant and they're not warm? I think that's how she is. I've never felt that she's interested in me. She never wants to know how I am, it's just Terry really. (Rachel)

I had a good relationship with my mum and dad and my in-law relationship has been pretty grotty. And I just wish it hadn't been like that. I regret it. And I've tried to work hard at it because I thought, if it works it's worth the effort. Not to give up easily, and get it to work like a marriage. You can easily give it up but you've got to be determined that you're going to do it. I've tried many, many times because I've thought that eventually I would succeed in getting a happy relationship. And I failed. (Annette)

People say, 'how can she not get on with you?', but there you are, you can't get on with everyone. But you do hope to get on with your daughter-in-law. And I wanted to be friendly with her but she wouldn't let you near her. She always had a barrier and kept you at a distance. I tried very very hard to like her and make things... but now I know she doesn't like me and I know she doesn't like Henry. But we don't like her now. It's very sad isn't it? (Mrs Swann)

In the past, sociological studies have tended to emphasize the positive functions of kinship (Goode, 1964; Parsons, 1964) thereby contributing to what Morgan (1975, p. 73) has called the 'family as a success story' theme. A shortcoming of these accounts is that they overlook the contradictions of kin relationships which allow for warmth and support but also place considerable limitations and stresses upon individuals. This neglect of conflict is particularly evident in analysis of generational relationships which, as Morgan points out, are central to kinship in urban society and which 'seem to have a fair degree of conflict embedded in them' (1975, p. 74). Indeed, given the amount of physical and emotional investment by women and the range of expectations which may or may not be realized, it is perhaps not surprising that conflict is a significant feature of family life. Conflict, when it is acknowledged, is frequently attributed to individual failure even in those relationships where its potential is recognized and anticipated. In relations with the mother-in-law, for example, conflict may be attributed to her personal failings. By placing blame on the individual, the contradictions between generational relationships and marital relationships as sources of strain and tension are conveniently overlooked.

The women interviewed were aware of the potential for conflict in mother-in-law and daughter-in-law relationships and many were concerned to manage tension in a way which would prevent an outbreak of overt hostility. This accords with Simmel's (1955) view that conflict is not always a sign of dislike. He suggests that preventing conflict indicates a lack of genuine affection in relationships which motivates those involved to compensate by utmost self-control and consideration. The degree of formality between mothers-in-law and daughters-in-law often precludes open dialogue and self-disclosure, thus generating unspoken conflict which neither can acknowledge. Unlike that in close relationships – say between mothers and daughters – conflict is seen as threatening and destructive. Conflict between mothers and daughters stems from an intimate knowledge of each other but mothers and daughters-in-law do not have this knowledge to draw on and, given their social boundaries, any conflict may be interpreted as an outright rejection of each other. Consequently, even where negative feelings ran high, there was little evidence of major disagreements or long-term rifts. Most women avoided family arguments at all costs, operating as peace-keepers and conciliators in their own interpersonal relationships and those between other people. Arguments, when they did occur, were generally short-lived, rarely fully resolved and often marked by lingering resentment. Only one woman felt able to disagree with her daughter-in-law without fear of the consequences, probably because in her view the younger woman was 'just like a daughter'. Others were adamant that conflict of any kind was extremely damaging with no possibility of a positive outcome.

> Me and Sally have had many an argument. She's the only one as we have. I think we understand one another as we can do that. (Mrs Jones)

> There's not an awful lot of love lost between my mother-in-law and myself, although we don't argue all the time. I don't think I could handle that anyway. I can't stand aggro with anybody but it would hurt me if it was his parents because even though there's not a lot of love lost, there's feelings there. (Wendy)

> I'm very forthright and if I have something to say I say it. But I don't with her. I've no idea why I don't. Perhaps I think that if I did it would be a step too far for Nick, and if he upset my mother like that I wouldn't like it. I think it comes from us both being second marriages, you tend to think things out a bit more and perhaps give more. You know, 'If I did that it could cause a row and is it worth causing a row over?' (Elaine)

> We've never quarrelled, there's never been any reason for it. But personally I wouldn't have a quarrel. I just don't think it's worth it at all. (Mrs Harris)

Although women go to considerable lengths to avoid conflict it is hardly surprising, given the ambiguity in in-law relationships, that arguments occasionally erupt. Indeed, some older women believed that in the last resort, arguments clarified and strengthened the relationship although these were mainly expressed views and not often practised. Most women were inclined to maintain peaceable relations by non-controversial behaviour but when conflict occurred the mother-in-law's age and experience assigned her the conciliator's role.

> I would say it there and then if necessary. I wouldn't keep it because you can make so much more of it if you hang on to a thing. You can make such a lot more of it and have a real good row and perhaps not see them anymore for a while. I would say something there and then, I'm sure I would. But I'm like that, I speak my mind. (Mrs Tagg)

> We agree to most things but if I don't agree I just say so and then it's finished. I don't carry nothing on, I just let it stop at that. (Mrs Brown)

> I've always thought that if there is anything wrong it's up to the older person to put it right. Because if it doesn't get put right it can go on out of all proportion and I think because you're the older one you're more experienced and if necessary back down and put things right. (Mrs Richardson)

Women often find it difficult to express or accept anger in personal relationships because the risks seem too high. Anger may be possible in marital relationships because it can be diffused by emotional and sexual intimacy, although this is precarious. Many women avoid expressing anger to their husbands because they are afraid to risk losing a relationship which has high status and on which they are dependent. Feelings of anger towards a husband or friend may also be suppressed because it seems incompatible with caring for someone or being cared for in return. Therefore, the mother-in-law who perceives her daughter-in-law as a friend may feel that she cannot afford to express anger because it is too explosive and may destroy her friendship.

Women's identities as peacemakers create a fear of confrontation which does not allow for openness in their personal relationships. Avoiding conflict with your mother-in-law or daughter-in-law necessarily means avoiding self-disclosure so that women's innermost feelings are obscured even to themselves and their needs are largely unrecognized and unmet. This makes it difficult for them to engage with their differences or express their feelings in a positive way.

> This is the trouble, really, I've not sat down with her and sort of sorted anything out definite. It's how I feel and how I think she's feeling. There's a lot unspoken ... It's not very often you sit down with someone is it, and say 'This is how I feel...', but then again, it's not helping our relationship at all because we don't get any further. I just let her get on with it but she obviously doesn't know how I feel and if I don't tell her she never will. (Rachel)

Few women could depend on their partners for support in conflict-ridden situations. Men, it seems, are uncomfortable when faced with the emotional problems of others. They tend to distance themselves from disputes between their mothers and wives because outward displays of emotion embarrass them and they are unsure how to react. Some take up an ostrich position, doing and saying nothing in the hope that the women will resolve the situation themselves. Others justify non-involvement by trivializing the problem or by victim-blaming, attitudes which particularly distress their wives. They are, however, effective, since it is less difficult for men to remain aloof if they can dismiss female conflict as emotional, illogical and unnecessary.

> He knew I felt upset. But Stuart is not a particularly emotional person. I mean, if you got emotional you were probably being silly. His attitude was, 'Well, you know what she's like, that's how she is, if it upsets you keep away'. His attitude was, if I went I went, if I didn't I didn't. He didn't ask me to go. (Annette)

> My husband takes the attitude that it'll all come out in the wash, and this also keeps the peace. You know, 'don't tell her how you feel...' because he doesn't want to take sides, you know. (Joyce)

Even those women who were confident of their partner's support rarely put it to the test. Perhaps doubtful of the outcome, they also followed strategies of non-confrontation and peaceful coexistence.

> He'd stand up for me. I mean, he won't have his mother browbeat him down. I mean, he won't have her talk about me. If she's in the wrong he'll stand up for me, he's never took her side against me. But I mean, sometimes if we're down there and something's been said, he'll look at me, 'don't say anything', you know. And then when we come home he'll say, 'you don't have to take any notice of my mum'. But I don't. Now it just goes over the top of my head unless I really think she's interfering. (Frances)

> I suppose if she did hurt me I'd let it lie but wail to Andrew. And he'd be my champion so I'd always win in the end. But I wouldn't really expect him to do anything about it... confront his mother or anything. Although if he wanted to I wouldn't stop him. (Deborah)

Although women might 'wail' to their husband to obtain his reassurance and support, they rarely expected him to mediate, or still less, disagree with his mother on behalf of his wife. This is just as well, since for most men mediation between family members is not one of their strongest points.

> I think at first I wanted him to do something. Yes I did, because I felt... I thought, 'You're afraid of your mother, to stand up to her'. He is, and it annoys me. (Rachel)

> I think it's reassurance you're looking for. 'Yes, I agree she is wrong...' You want your husband to recognize that something's not quite right even if he can't do anything about it... (Wendy)

> Some times the little remarks she's made have cut me and hurt me, and I haven't come home and cried or kicked the cat but it has upset me.

And maybe if he had said, 'Oh, never mind...' but his attitude has always been so abrupt, 'Well, it's your own stupid fault for going'. But I'm only trying to keep a connection. And once when he did say 'I don't know why you bother', I said, 'Well, I can't bear the thought of you and your mum not having any contact'. (Annette)

As we have seen, even when the women themselves have poor interactive relationships, daughters-in-law are concerned to maintain those between mothers and sons. Consequently, daughters-in-law were united in their opinion that conflict should never be allowed to reach a level where it provoked estrangement. There was little evidence of this but where it had occurred in mother/son relationships, the wife tried to act in the interests of both parties in an effort to reunite them. Although some felt that one should never interfere in other people's disputes, most women agreed that the wife had a responsibility to keep the lines of communication open.

A couple of years ago they had a big row and he said he wasn't going to speak to her again. I sent him up the weekend before Christmas to apologize. And he went, under pressure, and he did apologize. (Valerie)

They had a big row and he said he didn't want to go there again. It was weeks later when he discussed it so it obviously upset him a lot but he wouldn't go down. This went on for nearly twelve months. I continued to visit and so did the children but she never mentioned the fact that they'd had an argument or asked where he was, so I never got involved. In the end I think he went because it was Christmas... (Annette)

Again, these comments show that there are some aspects of kin-keeping which women will not be responsible for. Although the women encouraged their husbands to resolve conflict with their mothers, as wives they would not intervene directly between them. In other words, daughters-in-law can exercise their right to choose not to mediate if they so wish, unlike mothers-in-law who have no choice because they are restrained by the dictum not to 'interfere'. On the other hand, a daughter-in-law must maintain her own relationship with her mother-in-law even if mother and son are estranged, for avoidance looks like neglect and subjects the wife to the same criticisms as her mother-in-law.

It appears, therefore, that women are inclined toward peaceful coexistence even if peace comes at a price which involves suppressing personal feelings. In precarious relationships between in-laws confrontation seems dangerous and destructive and motivates women to resolve conflict in a way which, in reality, avoids it. This is not to suggest, however, that the mantle of conciliator rests easily on their shoulders. Women expressed considerable ambivalence about peace-keeping: they did it for their own sake and for the sake of others but it was fraught with contradictions.

Jealousy between mothers and daughters-in-law

One of the most negative and potentially destructive emotions in the mother-in-law/daughter-in-law relationship is jealousy. It is also one of the most public and stigmatized emotions and underpins the meanings which individuals attach to concepts of 'interference' and 'possessiveness'. Simmel (1955) suggests that jealousy occurs when a person feels she has a rightful claim to possess a desired object but is prevented because it belongs to someone else, although if it did not the jealous person would possess it. Furthermore, the claim to possession is frequently grounded in legality, as the legitimate claim of mother or wife, but because legal claims to love are inadequate and unenforceable, the person concerned inevitably appeals to duty and obligation. In this study women were asked a hypothetical question which required them to consider jealousy between family women and, although all of them acknowledged its existence, the majority were so conscious of its damaging effects that they strongly denied jealousy within themselves. However, women did recognize the emotion in each other and those who believed they were the target of jealousy had tried to understand and cope with it. Simmel suggests that recognizing jealousy in the other often produces a sort of unity based on the subjective need of the third party – in this case the husband/son. Certainly, women expelled a considerable amount of emotional energy in coming to terms with the other's claim and tried to create a balance in which all parties were satisfied. Unfortunately, however, in mother-in-law/daughter-in-law relationships women are separated by the person who also connects them so that one does not easily recognize the emotional work of the other.

> There was no jealousy. I could see that she loved him a lot and Douglas obviously loved her. But there was never any atmosphere between her and me. I think we had a lot of respect for each other. (Susan)

> I never felt jealous. I don't think you do when you've got sons. Your first thought is, 'isn't it nice to have girls around the house'. Because we'd got all boys so it was nicer for me than if we'd already got a girl. (Mrs Richardson)

> When I first saw them with their girlfriends I was very pleased for them but I was very jealous. You find this with mothers-in-law with sons. Because you know once they're married that's it. Even though they do think a lot of you and they come home, the mainstay is the wife. Which is as it should be, it should be that. But you still can't help being put out. You always will, you'll still have the jealous feeling and sometimes you think that you should be put first. You can't help it, but you've got to bury it, you haven't got to let them see this. (Mrs Jones)

In our society, patriarchal ideology is powerful is assigning unequal status to men and women. As a consequence, women's interests and their relationships with each other are devalued, leading them to compete for highly prized relationships with men – lovers, husbands, sons. Between mothers-in-law and daughters-in-law, therefore, jealousy may be attributed to rivalry for a man's affections but has little to do with personal antagonisms. Rather, it stems from contradictions and insecurities in the roles of wife and mother and women's pivotal relationships with men.

> I'm sure the majority of mothers-in-law must feel a twinge of jealousy because they're taking the baby away aren't they? That's probably why they're so critical, because they're jealous. (Laura)

> She's a very jealous person which gets to me a bit because I don't like jealousy and she is very jealous of me. I don't like to think I'm the object of it but the chances are that I am. And I do wonder whether part of it's jealousy on my part as well, although I've always said I'm not a jealous person and I don't think I am. But I do wonder sometimes whether it is a jealousy thing between me and my mother-in-law. (Wendy)

> Daughters-in-law do and say things that you don't really know why they're like that ... you don't know what you've done to make them behave as they do. I think some of it is to do with this word called 'love'. I think wives, some wives anyway, think the only love the husband should have should be for them. If the husband has any love for his mother, for instance, it's taking it off her, whereas in actual fact it's a completely different love. (Mrs Swann)

Jealousy, then, is subject to a number of interpretations. For example, the sense of loss experienced by some women when their sons marry may manifest itself as 'jealousy' and may be perceived as such by daughters-in-law. Mothers-in-law, however, rarely admit to jealousy because of its negative connotations but they will admit to loss.

When people talk about jealousy in in-law relationships the influence of stereotypes becomes increasingly apparent. Stereotypes of mothers-in-law are overwhelmingly negative: intolerant, interfering and possessive are just a few of the adjectives applied, so that mothers-in-law as a group have become degraded and discredited. Evidence from the study suggests that most people were influenced by stereotypes to some extent – a point to which we shall return in the next chapter. What concerns us here is the kind of stereotype: the 'possessive' mother-in-law, the 'interfering' mother-in-law and so on. For example, when discussing conflict-producing emotions, mothers-in-law were particularly concerned about the dangers of possessiveness.

> I should tell any woman not to be so selfish. Because that's all jealousy is. It's just selfishness and possessiveness. (Mrs Orchard)

> Try not to be jealous. But you can't because some people are built like that. I'm not, I'm not that type. In other words, it means she's been overprotective doesn't it? Which is all wrong. (Mrs Tagg)

> As for letting them go, I think you start doing that when they first meet a girl. You know, you don't have to be possessive. That's the biggest mistake, when you demand their attention too much. You've had your life, you know ... (Mrs York)

> You see, it's lovely to love your children but I think some people mix love up with attachment and possessiveness. That's a terrible thing,

possessiveness or jealousy. It destroys marriages, it destroys lots of things. So I think that's what you've got to keep away from if you can. (Mrs Harris)

'Possessive' mothering is something of a misnomer which contains negative overtones masking complicated feelings. It is a social and psychological construct relating to women who have devoted their adult lives to marriage and the family. Many older women have been socialized into their primary roles as wives and mothers and, as a consequence, they have a vested interest in their families and an expectation of involvement in the lives of their grown-up children. If this is not realized they may suffer loss-related feelings which make them anxious and insecure. Whilst I do not wish to suggest that all middle-aged women are inextricably bound up with family life, there are few realistic alternatives for those in this age group who have spent their adult lives looking after children. This gives rise to an image of the 'possessive' mother, although in reality no such person exists. It is a stereotype which, although false, influences the way people think about a particular group of women and, therefore, appears to be true. Consequently, women in the daughter-in-law group referred to the stereotype when talking about mothers whose love for their sons seemed exaggerated and emotionally constricting. Some daughters-in-law spoke of their husbands as men 'caught in the middle' who, finding it difficult to take action which seemed to reject their mothers, inevitably took no action at all. From the wife's point of view, especially in the early years of the marriage, such behaviour may be interpreted as reluctance on the part of her husband to put her interests before those of his mother. In short, what is perceived as 'possessive' mothering by the wife is often related to her own sense of rejection and insecurity.

> I think you can feel a bit jealous of that closeness between mother and son. And feel a bit left out, you know. You do feel something like jealousy at first. I used to think I did, being young and newly married. I always felt she was a bit of a threat. You know, she'd got this hold over him. (Gaynor)

> I did wonder if I'd be number one ... You know, if it came to the crunch would I be the one he chose. I did worry about that because you don't know do you? I mean, there are some where their mother always comes first. (Deborah)

> Well, there have been times when it's been very difficult to see them together because ... It does hurt sometimes because Tom's the only child and he does think a lot of his parents and I wouldn't have it any other way. And he makes a fuss of them. But she's so all-engulfing that sometimes it is difficult. (Wendy)

'Possessive' mothering is a construct which seems to make sense in relation to sons more than daughters. In the process of establishing gender identity a girl retains her identification with her mother and although the process of separating and defining herself as an autonomous individual may be difficult, the mother and daughter do not 'lose' each other because importance is attached to the mother/

daughter bond. For a boy, however, the process of establishing an independent sense of self is wholly different. In order to establish his gender identity he must separate from his mother and, importantly, she must make it possible for him to make the break. In other words, 'successful' mothers raise sons to be autonomous adults able to function in the adult world, form relationships with women and eventually marry and have children. Even so, the mother remains an important and obvious presence who essentially relates to the child in her son. The wife, however, relates to the man not the child, and therefore may deny the mother/son bond because masculinity rejects childishness. Therefore, masculinity is not only achieved during childrearing in mother/son relationships but is reproduced by wives in heterosexual relationships. Moreover, if 'successful' mothering means raising sons to become husbands it questions the notion of 'possessiveness' when the goal is achieved. It may be, therefore, that accusations of 'possessiveness' reflect the wife's insecurities because her need for support and reassurance from her husband is not being met. This is not to dismiss the views of those daughters-in-law who experienced their mothers-in-law as 'possessive' but rather to suggest that 'possessiveness' as a construct and an experience has more meaning for wives than for mothers.

> I think she was just a selfish and possessive mother. I mean, she probably must have known that it was ridiculous to expect her sons not to get married and stop at home forever but I think that's what she would have liked. And I'm sure if she'd have thought there'd been any problems in our marriage, you know, he would have been welcomed back with more than open arms. I think she'd have been quite pleased if any of them ever did run back home. (Gaynor)

> She wants him to live closer to her. Oh yes, she wants him to move to where she is so she can have more contact with him. She's just what you call possessive. She definitely is a possessive mother. She's always saying, 'Why don't you apply for a job down here'.... I mean, it isn't 'How do you feel, Rachel, would you like to come and live here?' It's 'Would you Terry?', and you can drag her with you if you like. But that's it. I just don't think she sees me as his wife yet, and as part of the family. I don't think she's accepted me at all. (Rachel)

On the other hand, Mrs Swann, who described her relationship with her daughter-in-law as disappointing and sad, held a view which contradicts those expressed above but which reflects those held by all the women in the mother-in-law group: that the stability of a child's marriage is all-important even if it means parents making sacrifices that are personally distressing.

> I hope with all my heart they stay as a family. I'd hate them to break up or have a split of any sort. I feel that we're better to keep out of it and let them live their lives. And that's what we do. We just don't know what's going on. (Mrs Swann)

Despite the negative message in stereotypes, the majority of mothers-in-law seemed to have established warm, friendly and easy-going relationships with their daughters-in-law. They had very few criticisms, and still less any expressions of outright dislike. This accords with Forcey's (1987) study of mothers of sons, who says that the few negative comments she received about daughters-in-law usually referred to personality differences or class biases which probably held for others too. Generally, most tension seems to be felt by daughters-in-law and this, as might be expected, tends to diminish as the marriage develops and grows stronger. Consequently, daughters-in-law who said they disliked their mothers-in-law were either in the early stages of marriage or still had a number of unresolved differences, but these were the minority. Most women, daughters-in-law and mothers-in-law, mellowed over the years and in time developed a remarkable degree of tolerance and sometimes genuine affection towards each other.

The 'interfering' mother-in-law

As we have seen, potential for conflict between parents and children-in-law exists because these relationships are not clearly regulated in our society. We have no formal rules governing interaction between in-laws, only rule-guided behaviour (Cunningham-Burley, 1985) to which people refer in order to interpret and explain their actions. For example, there is a widespread ethos that married children should be independent and allowed to lead their own lives, a belief which finds expression in that most common of in-law stereotypes – the 'interfering mother-in-law'. The influence of this stereotype is pervasive. It warns women about the dangers of interfering in the lives of married children and leads some to practise self-imposed avoidance to a degree beyond that which they or their children prefer. However, by restricting their involvement, women may find themselves accused of neglect and blamed by their daughters-in-law for not caring enough. Thus, the fine line between interference and neglect represents a classic 'double bind' for mothers-in-law who, by self-regulation, make themselves vulnerable to criticism and blame.

The rule prohibiting interference is the most influential in mother-in-law and daughter-in-law relationships and was frequently referred to by the women interviewed. Generally, 'not interfering' was an umbrella term used to identify any number of restraints which mothers-in-law should impose on their behaviour including action and non-action, advice-giving and verbal criticism. Not surprisingly, mothers-in-law themselves are particularly conscious of these restrictions. As a group they were extremely sensitive to negative stereotypes and how mothers-in-law are portrayed by the media generally. Anxious to be 'good' mothers-in-law, they drew upon a repertoire of resources to guide their behaviour including normative rules and personal experience.

> I can't remember consciously thinking when my eldest son got married, 'Now, I must be careful not to be like my mother-in-law', but that's not to say I didn't. Subconsciously I probably did. (Mrs Richardson)

> I wasn't conscious of the interfering mother-in-law when I got married because my mother-in-law didn't interfere. But I was when my son got married. You tend to think, 'Oh, I mustn't say this, I mustn't say that'. So yes, you are conscious of it. You know, perhaps being a bit

domineering and saying what you think. Yes, it's important not to interfere. (Mrs Orchard)

The combined influence of stereotypes and experiences had not escaped women in the daughter-in-law group, particularly those with adult children of their own. Although not asked a direct question, they frequently volunteered information about their projected role as mothers-in-law, describing their intentions in a way which clearly demonstrates how women anticipate critical life transitions and construct appropriate forms of behaviour.

Oh, I've been very influenced by my mother-in-law. Definitely. I'm absolutely determined to be nothing like her. In fact, I think I shall be so bending over backwards not to be interfering they probably won't even know they've got a mother-in-law. They'll probably think I don't care about them. (Gaynor)

Gaynor's comment illustrates women's awareness of the boundaries between interference and neglect and the dangers of appearing not to care. Indeed, although individual definitions of the boundary line varied considerably, they all stemmed from the need to strike a balance between distance and closeness in a way that satisfied both women. The concepts of interference and neglect tend to become more ambiguous after the birth of a grandchild because new mothers, anxious to appear competent, are often reluctant to seek help and yet feel neglected if none is offered. On the other hand, restraining factors in family relationships tend to continue into grandmotherhood, so that mothers-in-law sanction their involvement, assistance and advice. Indeed, one of the problems mothers-in-law find difficult to resolve is how to express concern about grandchildren which is not interpreted as criticism. Mothers-in-law often refrained from voicing anxieties or offering advice in case they were seen as 'fussy' or worse 'interfering', although, again, by practicing restraint they risked being though of as uncaring. Furthermore, it seems these fears are justified given that expressions of concern are sometimes perceived as undermining the mother's ability to care for her child.

We crossed swords when Varena was about 2 and she stopped eating. Varena went ten days without eating anything and she [mother-in-law] used to beg me to give her a biscuit. I said, 'I will not give her a biscuit. If she's not prepared to eat meals she will not have biscuits. There is no point in me struggling to get this child to eat if you are going to fill her up with biscuits and sweets'. So she didn't. She wasn't very pleased about it but she took my point. (Valerie)

In relation to children the notion of non-interfering, which restricts advice-giving to the mother and overindulgence of the child, is linked to perceptions of a positive grandparenting role. A frequent source of irritation for daughters-in-law focused on 'spoiling' grandchildren. Much of this centred on food and the grandmother's persistence in providing treats against the mother's wishes, and is a particular conflict arising from the women's joint orientation around the child.

> She was always buying them rubbish, sweets and chocolate which were no good for them. I did have it out with her but she took no notice, she kept buying. (Marian)

> She spoiled the children giving them rubbishy sweets all the time. I used to really create about this because she would not give them to me so that I could give them to the children a few at a time. She used to give them straight to them, and you know what that's like, trying to take chocolate off little children. (Janet)

Food occupies a unique position in concepts of the mothering role, for not only must the mother plan and provide a well-balanced diet, she must also ensure that her child eats it. Given that many children have a marked preference for 'junk' food, persuading them to eat 'proper' meals can be an uphill task. Consequently, mothers try to discipline and control the child's eating habits by limiting sweets to rewards for good behaviour and occasional treats. However, the grandmother may take a different view. She has no direct authority or responsibility for the child and, therefore, no interest in a disciplinary role. Whilst rule-guided behaviour warns her not to spoil her grandchild, in practice she expects allowances for a grandmother's indulgence. Because access to grandchildren is limited and controlled by the mother, most daughters-in-law are tolerant of indulgent behaviour provided their own rights are not subverted. In this respect, food is highly significant for it is an effective means of controlling adults and children. Consequently, the grandmother's refusal to cooperate over restricted foods subverts parental authority and controls the mother via the child.

The majority of daughters-in-law said that, at some point in the relationship, their mother-in-law had behaved in a way they construed as interference. Interference, as experienced by the daughter-in-law, seems to be related to the mother's need to maintain a role after her son marries. She may not object to the marriage or his partner but fears relegation to the periphery of his new life. Interference can also occur when the mother perceives her daughter-in-law as very different from herself, or if the couple's life-style fails to comply with traditional family forms. On the other hand, because mothers-in-law are always mindful not to interfere, it is unlikely that suggestions or opinions expressed in ordinary conversation are intended to influence the couple, although they may be perceived as such. Manipulation, real or imagined, is a source of irritation for daughters-in-law, even though it is largely unsuccessful. Most women, self-confident and secure in their marriage, neither complied with nor opposed their mother-in-law when their opinions differed. As a strategy for avoiding conflict there seems to be maximum advantage in taking the line of least resistance, listening politely and then continuing as before. Indeed, most daughters-in-law had a remarkable amount of tolerance for verbal 'interference', as long as it did not go beyond the level where their own position was subverted.

> Yes, she does interfere. On occasions she will put her own opinion as to why we haven't got kids, why we keep going around on motorbikes instead of buying a nice little car. And in that way she interferes because it isn't just commenting, it's sort of, 'why don't you grow up?', which I take as interference. But we wouldn't let her actually interfere in our

> decisions and because there's distance between us, that's fairly easy. So she tries to influence, but we are not influenced. (Ruth)

> She does meddle a bit. Occasionally I feel really cross but I don't tackle her about it. Well ... she considers it to be done for the best of reasons, to help us out. So I don't really see it as a problem ... (Nancy)

Some behaviour, however, ignores interpersonal boundaries and even goes beyond those of normal politeness.

> I think a lot of things niggled me more when we were first married than they do now. I mean, she would come in and wash the dishes and move the ornaments to where she thought they ought to be. And that sort of thing does niggle. Now, if she comes in and puts the apron on and washes the dishes, fine, I'm able to let her do that. It doesn't irritate me anymore. But I don't think anybody should do that, I think it's very rude to come into somebody's house and start moving the ornaments around or whatever. But with my mother-in-law, it's to do with possessiveness – 'It's Tom's house and I'm part of it'. (Wendy)

Whilst such behaviour looks like 'possessiveness' and is, indeed, tactless, it often stems from interest or a desire to be helpful. However, it is an understandable source of irritation for daughters-in-law because it seems to imply criticism of their home-making abilities and, importantly, infringes on the couple's right to privacy.

Interference, then, is the greatest taboo in in-law relationships, and awareness of its dangers emerged clearly from women in the study groups. Generally the rule prohibiting interference is inflexible, although in individual relationships both interference and advice are relativistic and open to some negotiation. Importantly, the recipient defines the status of what is being offered, so that another's opinion when it is welcome is interpreted as advice but when it is not is construed as interference. As older women, mothers-in-law have little power and influence in our society, but they do have considerable expertise in domestic matters and, therefore, their knowledge is valid and important to them. They may genuinely wish to share this knowledge by offering advice to their daughters-in-law but it is the younger woman who has the power to define its status and to choose whether to accept it or not.

Quite simply, parents should never 'interfere' in the lives of married children and, in extreme cases, such behaviour justifies severely curtailing contact. However, women did mention rare instances, such as serious financial or emotional difficulties, when it was felt that mothers-in-law might legitimately interfere. It is difficult to estimate how frequently these events occur in the 'average' marriage and, indeed, whether parents would know about them if they did. Clearly, if something is badly wrong parents might be justified in assuming that their intervention could hardly make matters worse and might do some good, but, in normal circumstances, mothers-in-law agree that married children should be left to lead their own lives, make their own decisions and bring up their children as they see fit. On the other hand, the 'good' mother-in-law is always ready to provide emotional and practical support when asked, for failure to respond at this juncture marks her out as uncaring. Normative rules which prohibit interference also allow a positive role in circumstances defined by the daughter-in-law and, to some extent, the son. Therefore, the limits of in-law involvement are both self-regulated and regulated by others.

Warmth, affection and positive regard

This chapter, thus far, has concentrated on negative aspects of the relationship and the reader might be forgiven for believing that positive emotional interaction between mothers and daughters-in-law barely exists. This, of course, is a mistaken belief, although it is clear that the realities of mother-in-law relationships are far more complex than, for example, popular media images and stereotypes suggest. Consequently, whilst some are clearly beset by conflicts and hostility, others contain high levels of tolerance and real affection. Indeed, it is fair to say that, at some time and to some degree, the majority of relationships contain all these emotions. Ambivalence and uncertainty mean that women must constantly assess and reassess their feelings for each other. These rarely remain fixed for a lifetime, and hostility usually gives way to tolerance and peaceful coexistence. Even when conflict remains, time has a softening effect making sadness and disappointment the primary emotions in unfulfilled relationships.

The first point about opportunities for positive relationships is that there is some descrepancy between attitudes towards affinal roles generally, and attitudes towards individual relationships. The first fall roughly into two categories which represent the views of mothers-in-law on the one hand, and daughters-in-law on the other. For example, mothers-in-law held mainly positive views, which certainly did not reflect any desire to hold on to sons. Mothers want their sons to grow up, form adult relationships and eventually marry, not least because becoming a mother-in-law has the potential of becoming a grandmother. Daughters-in-law tended to be more circumspect. They spoke of individual incompatibilities but also recognized that tensions arose from the structure of the relationship.

> I don't think there are many positive aspects, it's a relationship that's fraught most of the time. I suppose that's positive, having an older woman you can turn to, hopefully be friends with. I think it must depend a lot on the personalities involved. You know, if you can break down these rigid roles, 'I'm a mother and I know best because I've been through it all', sort of thing. (Pauline)

> I really can't think of any positive aspects. I suppose you've got a duty. They're your husband's parents and you've got a duty to get on with them. And see them when you can, especially if there are grandchildren. (Vicky)

Individual relationships reflected a wide range of experiences but in the majority of cases women got along tolerably well, or had developed very positive feelings for each other.

> I don't think there are any particular benefits for me at all, to be honest. It's beneficial to Tom and indirectly to the children. But all I seem to get is a load of aggravation... (Wendy)

> Well, in my relationship we don't have anything positive. It's as simple as that, we don't have any at all. It exists on my side from a sense of duty and hers to keep contact with her son. (Elaine)

> We have a close relationship. Not stifling, but close. (Sylvia)

> I'm very, very fond of her. She's a very fussy person and you always have to go overboard and make a fuss. Now, I don't feel false doing that although I'm not a fussy person at all. But I've always tried to go out of my way to be nice to Patrick's mum and we've had our ups and downs but... (Dianne)

> The thing I like best with me and Caroline now is friendship. I mean, if I go to the cottage on Sunday she'll bring me back and she's supposed to go straight back. I leave about eightish and she's here at eleven and half past chattering away. So the relationship is nice. (Mrs Brown)

The warmth of feeling between Mrs Brown and Caroline has not been easily achieved. First impressions were not favourable and suspicion further impeded the relationship but with time the women reconciled their differences and established a positive concern for each other.

> Since we've got to know one another better we say what we think now. We get it off our chests and we get on very well. And she's said, 'When you think, Mother, all these years we've edged one another. One hasn't known what the other's been thinking. We've never got underneath it'. But these last few years... we say what we think and we don't hold back. And I think that's just with the years and getting used to one another. (Mrs Brown)

The concept of 'talk' was frequently mentioned and seems to be a significant factor in the way women assess their relationships. Studies have revealed gender-related differences in male and female conversation and suggest that talk is the substance of women's relationships (Johnson and Aries, 1983; Spender, 1980). Women are more self-disclosing about intimate problems, family concerns and personal doubts and fears and often prefer to talk to each other rather than to men. Although women put high value on marital relationships and may confide in their husbands, most have at least one female in whom they trust. Women also attach more importance to kinship than men, particularly ties with female kin and significantly with mothers and daughters. Bonds between women kin and friends are often formed as a consequence of their responsibilities for childcare and domestic management. Thus in the private domain female bonds are a resource for mutual aid and emotional expression (O'Connor, 1992; Willmott, 1987; Rubin, 1976; Young and Willmott, 1957)

Given this, it seems reasonable to suggest that women use talk to assess the

Emotional Investment

quality of their relationships. As we have seen, stresses occur when rigid communication patterns prevent a common understanding and, therefore, it is not surprising that both mothers-in-law and daughters-in-law attach considerable importance to talk. They acknowledge the limitations on simulating mother/daughter bonds but hope instead to become friends and, for women, the fabric of friendship is self-disclosure. However, there is another dimension to friendship or friendly relations between mothers and daughters-in-law for they are linked together in a kinship network. Part of the lay understanding of kinship is an affective element which allows for positive concern and mutual interest in each other's welfare and, therefore, even where women described their relationship as friendly rather than intimate, significant levels of confidence existed between them.

> Yes, I can talk to her about anything you know. In fact at one point when we were going through a bad patch... we ended up going to marriage guidance. And if anything she took my side more than his. Which I must admit I found very strange with a woman with an only child. But she did. (Valerie)

> Oh yes, I can confide in her. Very much so. We confide in each other. I don't think there's anything I wouldn't tell her. I've certainly not kept anything from her so far. (Mrs York)

> I don't think she'd keep anything back for fear of worrying me. I hope she wouldn't. And I tell her most things... (Vicky)

Some daughters-in-law had mothers-in-law whose traditional domestic role had prevented opportunities to form close friendships outside the kin network. The younger women were quite prepared to act as confidantes but, sometimes with good reason, had reservations about making personal disclosures themselves.

> She confides in me, but I think she does that because I think she feels closer to me than the other two [daughters-in-law] and she's got no daughters. I don't mind. She's got nobody else. But no, I don't share confidences with her, I'm not a confiding person. I tend to go in on myself and deal with it myself. If I can't I talk to my mum. If there was anything wrong between me and Jeff I'd tell my mum. Anything else I'd talk to Jeff. But it would be my mum, it wouldn't be his mum. (Frances)

> I used to tell her all my problems until my daughter became pregnant. And we didn't want it broadcast really, because she was very young and... Well, we might as well have told the town crier. So these days I hold back a bit and only tell her what I think she ought to know. (Nancy)

Privacy and self-disclosure are, of course, relative concepts although everyone has a final boundary beyond which they cannot reveal themselves to others. Individuals have a right to withhold personal emotions and feelings from some people and to choose to disclose them to others. Bates (1964) suggests that one form of privacy is a response to an unwanted actual or potential intrusion, that is the exclusion of some people whom we wish to prevent having certain information about us. Another form of privacy is that which protects the self from revealing thoughts or actions, which to have known would damage existing relationships.

> Well, I wouldn't talk to her about men. I mean, I've had one or two offers and I have been out with one since I've been married. There was nothing in it ... but, Oh no, I'd never tell her about that. (Tracey)

> There are lots of things that relate to my upbringing and my relationship with my mother and father. And I don't like discussing that with Lily. It feels very disloyal to my mother ... I just don't want her comments on my upbringing. I'm sensitive to that. (Pauline)

Restrictions on self-revelation are also imposed to protect others and may prevent one woman confiding in another even when she would wish to. For example, many women concealed anxieties about their health out of a concern not to worry their families. Bates suggests that such behaviour reveals the taken-for-granted nature of privacy, since people only become aware of the boundaries if they want to remove them but fear doing so.

> I do confide in them and they confide in me. I don't think there's anything we wouldn't tell each other. I don't think so. A few months ago I was worried because I'd got a lump on my breast and I didn't tell anybody only Len until I'd got it sorted out, because I didn't want anybody to worry. I wouldn't because it's unfair to worry somebody else. (Mrs Richardson)

Of course, not all women confided in their mother-in-law or daughter-in-law. Obviously, women whose relationships lacked an affective dimension saw little advantage in self-disclosure, believing that concealment at least limited their vulnerability to disapproval. Personal characteristics were also significant since some women were inclined towards secrecy whilst others described themselves as 'open books'. And again, protection of others figured strongly, particularly the desire to protect one's own parents from unnecessary worry.

> I don't confide in my daughter or my daughter-in-law because I don't want to pile my worries on them. I wouldn't pile my worries on them because they've got enough of their own. But they tell me. If anything isn't going right they let me know, and they tell me anything that does. (Mrs Brown)

> No, you couldn't trust her. I mean, she talks about other people to us so she must do it back. So no from that point of view and no because she's not sympathetic. I don't think I'd confide in my own mum either because I think of my mum as somebody who has to be protected. She's had enough problems in her life so she's the last person I'd confide any sort of problems or upheaval. (Elaine)

On no, I could never tell her anything at all. But I've never confided in my own parents because I didn't want them to have the worry. I do confide in my twin sister. And I confide in my husband except regarding his mother of course. (Joyce)

One positive aspect of the mother/daughter-in-law relationship is having another woman with whom to share concerns about the husband/son. For example, daughters-in-law are often reluctant to discuss their husband's faults with outsiders because to do so seems disloyal or inflates the problem more than they would wish. Very often all that is required is a sounding board which enables the wife to work through her feelings without leaving herself open to unwanted criticism or advice. Here her mother-in-law is a valuable resource since an intimate knowledge of her son's qualities and failings allows her to take a balanced view but is unlikely to alter her feelings for him. This represents a rare circumstance when mothers-in-law are more highly valued than mothers. Daughters are particularly sensitive about their mother's view of their husbands because they often criticize beyond an acceptable level. Furthermore, an excessively partisan view reflects on the daughter herself since it implies that, ultimately, she chose the wrong partner.

I do confide in her. Well, I often have a moan about Russell. (Sylvia)

If I'd got a moan about Andrew... I know I could have a jolly good moan to my mother-in-law and it wouldn't matter because she loves him as much as I do, and it won't turn her against him. But I couldn't go to my mother because she would be totally on my side and that's not always what you want. I could go to my mother-in-law and say, 'Do you know what he's done...?' and she'd sympathize but it wouldn't turn her against him. Now if I told my mother she'd go mad and I wouldn't want that. (Deborah)

An important reason for choosing not to confide marital problems to outsiders is reflected in the nature of the marital relationship itself. Oakley suggests that marriage is governed by an 'ethic of privacy' (1976, p. 83) which conceals much of what happens within it. Husband and wife live together in domestic privacy and, unless there is a gross disturbance, they are protected from criticism and the success of their marriage is unquestioned. They are expected to be loyal to each other even under the most stressful circumstances and to disclose little, if anything, about their intimate relationship to others. Consequently, stresses and conflicts are concealed and people faced with marital problems hesitate to share their anxieties in case they seem disloyal. Furthermore, it has been suggested that women more than men are bound by a 'coercion of privacy' because of their primary location in the domestic sphere (Dahl and Snare, 1978). Here much of their responsibility is to protect men from the discomforts of domestic life, so that women internalize problems and blame themselves for the failures of others. Furthermore, inequalitites in the marriage relationship and their economic dependency on men mean that women are expected to tolerate a great deal from their partners, yet feel bound to 'keep it in the family' and thereby protect their partners' reputation.

Friendly Relations?

> I wouldn't go to a friend with it because I would feel that's disloyal to him. If somebody said to me, 'Well, I'm just about fed up with him, he really is getting on my nerves. We're not getting on, we're going through a right bad patch...', I would think that's being disloyal to her husband. It's just a sticky patch and it seems disloyal to blame your husband. But I think the main reason is my mother-in-law's not going to interfere. She's not going to come out with constructive advice. She would never do anything like that. So those are the reasons. It's keeping it in the family and all I need is a sounding board, no more than that. (Valerie)

It seems clear that talk is not only gendered, it is situational even between those of the same gender. Although self-disclosure is a test of intimacy between women talk is always rule-governed, and even in relationships described as 'close' there were some topics which could not be discussed and some emotions which could not be expressed.

This chapter, then, has been concerned with women's responsibilities in three important areas: kin-keeping, peace-keeping and tension-management within the family. It has shown how women, as wives and mothers, keep contacts and maintain links between their own and their husbands' families and how, in the emotional realm of family life, they mediate between family members, sustaining relationships and improving the quality of those relationships. The chapter has also examined women's identities as conciliators in their own interpersonal relationships and those between other people, revealing how an inclination towards the ethic of peaceful coexistence subverts expression of their own individual needs. And in the area of tension-management, analysis has endeavoured to discredit the notion that personal characteristics – the 'selfish' daughter-in-law, the 'possessive' mother-in-law – are to blame for conflict between affinal women by revealing the structural patterns which underpin in-law relationships.

In the triad of mother/son/wife activated by marriage, the two women provide a convenient scapegoat for family tensions past and present. We have seen how men control their availability in an emotional and physical sense, thereby limiting their support for both wives and mothers and giving neither woman 'what she wants'. But because the women share an intimate bond with the man which they want to maintain at all costs, they sometimes find it easier to blame each other for his faults. Consequently, mothers blame their daughters-in-law for keeping them from their sons rather than admit the sons do not respond in the way they would like; and wives blame their mothers-in-law for 'possessiveness' and 'interference' rather than confront their husbands for not supporting their own definition of the marital boundary.

Chapter 4

Humour and Social Control

Humour is an important dimension of in-law relationships in Western society because of the special cultural framework set up by the mother-in-law joke. This is a unique phenomenon as no other family or domestic relationship is institutionalized in popular culture in the same way.

Although humour is only one dimension of social control, it is particularly effective in regulating potentially stressful relations between in-laws. Its controlling function in such relationships can be understood by examining two broad areas: joking behaviour and joking abuse, and the implications of negative imagery portrayed in mother-in-law jokes and its influence on perceptions and conduct. What follows, therefore, is a consideration of the form and meaning of joking relationships between family members, and also the cultural stereotype of the mother-in-law as illustrated in jokes made by popular entertainers.

Joking relationships and joking behaviour

Many writers concerned with the meanings and effects of joking behaviour and jokes have commented on the conspicuous lack of analysis within the sociological literature (Powell and Paton, 1988; Whitehead, 1976; Zijderveld, 1968). Therefore, it is necessary to refer, like them, to anthropologists whose writings on joking relationships are more prolific (Rigby, 1968; Christensen, 1963; Radcliffe-Brown, 1952), and whose analysis will provide a useful background for what is to follow. Also as with them, the most productive starting point seems to be Radcliffe-Brown's analysis, since it allows us to draw parallels with forms of informal joking behaviour between men and women in industrial societies. Radcliffe-Brown suggests that joking relationships are a peculiar combination of pretended hostility and genuine friendliness associated with relations of conjunction and disjunction. They are founded on 'permitted disrespect' between specific people in specific relational positions to each other, generally those who may treat each other as equals. In stateless societies[1] this usually means people of the same or alternate generations. The first are potential sexual partners and joking relationships between these individuals often coexist with formal avoidance rituals prohibiting sexual relations with certain related others. For example, in many societies it is desirable to marry a cross-cousin, that is, the daughter of the mother's brother. Consequently, cousins of this kind are potential wives or brothers-in-law. This type of marriage is often accompanied by a joking relationship between cousins in which no-one may take offence. The persons involved are of the same generation and are classified as equals. Therefore, mutual disrespect and licence is perfectly acceptable (Radcliffe-Brown, 1952).

The other acceptable joking relationship is between grandparent and grandchild and this allows some comparisons with grandparental relationships in industrial societies. Both are founded on the principle of asymmetrical relations between parents and children, bound by considerations of respect for those of proximate generations. Relations with grandparents, however, are relatively free of restraint and marked by attitudes and behaviour approaching friendly equality. Frequently, these take the form of joking relationships: institutional bantering and reciprocal horseplay which is not meant seriously and must be taken in good part.

The customs of joking and avoidance are frequently associated in stateless societies and have the same social function. They provide a means for controlling potential conflicts, particularly those which arise from the divergence of interests associated with marriage. Neither avoidance nor joking must be looked upon as signs of hostility. The mutual respect between a man and his in-laws is based upon friendship and designed to prevent conflict. As Radcliffe-Brown points out, quarrels spoil friendship but it is impossible to quarrel with someone with whom your contacts are regulated by convention. Given this, it does seem that extreme avoidance often practised between son-in-law and mother-in-law is less concerned with incest taboos (Aberle, 1961; Freud, 1953) than the measure of respect for those in proximate generations – that is, appropriate behaviour prescribed between parents and children and extended to other relatives and non-relatives. Even so, in those societies where joking and avoidance relationships coexist, anthropologists appear generally to accept that joking relationships between persons of different sex indicate they are potential sexual partners, whilst avoidance relationships indicate they are not. However, this does not hold true for industrial societies, where informal avoidance practised by in-laws frequently coexists with joking relationships between them.

It is worth mentioning at this point that 'joking relationship' is something of a misnomer when discussing this particular form of interaction and exchange between sons and mothers-in-law. Certainly, it is very different from that described by Radcliffe-Brown. Here, the joking relationship is a permitted and mutual aspect of social action, involving reciprocal exchanges between people who consider themselves equals. We shall discover, however, that joking between sons and mothers-in-law is not based on friendly equality but, in a very real sense, is used by men to regulate their mothers-in-law and also their wives. Therefore, as far as the study is concerned, it is more accurate to say that *some* men control their mother-in-law relationships by jokes, joking behaviour and joking abuse, than to imply that mutual and reciprocal joking relationships between sons and mothers-in-law are commonplace. Nevertheless, the term 'joking relationship' is retained but is used as others have used it in sociological studies of humour between gender and generations; that is, with specific reference to power relationships and social control (Whitehead, 1976; Zijdverveld, 1968; Sykes, 1966).

Sykes' (1966) study of cross-gender relations in a Glasgow print works is a useful analysis of informal behaviour between men and women and provides relevant insights into joking relationships in the family context. In his study,

Sykes draws on the work of Radcliffe-Brown but extends his analysis to show that, in industrial settings, joking behaviour is found between both potential and prohibited sexual partners. However, patterns of behaviour differ significantly in relation to particular cross-gender groups depending on their sexual 'availability' to each other. Between young men and young women, for example, exchanges were initiated by the men and encouraged by the women. Their behaviour was light-hearted but always restrained and marked by an avoidance of overt obscenity, indicating in, Sykes' view, their potential as permitted and available sexual partners. Between 'old' men and young women, who were prohibited sexual partners, all forms of obscene banter and horseplay including publicly kissing and petting were permitted, initiated by the men but, again, often 'led on' by the women. Relations between men and young women, therefore, consisted almost entirely of joking relationships with the distinction that open obscenity between young men and young women was not permitted. Furthermore, Sykes observed that men and young women did not engage in serious conversation but that all exchanges between them were conducted in terms of the joking relationship.

Joking relationships in other cross-gender categories were somewhat different. Both old and young men and old men and 'old' women exchanged obscene banter but their behaviour was marked by an absence of physical horseplay and, significantly, people in all three groups also engaged in serious conversation. Symmetrical relations existed between old men and young men, and old men and old women, in that persons of either sex could initiate banter, but between old women and young men such exchanges were acceptable only if initiated by the women. Furthermore, their behaviour was restricted to verbal banter; open displays of physical contact between the two groups were prohibited.

These observations underpin Sykes' assertion that joking and joking behaviour is found not only between people who are potential sexual partners, but also between those where a sexual relationship is prohibited. This is a marked departure from Radcliffe-Brown who suggests that joking relationships generally exist between people who may marry, whilst avoidance is practised between those who may not. Furthermore, in stateless societies, permitted horseplay found, for example, between cross-cousins who are desirable marriage partners, is absent in joking relationships between those of marriageable age in industrial societies, that is, young women and young men. Indeed, according to Sykes, physical contact is most commonly found in one of the tabooed relationships as regards marriage, that between young women and old men. This, then, is the converse of joking relationships and avoidance rituals referred to by Radcliffe-Brown. In industrial societies, courtship behaviour between young people is marked by restraint particularly on the part of the female, whilst 'permitted disrespect' is often found between people who are unlikely sexual partners. Furthermore, Sykes suggests that the joking relationships in the print works were generally much cruder than those men and women displayed in their private lives. The reason for this is that the factory provided an opportunity for sexual contact not available in other settings. Therefore, in Sykes' view, 'In these circumstances the behaviour patterns that regulated sexual relations required strong emphasis. Hence the crude but powerful nature of the joking relationship' (1966, p. 193).

If we draw on Sykes' observations to analyze joking relationships between in-laws, a number of contrasts and comparisons can be identified. Sykes suggests that exchanges of obscene banter between old women and young men were acceptable to both but only if initiated by the women. However, in relationships between men and their mothers-in-law, women do not appear to be the primary initiators of such conduct and when banter does take place it is invariably initiated by the man. Furthermore, unlike in the print works, banter between mothers-in-law and sons-in-law is not overtly obscene, although some people feel able to exchange risqué jokes. Rather, it seems to reflect the socially and individually imposed boundaries between in-laws which prohibit or prescribe certain forms of behaviour. Indeed, jokes and joking behaviour are themselves powerful means of boundary maintenance, for in any joking situation there is a joker and a victim, and the former, if only momentarily, controls the latter. There is also a significant difference between 'telling a joke' and 'making a joke'. Telling a joke to someone is inclusive and breaks down barriers. For example, if a man tells his mother-in-law a joke his behaviour suggests a shared understanding and, if only temporarily, a sense of equality between them. On the other hand, making a joke which is intended to ridicule an individual or a group of individuals is exclusive. Therefore, mother-in-law jokes which target a particular female group and rely on simplistic and unflattering stereotyping are powerful precisely because of their excluding effects on women.

> They joke and can by very sarcastic with one another. They banter together quite a lot, but that's just the way they are, you know. It's not serious. (Sylvia)

> We went to a wedding reception and she'd borrowed one of my dresses to go in and Bill said, 'You look very nice in Sonia's dress mother-in-law'. She said, 'shut up', but she was laughing. He said, 'She's had that dress for ages...' and he wouldn't let go of it you see, that was his way of ragging her. But I think it's affection really. I mean, whether my mother took it that way I don't know. She kept saying 'shut up', but she was laughing the whole of the time. (Sonia)

> He can have a laugh and a joke with my mum, but he is so awfully rude to her that she can't believe it. So she thinks it's all part of 'he loves me very much'. I mean, at times he's so rude in quite a familiar way, in a way that he wouldn't dare be to another person. So perhaps that's his way of coping with her. I mean, he wouldn't dream of saying some of the things he says to my mother to his mum... (Laura)

These comments appear to deny that the woman is the victim in joking situations between sons and mothers-in-law. This suggests a complex use of the language and questions what people mean by words such as 'banter' or 'sarcasm'. For example, banter implies verbal exchanges between two people of equal status both adept at retaliation, and this is clearly not happening in some of the situations described above. It seems, therefore, that the daughters-in-law recognized that their mothers were victims of the joke on one level, but denied it at another by referring to their husbands' joking behaviour as banter.

Our society accords high status to heterosexual relationships and the status of most others depends upon whether they support or deny unions between men and women. The other high-status relationship (albeit somewhat idealized by male sociologists) is that between mother and daughter: hence pejorative mother-in-law stereotypes expressed as conflict-producing relationships between mothers and sons-in-law. Clearly some men do perceive the mother-daughter bond as potentially invasive and a threat to their authority. Their fears are expressed in jokes made by popular comedians which devalue and ridicule mother-daughter relationships, and in the joking behaviour and abuse some men employ to regulate their wives and mothers-in-law. For example, daughters-in-law mentioned various derogatory names used by men as terms of reference and address for their mothers-in-law and, although they were professed to be based on affection and liking, women were not unaware of their controlling function. Joking behaviour designed to make the other party feel foolish, incompetent and subordinate was also used by men in relations with their mother-in-law. This is a paternalistic device which, by reducing the woman to a childlike state, allows the man to control the relationship and assert his dominance within it. It also demonstrates his right not to accord his mother-in-law the same respect he has for his mother.

> He calls my father 'sir'. He calls all men older than he is 'sir'. And my father thinks it's marvellous. But he just gives that deference to people that much older ... With my mum ... He calls her all sorts of things like 'the old dragon' ... He calls her the old dragon and my brother-in-law calls her a trout. But with Simon, they have this sort of relationship where my mother thinks he must really love her because nobody could possibly be that rude and mean it. And she's quite happy thinking that. (Laura)

> I know when we were first married, for the first couple of years, Tom used to make jokes about my mother until I started to say, 'Tell me when that happened. When did my mother do that?', and it turned out to be never, because my mother just isn't the sort. And I knew that. And he hasn't done it since. Because he hasn't got cause to you know, because if anything my mother distances herself too much. But the fact remains, he would never do it about his own mother. (Wendy)

Much of this accords with work-based gender relations where 'good-natured' humour is also used as a controlling device. Studies of women factory workers suggest that joking relations between management and shop floor specifically promote female subordination in the workplace (Westwood, 1984; Cavendish, 1982; Pollert, 1981). Supervision methods relied on a mixture of jokes and sexual innuendo, whilst referring to the workers by their first names suggested a spurious equality that was, in fact, patronizing and sexist. In particular, the collective term 'the girls' was applied to women operatives regardless of their age and, with its connotations of school and discipline, effectively reinforced management control.

Zijderveld (1968) refers to joking behaviour of this kind as 'joking up' and 'joking down', and says it is an important indication of power relations in stratified societies. Thus the powerful may joke with those of lower status, in a pretence of equality which effectively reinforces their positions vis-à-vis each other. Consequently, 'joking up' is only possible in circumstances which allow the powerful to retain control, and does not threaten or alter the asymmetrical relationship

Friendly Relations?

between the participants. These joking relationships, paternalistic in nature and intent, are designed to keep the inferior in their place. Like many joking relationships in industrial societies, they are based on taken-for-granted assumptions within a hierarchical social structure, yet have an 'equalizing' function (Coser, 1959) in creating a consensus that jokes are good-natured and harmless. Provided these assumptions are unquestioned, powerful status groups are not required to justify their behaviour, but if the less powerful resist the situation becomes problematic. In relations between mother-in-law and son-in-law, for example, if the woman resists the man's jokes his response may be defensive. This effectively turns the tables on the older woman by implying that she is too sensitive and cannot take a joke. Consequently, although women said their mothers accepted jokes in good part, they sometimes doubted if this attitude reflected their true feelings. Others said joking was acceptable provided women were reassured that it was 'only a joke', and it did not become overtly offensive. At first sight, therefore, neither women in the mother-in-law group nor the mothers of women in the daughter-in-law group appeared to object to joking behaviour, either reciprocal banter or asymmetrical jokes, in which they were the victim. This, however, is not surprising given the powerful sanctions explicit in the accusation that one lacks a sense of humour. Women, then, are in a classic 'double bind' for whether or not they approve of the joke, refusal to respond positively marks them out as deviant. Thus, humour is to do with testing and therein lies its power to control. A mother-in-law who will not laugh breaks the rules of humour by refusing to be the butt of the joke or to accept derogatory images of women generally. She is also trapped by the social pressures on women to smile. Exhortations to 'give us a smile' or 'smile and look happy' demonstrate how men have the power to police and correct women's facial expressions in a way which they themselves would never accept. It is hardly surprising, then, that women often find it easier to conduct their relations with men in a joking manner than attempt overt resistance against sexism. We know that women are uncomfortable with anger, their own and other people's, and do all they can to avoid it in their interpersonal relationships particularly if it risks alienating their children. Given this, 'cheerful' acceptance of joking behaviour may be a further example of the ways, in which women subvert their own feelings in order to sustain relationships within their families.

> She takes it well I suppose. But she doesn't give as good as she gets because there's not a lot she can pull his leg about really. And probably she realizes that if she went too far she'd get me on her back as well... I don't know what would happen if she reacted badly to his jokes because it's never happened. I hope we would both be aware of it and it would be smoothed over. Unless it really was a matter of principle and then I don't know whether Simon would back down. But it's never really happened, or we've never been aware of the fact that he's hurt her. But then I don't really know what she's feeling when he puts her down. She could be feeling terribly, terribly uptight and cut up about it... (Laura)

> You see, it's all right for the man to call his mother-in-law 'the old battle-axe' or whatever, but it wouldn't be OK for that women to turn round and say, 'You've upset me by saying that'. Because that would be the next tack, 'What's the matter with the woman?' But my bet is she

doesn't like it. I'm sure she doesn't. And what probably hurts her most is that her daughter allows it to happen. (Wendy)

Although some men indulged in joking abuse which contained a considerable amount of barely disguised criticism, 'serious' comments about their mothers-in-law were usually reserved for her daughter. Fault finding by the husband effectively controls both mother and wife since the older woman cannot reply and her daughter may hesitate to defend her. If she does, she is placed in the difficult position of having to challenge her husband in order to justify her mother (and herself for supporting her). Criticism of the mother-in-law also regulates the wife because it warns her of the consequences if she becomes like her mother. Therefore mother-in-law jokes are effective in their ability both to devalue mother-daughter bonds and to assert the importance of the mother/son relationship. As might be expected, men did not censure their own mothers as strongly as their mothers-in-law, nor resort to derogatory names or joking abuse. These attitudes are also reflected in cultural stereotypes which idealize mothers and discredit mothers-in-law, a point to which we shall return.

I mean, sometimes Adrian would say, 'Your mother, no wonder she's fat, she's always eating fish and chips'... you know, always criticizing her for being overweight. Because really it was trying to be constructive criticism he was making because if she hadn't eaten so much she wouldn't have been overweight. She would have been able to move about a lot better and enjoy things a lot more. Because she couldn't hardly walk because of her weight. So I could see his point, but I used to think 'Oh, I wish he'd keep it to himself though', because I could see it for myself. And I think this is why I try and keep a bit fit, keep the weight off as well, because I don't want to get like my mum in that respect. (Jenny)

There are, then, significant differences in the joking relationships between mother and son-in-law and the ones between old women and young men described by Sykes. In the print works, men and women exchanged obscene banter but only if initiated by the women: young men were expected to reciprocate but rarely initiated the exchanges themselves. Between mothers and sons-in-law the opposite holds true. Women do not usually initiate such conduct and whilst some exchange banter, others are victims of joking abuse to which they may not respond in kind. They are expected to accept derogatory names and other insults good-naturedly, for to do otherwise makes them vulnerable to accusations that they lack a sense of humour. Exchanges of banter are also different from those which occur in the print works. Again, women are not the primary initiators nor is banter overtly obscene although some of it may be slightly risqué or suggestive.[2]

Frequently, cross-gender joking between in-laws is a paternalistic device designed to allow one participant control over the other by reducing her to a childlike state. This is the significant difference between these joking relationships and those referred to by Radcliffe-Brown. Joking relationships in stateless societies are acceptable only between persons who may treat each other as equals. This is marked by reciprocal joking behaviour which is not intended as an insult but is offered and received in the spirit of real friendliness. In our society the relationship between son-in-law and mother-in-law is based on conflicting components. As previously mentioned, the role model for the relationship is provided by that for parents and children which is essentially asymmmetrical. The alternative role model, found in all gender relations, is one which stresses male superiority and female subordination. It would appear that the latter role model informs in-law relationships between men and women and provides the framework within which joking behaviour may be used by men to disarm the disadvantaged but potentially threatening older woman.

Stand-up comedians and mother-in-law jokes

Although we have no clearly defined avoidance or joking practices specifically designed to reduce conflict between affines, we do acknowledge mother-in-law jokes. Research into the social functions of humour and laughter tells us that while laughter is a distinctively human activity, what makes people laugh is culture-bound and peculiar to different societies and groups (Leech, 1979; Zijderveld, 1968; Coser, 1959). Laughter is also situational. There are occasions when people are expected to laugh and are sanctioned if they do not, just as there are others when jokes and humour are inappropriate. Laughter is essentially an interactive process which presupposes that other members of the group recognize the situation to which the joke refers. It also involves the notion of sharing, so that refusal to join in the common laughter denotes a humourless person who cannot 'take' a joke.

Humour and laughter must have social significance and are only understood when relating to specific situations. For example, Leech says that although people believe they laugh at the unexpected, genuinely unexpected happenings are more likely to frighten than amuse. People actually laugh at jokes which deviate from standard situations without changing much of the original logic. This is the reason why some women say that mother-in-law jokes are grounded in truth: a point to which we shall return. Moreover, joking situations and laughter are not as spontaneous as they appear at first sight. Zijderveld suggests that jokes have a coercive nature and points to 'canned laughter' in situation comedies which reminds the audience that they should laugh too. This has the same effect as shared laughter in a mixed audience where one group is the target of the joke. Thus women are expected to laugh at mother-in-law jokes even if, to them, the joke is not funny.

The significance of culture-bound humour is not lost on the professional stand-up comedian for whom mother-in-law jokes are a stock-in-trade. His job (for they are still usually men) is to make his audience laugh and he does so by telling jokes about common experiences and concerns. Therefore, the successful comedian must understand the cultural background of his audience and use this knowledge to devise jokes which its members will find humorous (Paton, 1988). Much of his material will articulate the anxieties of his audience and allays their fears by stripping events of their threatening features. Thus, in mother-in-law jokes, relations with the mother-in-law, potentially stressful and problematic, are temporarily removed from reality and rendered harmless. Jokes provide a vehicle for the professional comedian to express opinions which in real life are prohibited and unacceptable. They allow him to overstep socially recognized boundaries, yet, at the same time, confirm and reinforce those boundaries. In short, the professional comedian is in the business of tension-management, just as the laughter he evokes from his audience is a form of tension release.

In his discussion of the comedian and social morality, Paton (1988) suggests that professional comedians can be identified as role-types who conduct their joking behaviour within particular joking frames. 'Conservative' comedians establish a 'category-routinized' joking frame which is rooted in generally recognized social traditions and stereotypes of particular groups. Stand-up comics whose repertoires of jokes rely on unflattering images of women are representative of the 'conservative' role-type. Their material maintains comic traditions established in the music-hall and is equally outmoded. It draws on tried and tested themes, periodically updated, so that variations of the same jokes are repeated over and over again. Nevertheless, the portrayal of negative imagery in such jokes has a powerful controlling function and continues to reinforce the influence of stereotypes which in reality no longer exist.

Leech suggests that 'stage stereotypes have a remarkable longevity and often survive well after the social situation which first brought them into existence has faded into oblivion' (1979, p. 8). He points to images of shy curates, parsimonious Scots and ultra-stupid Irishmen which continue to appear on stage yet no longer (if they ever did) exist in real life. So it is with mothers-in-law. Negative imagery of the mother-in-law is not a modern phenomenon. Firth *et al.* (1970) quote a seventeenth-century citation which speaks of 'the everlasting Din of Mothers-in-Law' (p. 413), and there are numerous references to in-law relationships in English literature (Wolfram, 1987) but it was in the nineteenth-century music-hall that mother-in-law jokes became a popular form of expression. It is no coincidence that their popularity corresponded with the development of working-class communities where married couples lived in close proximity to the wife's mother. Ties with daughters strengthened as a consequence of domestic and childcare responsibilities and meant that women spent much of their day visiting in each other's homes. In the private domain female bonds were not only an important source of mutual aid: mothers in particular were a fountain of knowledge on all personal and domestic matters and it was to them that wives turned for reassurance and advice (Roberts, 1984; Meacham, 1977; Rosser and Harris, 1965; Young and Willmott, 1957).

It is, perhaps, not surprising, given married women's attachment to their mothers, that husbands resented the older woman, and if tension was not to break out in overt hostility ways of controlling it had to be found. One way, developed and utilized by popular comedians of the day, was to ridicule and discredit the private world of women and particularly the mother-daughter bond. Thus mothers-in-law along with other familiar phenomena, 'lodgers, chuckers-out and booze',[3] were themes which had a place in the 'culture-code'[4] of working-class communities. Humorous observations about these often stressful situations were the stock-in-trade of comics in music-hall and old-time variety theatres, both reflecting and reinforcing the fabric of traditional community life.

Today demographic changes have led to a breakdown of many traditional working-class communities and people expect to put at least some geographical distance between themselves and their in-laws. Nevertheless, whilst the conditions which created mother-in-law stereotypes have changed, jokes continue to thrive because they observe institutions enshrined in our social and political systems. Idealism about family life is reflected in the high status accorded to heterosexual relationships, especially those sanctified by marriage. All other relationships, including those between members of the same sex, are secondary to these. Consequently, it is unlikely that friendships between women (including those between daughters-in-law and mothers-in-law) threaten men or undermine their authority in the home. Indeed, by sharing intimacies with female friends, women support the marital status quo and help make male inexpressiveness possible and, as far as wives are concerned, more bearable. Because the language used to describe women's talk is in itself degrading – gossip, whinging, nagging and so on – women may doubt the legitimacy of their complaints. Female friends and relatives understand this and are able to provide a valuable outlet for each other. However, relations between mothers and daughters are somewhat different. Parent/child relationships also have high status in our society but, unlike those between mothers and sons, mother-daughter bonds are expected to continue after marriage. Although these bonds are in themselves more complex than traditional studies of the family suggest,[5] from the husband's point of view, the mother's influence may indeed threaten his authority over his wife. This contradiction between generational and conjugal relationships finds some outlet in cultural representations and humorous treatment of mothers-in-law. The jokes survive because they are a legitimate means of discrediting the only socially recognized tie between women which has the potential to undermine heterosexual relationships.

> I don't know why men make jokes about the mother-in-law. Maybe because it's generally thought that the wife's mother will interfere. Perhaps men think that because mothers and daughters are usually close. (Dianne)

> Perhaps when a man gets married he's got two women to contend with. He's got the wife's mother to put up with as well, in a way, hasn't he ... as well as the wife. So perhaps he thinks he's going to be dominated by women. So perhaps he thinks he can stand up for himself if he cracks stupid little jokes. (Jenny)

Freud (1960) also sees jokes as a way of relieving tension in a potentially difficult relationship which is why, he suggests, mothers-in-law are a favourite subject. Humorous treatment of the mother-in-law can be a safety-valve providing an outlet for discontent which might otherwise be suppressed, given that overt conflict or extreme avoidance would have serious consequences for family relationships. Therefore, Zijderveld notes that joking is often instituted in 'oppressively fixed relationships' (1968, p. 305). Without actually altering the relationship it allows one party, at least, a means of expression which evokes sympathy from others in the same situation.

It is an inescapable fact, however, that jokes about the mother-in-law overwhelmingly channel *male* discontents. We know, for example, that jokes are almost always told by men about the wife's mother and, like all jokes and joking behaviour resorted to by men to control women, are based on components of hostility and rejection (Phillips, 1986; Rogers, 1981; Whitehead, 1976). Although many people attribute this to the fact that stand-up comedy is a male-dominated profession, the simple truth that there are fewer female comedians does not explain masculine propensity for mother-in-law jokes. For example, contemporary forms of comedy (loosely labelled 'alternative' comedy), although still dominated by men, have more than usual numbers of female performers whose success seems not to rely on outmoded images and stereotypes. In order to understand the art of the female comedian, it is useful to return briefly to Paton's analysis of comedy role-types. Contemporary female artists can be identified as 'radical category-routinized' role-types whose jokes protest against current social arrangements, whilst 'conservative category-routinized' role-types utilize humour to reinforce traditional social morality. On a merely speculative note, it may be that women comedians see mothers-in-law as an irrelevant topic for jokes when compared with more pressing female concerns, although this seems unlikely since other relationships do not escape humorous treatment. A more plausible reason lies in the negative imagery of the mother-in-law entrenched in our culture which, in effect, insults all women. Thus mother-in-law jokes, emphasizing the physical and mental ugliness of a specific group of women, would seem particularly tasteless if included in the female comedian's repertoire. Given that humour is essentially an interactive process and requires the performer to carry out negotiations which ensure her audience is on her side, jokes of this type are a particularly potent means of alienating both men and women. In a patriarchal society noted, historically, for idealizing 'mothers'[6] (Dally, 1982; Badinter, 1981), jokes about the woman's mother-in-law, that is, the husband's mother, are unlikely to receive a positive response from men, whilst women, who feel uncomfortable when confronted with a male comedian of the genre, are likely to feel betrayed if the jokes are made by a member of their own sex.

Although cultural expressions overwhelmingly refer to poor relations between mothers and sons-in-law, it seems that from the man's point of view, there are few grounds for conflict in mother-in-law relationships. Generally, men have manageable relations with their wife's mother because they conduct them within informal joking or avoidance frameworks which effectively allow them to control interpersonal boundaries. Conversely, Firth *et al.* (1970) suggest that the absence of parallel images for mother and daughter-in-law relationships may be because 'wives suffer their mothers-in-law more patiently than do their husbands' (p. 412), a view supported by evidence from women in this study. Certainly they appear to take their in-law relationships more seriously and the emotional work this involves makes boundary maintenance an ambivalent and difficult process for women. To take just one example, women's identities as peace-keepers would suggest that their responsibility for managing tension between family members is not an obvious cause for humour and jokes, a fact often mentioned by the women themselves.

> I think it's women who deal with all the emotional side, all the big responsibilities. I mean, you've got your children and the house and you're looking after your husband. And then you've got your husband's family. And I do think with men in relationships . . . women give one hundred per cent and men give ninety-nine point something. (Frances)

> I do think women take their relationships more seriously. I mean, don't you think that's a general thing with women and men, women are more serious about their relationships whether it's their mother-in-law or . . . ?

> Men aren't as serious are they? They don't take them as seriously, I don't think so. It just seems to be part of a man's make-up not to. It's like you were saying earlier about women keeping the family together. Well, women do take that seriously. I mean, it is hard work. So they're not going to laugh about it are they? They're not going to make jokes about it. (Dianne)

These comments demonstrate quite clearly that women are aware of their responsibilities for orchestrating family relations and, by contrast, the variation in the degree to which men do the same.

In the light of the foregone discussion it is not unreasonable to say that the cultural representation of the mother-in-law is one which most women will not be particularly inclined to find funny. Indeed, women revealed considerable ambivalence in their attitudes towards mother-in-law jokes. Some were disturbed by stereotypical images of the sexually unattractive and dominant mother-in-law in jokes; others rejected the notion that jokes are influential and damaging and felt that, whilst not particularly funny, they are generally harmless in intent and effect.

> I don't know why they have to make the jokes really. Why should mothers-in-law be the butt of this sort of humour? I think it's quite likely that they are hostile. You know, a bit chauvinistic. (Gaynor)

> I don't like jokes about women. I don't think most women do. But women through the ages have been used to being made fun of or ignored. What's the word I'm looking for... abused is too strong a word... I mean, to be inferior. (Mrs Harris)

> No, they don't make me feel uncomfortable. I don't honestly think that they're intended to hurt at all. I think they're just jokes, they're not done in a snide way. I suppose there are some cases when it is snide, but I mean as a source of public entertainment I think it's just one of those things that's an easy thing to do, and so successful that comedians carry on with it. (Mrs Swann)

> We laugh at them because we don't think the mother-in-law means us. We think we are different so we laugh at them as jokes. I don't think we ever take offence. (Joyce)

> I don't think they have any influence. They're only jokes, aren't they? (Mrs Colclough)

> They don't worry me at all, not a bit of it. If they're really funny I'll laugh, but if they're smutty... you do get a smutty one now and again. But I think I'm, broadminded enough not to mind. (Mrs Tagg)

It is interesting that mothers-in-law were generally more tolerant in their atitudes towards jokes than daughters-in-law. This may be partly related to the younger women's heightened awareness of how gender relations are structured but there are other equally plausible explanations. Comments from mothers-in-law suggest that the image of mothers-in-law represented in jokes is so gross that women cannot believe it applies to them and consequently they are not offended. Alternatively, some mothers-in-law may not have expressed their antipathy towards the jokes because, even in conversation with another woman, they were concerned not to fail the humour test.

Some women believed the masculine tendency to joke about relationships is a sign of real affection which men are otherwise unable to express. This seems to contradict previous evidence that joking behaviour between son-in-law and mother-in-law is hostile and controlling, even though it is overwhelmingly one-sided. Moreover, joking which involves insults seems an odd way of reassuring a person that she is liked, until one considers the contradictions in men's social attitudes towards women. Men's location in the public sphere requires expressions of masculinity which enable them to both compete and identify with other men and, as a consequence, a considerable amount of male-to-male contact involves joking exchanges which degrade women. Such behaviour is an assessment of the identity and cohesion of male groups and reduces conflict between individual men. However, within the private sphere, there are increasing demands on men to embrace feminine values by becoming more expressive and responsive towards their wives. For many men the conjugal relationship is the only exception to cultural expectations of male inexpressiveness and so, even when a man is motivated by warmth and affection, it may still be easier to conduct his mother-in-law relations within a joking framework.

> To be honest with you I think it can be affection. I think it's deep-rooted affection that men feel for their mothers-in-law but with men being unable to express themselves by talking, if you like, to actually say, 'I think my mother-in-law's great', I think they go the other way. So it's all down to men not being able to express their feelings. (Helen)

> I think men make jokes about their mother-in-law because, to be honest they don't like to admit just what nice people they are or can be. You know, in case somebody thinks they're a soft touch or sort of daft like that, so they sort of joke and call her the 'old bag' or 'she's got a mouth like ...' I mean, they really don't mean it. It's in good fun and I think it covers up the embarrassment that they feel because they've got an affection for her mother. I really do think it's that. (Nancy)

With the possible exception of jokes about wives, jokes about mothers-in-law are the only ones recognized in our culture which refer to family relationships. There are, for example, no jokes about fathers-in-law and there are certainly no jokes about mothers. Yet if jokes really are a means by which inexpressive males channel positive feelings, we might expect to find humorous representations of the mother. Previous discussion of communication patterns between mothers and sons suggests that men do find it difficult to express themselves emotionally, although physical contact between them is not unusual. For example, those daughters-in-law who were the mothers of teenage sons referred to reciprocal horseplay which is part of their relationship and, moreover, welcomed this type of interaction both as a sign of their son's affection and confirmation of their own self-worth. In interpersonal relationships between mothers and sons and between mothers-in-law and sons-in-law, therefore, joking behaviour can have positive meanings and may indeed be an expression of genuine regard. The only obvious difference here, although a highly significant one, is that between mothers and sons there is no evidence of joking abuse.

The absence of jokes about mothers seems to reflect Douglas' (1968) view that 'there are jokes which can be perceived clearly enough by all present but which are rejected at once'. She goes on to state that 'social requirements may judge a joke to be in bad taste, risky, too near the bone, improper or irrelevant' (p. 366), factors which the professional comedian knows well not to ignore. When an unacceptable and serious aspect of a joke cannot be successfully renegotiated, the comedian is likely to evoke a hostile response from the audience, and the need to avoid this danger seems to prohibit jokes about mothers. In our society images of mothers emphasize negative as well as positive themes, a duality reflected in tendencies to blame mothers on the one hand and idealize them on the other. This stems from a polarization of maternal behaviour which is expressed in images of the 'good' and 'bad' mother. In cultural representations the mother-in-law embodies all that is 'bad' about mothering behaviour – neglectful, possessive, manipulative and so on, whilst the mother embodies self-sacrifice, nurturance and accessibility – in short, all that is good. Both are distorted representations which ignore the realities of mothering in a society which devalues mothers and offers them few rewards. However, where jokes are concerned, such distortions are extremely powerful. Thus 'bad' mothers, that is, mothers-in-law, are a legitimate subject for jokes whereas 'good' mothers are not.

> People don't tell jokes about their own mother do they? Especially men. You know, it's 'my dear old mum...' (Mrs Colclough)

> Men never make jokes about their mother. But of course, the wife's mother is removed. The bond is missing. (Mrs Harris)

All humour is based on the unexpected or extreme in situations which are recognized and understood within a given culture. Therefore, a person who invites others to join in the joke creates an atmosphere of sharing which allows them to interpret together each one's experience. Because jokes encompass the views of others in a commonly recognized situation, men, and for different reasons, some women, are able to identify with and laugh at mother-in-law jokes. Furthermore, jokes do not admit to vulnerability. This is the difference, Coser (1959) suggests, between jokes or 'jocular gripes' and complaints. Complaints are made to a single person and may imply that, within a particular situation, the complainant is unable to cope. Jocular gripes made to a group perform a double function of complaint and joke. They overcome vulnerability through the group's shared experience and this, in turn, legitimates and justifies the complaints. Much of this accords with the views held by some women who feel uncomfortable in a mixed-gender group if someone tells a mother-in-law joke. Others, referring to popular comedians, commented on the 'conspiracy' between the man who relates the joke and the men in the audience whose laughter comes from a shared understanding. On these occasions women often perceive themselves as 'outsiders';

they recognize the unpleasantness of a joke which insults all women, but refusal to join in the laughter makes them vulnerable to accusations of 'sour grapes'.

> Well, I suppose the jokes are sometimes funny. But I don't know, I think they can be very cruel as well. But of course, if women don't take them in good part people say they have no sense of humour. (Mrs Harris)

> The jokes are about women really, aren't they? I mean, the women are expected to laugh but it's not very funny really. I don't think it's very funny. It certainly doesn't amuse me. (Gaynor)

> It's a shame isn't it? And also it's almost a bit like ... well, it's like abuse of women isn't it? I mean, they're knocking them on the grounds of their sex not necessarily their personality. In actual fact they're critical of yourself aren't they? (Laura)

Much of this evidence points to significant differences in male and female humour and the jokes and joking situations to which they will respond. For example, some women said that in single-sex groups women's humour often referred to their husbands and family situations, and sometimes to other women, but that a lot of self-deprecatory humour went on as well. This accords with Levine's (1976) suggestion that women indulge in self-deprecatory humour to a greater extent than men, a view also supported by a study of American 'put-down' humour. Here, Zillman and Stocking (1976) found that women were more inclined to laugh at jokes featuring a self-disparager of either sex than ones in which the central character puts down another. The fact that, in male-dominated cultures where hostile humour is the norm, women prefer jokes which disparage the self, tells us something about differences in male and female humour. It may be that cultural expectations which promote female inferiority enable women to laugh at their own expense, whereas a more pronounced sense of self-image prevents this in men.

> It is true that men engage in jokes that women are not part of. When I'm with my women friends we make jokes about husbands or situations ... family situations. But you see, I suppose it would only appeal to a few people to laugh at. We wouldn't all laugh at jokes that men make in the pub. I don't know, but I would imagine they're rather crude about women. But women's jokes are usually about other women and they don't mind telling them against themselves either. (Joyce)

> We probably don't make jokes in the same way because I think women are a bit more sensitive to 'I mustn't run my husband down'... Disloyalty. Whereas men, it just comes out as a joke. But in some situations with women it can sound a little bit, 'Well, I wonder if she's unhappily married...' you know? It can start being analyzed in a different sort of way. (Susan)

Normative expectations of appropriate gender behaviour promotes women (and men) to sanction the unacceptable in female humour and means that this, like any other form, has its limits and boundaries. Disloyalty toward husband and family is just one interpretation of bad taste; unseemly joking behaviour is another.

> It's like if a woman gets up and tells a joke a lot of the men find it embarrassing. Where I work there's a girl who comes in and ... well, she tells the most obnoxious jokes. But if a man had told it, you know, ha ha it's a giggle, and the women look at each other, you know, it's disgraceful but what do you expect. But because it's her, it's, oh, smutty and dirty and lowering her standards. And some of the men have said, 'Oh God, I hope she isn't going to start', because they find it embarrassing. But if a woman tells them the men don't like it. Because a woman shouldn't really say those sort of things. (Annette)

Women, then, are trapped by their gender and their behaviour is censored not just by men but by other women and themselves. Again, they find themselves in a 'double bind'. Constraints on their language prevent them from telling jokes as men do because it is unfeminine, but if they resist derogatory jokes in mixed-sex situations they are sanctioned for failing the humour test.

We have seen that humour can be a safety-valve and is utilized differently by men and women. Standardized jokes about mothers-in-law and forms of joking behaviour and abuse provide an outlet for men and enable them to control what some perceive as an invasive relationship. Women, on the other hand, are less inclined to laugh at mother-in-law jokes and often find them more offensive than amusing, whilst cultural prescriptions for feminine conduct restrict their own humorous observations and expressions. It is not surprising, therefore, that when women talked to me about jokes they did not relate mother-in-law jokes or mention joking behaviour when referring to their own relationships. This is not to say that the interviews with women were sombre affairs but it reflects their strongly-held views that emotional and physical investment in family relationships is not an obvious subject for jokes. There was, however, a great deal of humour (much of it self-deprecatory) in the way women described their interactions with mothers-in-law and daughters-in-law. Often they depicted the minor eccentricities of both women and showed how being 'able to see the funny side' can be an important coping strategy in otherwise tense situations.

However, being able to see the funny side of situations is not the same as telling jokes, and confirms that humour means different things to people in different settings. For example, humour is one way that people can relate to each other as equals. Men have more opportunities to relate to other men in the public sphere both at work and in the pursuit of leisure activities, but many of their jokes stem from a shared understanding of the private sphere. Women relate to each other in both the private and public spheres by seeing the funny side of life and finding pockets of humour in what are essentially difficult situations. If we look again at studies of female factory workers (Westwood, 1984; Cavendish, 1982; Pollert, 1981) we can see how 'having a laugh' together is an important form of female bonding and resistance against male control. Indeed, it may be easier for women to 'have a laugh' in the workplace than in the home, for if a woman initiates 'put-down' humour, say, in relation to her son-in-law she risks alienating the bond between herself and her daughter. This demonstrates how failure to initiate humour in one setting can have the same effect as taking the initiative in another. That is, bonds between women in the family are often reinforced by reversing the behaviour which underpins female solidarity at work. However, when men and women relate to each other humour does nothing to alter unequal relations between them. Joking behaviour in the workplace merely trivializes female workers and reinforces male power; joking behaviour between men and women in the family does much the same.

Negative images and stereotypes of mothers-in-law

This chapter, thus far, has been concerned with the functions of humour and control in two important related areas. Firstly, the humorous treatment of mothers-in-law in popular culture which overwhelmingly invokes negative images and stereotypes; secondly, the utilization of humour in interpersonal relationships according to gender and status. These observations provide the background from which to examine the third important area: the implications of negative stereotyping and its influence on perceptions of mother-in-law relationships.

Perkins (1979) argues that the strength of a stereotype is derived from three components: 'its simplicity; its immediate recognisability (which makes its communicative role very important and its implicit reference to an assumed consensus about some attribute or complex social relationships' (p. 141). Stereotypes also have a 'flexible range' (p. 146) in that they can be expressed in a simple, generalized way or more realistically. Professional comedians and cartoonists rely on simplistic stereotyping which emphasizes a few, commonly recognized features and excludes all diversifications. More 'realistic' versions of stereotypes are often found in film or television drama. For example, Seiter (1986) suggests that in family melodrama and some situation comedy, mother-in-law stereotypes are commonly associated with problematic family relationships and generational conflict. Consequently, images of women are particularly powerful because they reflect experiences which are shared across class barriers. Therefore:

> Many scenarios found in family melodramas are emotionally charged because they correspond to situations of conflict in the social order, in the family, in relations between men and women and in relations among women. Identification is made possible because they are social and shared, rather than merely emotional and individual. (Seiter, 1986, p. 63)

The simplistic and rigid nature of stereotypes appealed to by professional comedians is, in itself, deceptive. Perkins suggests that stereotypes are like symbols and are both simple and complex. She takes as an example the stereotype of the 'dumb blonde', and suggests that this tells us much more than the colour of the woman's hair and her intellectual powers. Similarly, the 'interfering mother-in-law' stereotype contains both simple and complex components. At one level it is a generalization which ignores individual differences; at another it specifies the woman's sex, status, approximate age, her gender and generational relationships and, importantly, her behaviour.

Another point which Perkins makes about stereotypes refers to differences in how they are acknowledged and understood. Some people accept stereotypes as accurate representations of reality, whilst others acknowledge them and know what they contain, but believe them to be false. However, these are not clear distinctions. The nature of stereotypes, for example, about mothers-in-law, is such that they are culturally expressed and therefore widely known. Consequently, whether they are believed in or not, they can be drawn upon to interpret or justify behaviour should the need arise. This in turn questions the assumption that stereotypes have no relation to direct experience and that they are always inaccurate. Perkins suggests that 'stereotypes are often "valid"; that they are often effective in so far as people define themselves in terms of the stereotypes about them' (1979, p. 155). Taking this a stage further, stereotypes are also 'valid' in so far as others refer to them in order to define an individual member of a stereotyped group. For example, where relations with the mother-in-law are strained, stereotypes in jokes and media images may be a distorted reflection of reality but, nevertheless, appear to be grounded in truth.

> I think when they're making the jokes about the mother-in-law there's probably a lot of truth behind what is said. From my point of view, but then I consider I've had a bad experience with mothers-in-law. And sometimes when they say jokes I can turn it round to fit my way. You know, I think, 'My God, that's true...' You know, you laugh but you think, 'God, that's true'. (Annette)

> I think stereotypes do have an effect. I mean, I would have said definitely that I wouldn't go for that, I wouldn't care and I wouldn't be influenced by anything. I'd just find out for myself. And I would have believed that. But I'm sure deep down some of it must come out. If she does something, 'Oh, it's true what they say...' and then you tend to believe it more. (Rachel)

Clearly, then, it is misleading to say that stereotypes are erroneous since, if they were totally false, they would be powerless in the socialization process and as a function of social control. Stereotypes are more accurately described as distortions because they select and exaggerate what is problematic in relationships. For example, women's central role as mothers may be increasingly difficult to maintain as mothers-in-law and, because this then problematizes mothers-in-law as a group, stereotypes about them inevitably arise. Therefore, in an important sense, stereotypes are both true and false, or more precisely, 'they are both (apparently) true and (really) false at the same time' (Perkins, 1979, p. 155).

Turning now to the influence of stereotypes on women's perception of mother-in-law and daughter-in-law relationships, it is possible to identify significant differences between mothers-in-law and daughters-in-law. Young women do not consider in-law relationships before marriage and it is only when they experience themselves as part of a wider kin network that the relationships have any meaning. Before marriage, the message in jokes and other images, if acknowledged at all, is perceived as external to the individual's expectations and is not considered influential. It is after marriage, particularly if the relationship proves difficult, that stereotypes become significant and appear to contain a 'grain of truth'.

> I don't think daughters-in-law are influenced at all. Not before they get married anyway. (Janet)

I was only interested in Adrian, I wasn't interested in what his mother looked like or what she did at the time. It's only when you've grown, when you're married and you've actually got to share your life with them as you come to whether you like them or hate them. But I think when you're 19 or 20 you're only interested in the lad, you're not interested in what his mother looks like. (Jenny)

Yes, people do have mother-in-law problems, but I certainly didn't go into it thinking, 'Oh my God, what's my mother-in-law going to be like?' That was the last thought on my mind... (Elaine)

Assessing the impact of the mother-in-law stereotype on older women is more complex. At first sight it appears to have no more effect than on women about to become daughters-in-law, although this is misleading. However, only one mother-in-law felt stereotypes might influence the older women's perceptions and conduct. The majority said that jokes, at least, had little or no effect.

Oh yes, they probably influence in the way the woman might think, 'Well, I'm going to do my best not to be like that'. (Mrs Richardson)

I don't think mothers-in-law ever think about jokes. Apart from having a good laugh at them. (Mrs York)

The fact that mothers-in-law recognize the stereotype of their own group but reject the notion that it is influential supports Perkins' claim that stereotypes 'can be "held" in the sense that we know that a stereotype exists about a particular group and what its content is, even though we don't necessarily believe it' (1979, p. 145). Paradoxically, if mothers-in-law as a group are socially recognized and one is a mother-in-law, it is impossible not to define oneself as a member of that group and, therefore, according to Perkins, 'because one's membership of a group is always present, so too is the stereotype of oneself' (p. 156). Moreover, if the group is an *oppressed* one (with which most stereotypes are concerned) definition of oneself as a member can also be self-derogatory and, therefore, an important instrument of social control.

It is worth examining, at this point, Perkins' definitions of dominant and oppressed groups and the main differences between stereotypes about them. The first observation is that, although stereotypes tend to be defined as negative, there are, in fact, both negative and positive stereotypes, or what Perkins calls 'pejorative' and 'laudatory' stereotypes (1979, p. 144). The majority of negative stereotypes are about oppressed groups (which is why there are more stereotypes of women than men). Oppressed groups give rise to stereotypes because they are frequently 'problematic', unlike dominant groups whose authority and status is generally unquestioned. It follows, therefore, that dominant groups are male and that one group (white, middle-class males) is the most well-defined in terms of laudatory stereotypes. However, there are also positive stereotypes about some oppressed groups. The most obvious example is the 'good' mother against which many pejorative stereotypes of women are measured. The significant factor here is that most stereotypes of women define them in terms of their relationships to men, that is, the dominant group. Therefore, according to Seiter, 'what is good for men (for maintaining a system of gender inequality) is presented as laudatory, and what is inconvenient, or conflict-producing, is presented as objectionable' (1986, p. 70).

Stereotypes, then, are defined by the dominant group and *self-defined* by individual members of the oppressed group to which a particular stereotype applies. They also confirm and reinforce the limits of that group's legitimate behaviour and, in this respect, are extremely influential. What is important, therefore, is the nature of he stereotype. It is hardly surprising that women reject the stark, blatant stereotypes appealed to in jokes because these are external to women's images of themselves. However, 'realistic' stereotypes are much more pervasive. For example, all the women in the mother-in-law group referred to the 'interfering mother-in-law' which warned them of the dangers of failing to adapt the mothering role to their married children. In this respect, therefore, women were extremely sensitive to 'realistic' negative stereotypes and to how mothers-in-law are generally portrayed by the media. Consequently, although many of them rejected notions that stereotypes are influential, the majority of opinions complied to some degree with media images and sometimes with those in mother-in-law jokes.

Conclusion

Jokes, joking behaviour and the negative imagery which surrounds mothers-in-law are all powerful functions of social control. Humorous treatment of mothers-in-law in interpersonal relationships and in popular culture discredit and devalue older women and, as a consequence, control women generally. Their behaviour is regulated in cross-gender joking between sons and mothers-in-law and in cultural representations which appeal to negative stereotypes in both simple and complex ways. Consequently, women's behaviour is simultaneously controlled and self-controlled. They are prevented from resisting blatant stereotypes because they know the result is likely to be punitive, whilst more 'realistic' stereotypes remind women of the need to constantly renegotiate and modify their conduct in respect of their married children.

Notes

1 Stateless societies refers to those characterised by the absence of clearly identifiable state institutions and bureauracies. Examples include hunter gatherer societies and tribal societies found in Africa, Asia, Australia and North America. Radcliffe-Brown (1950, 1952) refers to, among others, the Lendu of Uganda, the Wagonde of Nyasaland, and the Ojibwa Indians of North America.
2 Given that the most significant joking relationship in the print works was between 'old' men and young women, it might be expected that similar (although perhaps not obscene) joking behaviour might occur between fathers and daughters-in-law. This was not a topic for discussion in the interview schedule and, interestingly, was not mentioned by women during our conversations. Therefore I have no evidence to support or deny the existence of cross-gender joking relations between older men and young women related by marriage. However, anthropological literature suggests that such relationships are uncommon. In India, for example, a new bride

is always restrained with her father-in-law (Sharma, 1980), whilst in Mongolia, fathers-in-law have little to do with the daughters-in-law, although a woman must always maintain the utmost courtesy and respect in the presence of her father-in-law (Humphrey, 1978).

3 See Disher (1974), p. 60.
4 See Paton (1988), p. 216.
5 For example, Ann Whitehead has criticized researchers who have perpetuated the notion of the 'women's trade union'. Her study of a village in Herefordshire found that women do not always side together and that mothers frequently police their daughters and will refuse to support them if they disapprove of their behaviour. Whitehead says:

> It has been suggested to me that this does not have to be seen as the act of a woman who resents freedom which she does not have, but that the older woman may be more aware of the quite serious consequences for women if they do not toe the line. (1976, p. 198)

6 Of course, 'mothers' are not idealized *per se*. Mothers of sons are, as are wives who become mothers of men's children; mothers of women who become wives are not.

Chapter 5

Changes in Marital Patterns: Two Mothers-in-Law or None?

The previous chapters have discussed in-law relationships largely in terms of 'normal' families, that is, consisting of husband and wife with or without dependent children. However, in contemporary society the organization of domestic life is subject to a number of changes which disturb and alter the focus of family relationships. Social and demographic changes such as geographical mobility, divorce, cohabitation and retirement affect the structure of kinship networks and domiciliary units and change the nature of relationships established by marriage. A decline both in traditional extended and nuclear 'unbroken' families confuses the understanding of kin relations so that no unqualified conclusions may be drawn about the structure of the family or the meanings attached to it by individuals. These observations are reflected in two main themes in this chapter: the concept of the family life-course and the cohort effect on individual expectations.

Doubts have been raised about the value of the family life cycle approach to sociological research, given the increasing diversity in existing family structures (Murphy, 1987). The approach has been criticized for its normative element which makes implicit assumptions about an 'ideal' family form consisting of a predetermined sequence of stages through which individuals progress as they age. As Murphy points out, there are individuals and families whose family life does not conform with the ideal model and for whom circumstances alter the sequence of events or prevent progress through every stage. The approach is flawed because factors such as death, divorce, cohabitation and premarital pregnancy disturb the chronological order of life course stages and create family forms which differ from the ideal. Moreover, this is not a new phenomenon. There is no firm basis for the assumption that social changes and separations today are more significant than those in the past. For example, in contemporary society divorce is seen as problematic because marital breakdown disturbs the structure of the family but in the past the death of a partner had the same effect. Thus, in various ways demographic change throughout history has dissolved or fractured the model of the family in its ideal form.

Although the family life cycle is useful as a theoretical concept, its emphasis on an 'ideal type' of family suggests that it has empirical limitations as an aid to understanding family forms which deviate from this model. Therefore, the use of age cohorts has been forwarded as a more reliable means of tracing the movement of individuals through family transitions (Murphy, 1987). In this study, the term 'family life-course' is used in preference to 'family life cycle', and both the life-course and the effects of cohorts are highly significant. The family life-course is used because it encompasses social and demographic changes which affect all our lives, as well as the personal biographical events in each individual's life-course. This is important because the women interviewed made sense of their lives by referring to individual and family transitions. They anticipated future roles for themselves, for example, by looking forward to a time when they could re-enter the labour market, when their children married and when they, themselves, expected to become grandmothers. However, the cohort effect clearly demonstrates how individual circumstances and, importantly, the actions of others can disturb such expectations. This becomes clear when we consider how relationships between family women are made possible by the roles they play. For example, if a woman has expectations of becoming a mother-in-law or grandmother by a certain age, decisions made by others can delay or prevent these expectations being fulfilled. Thus, if a couple cohabit rather than marry or postpone having children, they delay the mother's own critical life transitions and prevent her from having a meaningful role. We can see, therefore, that whilst women anticipate important stages through their understanding of the family life-course, individual factors make it impossible to generalize about how and when these stages are reached. In this chapter, then, the two themes come together and overlap, as this combination seemed the most productive method of examining the impact of change on marriage and the family, and the experiences and expectations of individual women.

Living away

As previously mentioned, the social characteristics unique to Stoke-on-Trent include a high proportion of locally-born persons, close-knit kin relationships and residential proximity. However, among those interviewed, there were some women who had moved into the area or whose married children had moved away and for these geographical mobility had significant effects on in-law relationships. Because choice of residence is primarily associated with job considerations and the need to be close to one's workplace, the majority of people not locally-born live in Stoke-on-Trent because they work there, just as those married children who live elsewhere do so for reasons of employment. Bell's (1968) study of middle-class families questions the belief that extended kin networks are least important to the socially and geographically mobile as they are frequently isolated from their parental families. This view is not supported by Bell or by this study, which confirms that geographical distance only temporarily disrupts kin relations particularly when there is access to private transport and the telephone. Clearly, distance affects the frequency and duration of face-to-face contacts but relationships do not depend on these and unavoidable restrictions on family gatherings do not reduce commitments between parents and children. Contacts are maintained by regular visits, letters and frequent telephone calls, so that in absolute terms there is little difference in interaction between parents and married children who all live in Stoke-on-Trent and those where one couple live elsewhere.

Those who did not live near to each other spent occasional weekends together and exchanged longer visits during holiday periods. Attitudes toward spending lengthy amounts of time with in-laws varied considerably depending on the quality of relations between both women, although the actual number of visits were about the same in all cases. There was always a strong element of obligation involved in visiting and whilst some women experienced it as enjoyable, for others distance was important as a legitimate means of informal avoidance.

> You can't just go over for a weekend because it takes five hours to get there and it's awkward with a baby. So I don't see that much of her, perhaps twice a year something like that. So when I do see her I'm always very pleased to see her and I like her to enjoy her grandchild while she can. (Vicky)

> We'd love them to live close to us. We'd love to see more of him and of the boys if it comes to that. But when we reflect on it and realize it entails seeing more of Stella, we know how difficult it would be and feel, well, we're better to be far away. (Mrs Swann)

Distance restricts unexpected visits and prevents entirely the habit of 'dropping in' so much encouraged by mothers-in-law. Prior arrangements well in advance are almost always necessary, and thus the sense of voluntarism associated with interaction between kin tends to be diminished. Also, prevailing circumstances often dictate how much importance is attached to family visits. For example, attitudes towards visiting during holiday periods may depend on economic resources, for if there is no money available for 'real' holidays spending vacations with parents or adult children who live away is a relatively cheap substitute. There may also be increased pressure on the young to visit more often when their parents retire, because this reduces social life contingent on work relationships and contacts with the family become more important. Thus, parents and parents-in-law, often retired and perhaps in poor health, have an understandable desire to see their families more frequently than married children can comply and, whilst daughters-in-law were sympathetic, personal choice and parental demands often conflicted.

> We don't visit her very often although she comes here. We make excuses about the business which is true in a way, but we could go more often than we do. But that's Nick. He works six days a week and he says he's not going to spend his day off driving over there. (Elaine)

> I say, 'we come to see you', but she says, 'yes, but not very often'. But it's a hell of a lot more than we go and see anybody else, although yes, it's not good enough for her. But in comparison it's still pretty good because there's no getting away from the fact that we are very selfish as a couple. And I don't say it's good but that's the way we are. (Ruth)

> It's usually about every three months. Through the summer we perhaps see them more. We always get, 'don't leave it so long, it's a long time since we've seen you'. I suppose it's because his mother is only interested in family things. You know, everything is to do with the family. (Laura)

Changes in Marital Patterns

Reduced face-to-face contact does not appear to affect the mediating role many wives fulfil between mothers and sons. As previously mentioned, women who live in close proximity to their mothers-in-law encourage visits by their husbands, despite the reluctance of some men to make the effort. However, because short visits are impractical, men seem even more inclined to avoid their obligations when their parents live away. And since some do not communicate effectively with their mothers but rely on their wives to intervene, it is hardly surprising when daughters-in-law are blamed, or perceive themselves as blamed, for the son's neglect.

> We crossed that line once when we didn't want to go for Christmas, and she said we were very unreasonable and we did have a yelling match on the phone. And I was in tears and she was in tears. Because I was making excuses she said, 'It's unreasonable, I am his mother. Why don't you let him come?' Not that it was me, I mean he didn't want to ... But I didn't actually say that he didn't want to come because I thought that would upset her. (Ruth)

> They went to Durham on the day I went into hospital to have an operation. And I was very ill ... They'd only just moved up to Durham and of course, I suppose moving into a new job and a new house ... He used to phone me in hospital but it was eight weeks before he came to see me. But I don't think he could come until he'd done what she said he'd got to do, you know. (Mrs Swann)

It appears that where relations between mother-in-law and daughter-in-law are stressful, geographical distance and infrequent contact neither reduces tension nor makes it more manageable. Daughters-in-law in particular spoke of the strain involved in the exchange of lengthy visits with in-laws and the increased obligation to spend at least some of the holiday periods together. They felt that co-residence with parents-in-law, although only for a short time, disrupted the normal pattern of life and that temporary adjustments were difficult to make. The assumption that 'the grass is always greener ...' meant that, given the choice, some would have preferred to live closer so that visits, while more frequent, would be short and would dispense with the necessity to share the same roof. Others, however, felt that this was bearable, given that visits were soon over and the time in between relatively uninterrupted.

> I find when they come here for a few days or we go up there for a few days, I have to have my own space and somewhere of my own to hide away. The problem is we don't see each other for three or four months and then we have such a lot of time together, two or three days. I really would prefer it more frequently but for less time. (Laura)

> The visits are so intense. And I'm quite sure that a couple of times she's gone knowing that if she didn't go we'd end up arguing. So she's as sensitive to it as I am. Other times it's quite pleasant and you enjoy having her. So yes, you do have them for a long period of time but having said that, it's over and done with. You grit your teeth for a couple

of days and at the end of them you know you're not going to see her for a month or so. (Elaine)

These comments reveal the stresses in prolonged face-to-face contact when people are motivated more by a sense of duty than affection. They also demonstrate the contradictions which underpin the meaning of family life. At one level, the family is essentially private, resistant to intrusion from outsiders and, in many ways, from extended kin. At another, it creates ties with individuals by blood or marriage and sets of relationships which are supposed to be founded on love but are often not. When this affective element is lacking between mothers and daughters-in-law, their relationship depends on family obligations which prescribe a certain amount of interaction. If, however, this involves regular and prolonged intrusions into each other's private domain, relations frequently break down.

One significant cause of stress during prolonged visits is differences between the two women in their approach to domestic tasks. Previous discussion of domestic cultures suggests that difficulties arise when two women attempt to work in one kitchen because of the dangers of overstepping boundaries in someone else's domain. The image of two women occupying a kitchen, whilst simplistic, is nevertheless a pervasive stereotype which with mothers and daughters-in-law appears to resemble reality. According to Arcana (1981) 'the prevailing myth is that we all ought to be isolated each in her own kitchen' (p. 3) but since her home is the location of a woman's identity the very presence of another female in her kitchen may be threatening and disruptive. This tends to be more so for the daughter-in-law whose in-laws come to stay. Her domestic domain is immediately observable to her mother-in-law and she may worry about comparisons with the older woman's expertise developed during years of household management. Consequently, what may only be an expression of interest by the mother-in-law can be interpreted as criticizing and encroaching. Such misunderstandings occur because women are used to servicing others and, whilst the daughter-in-law wants to appear able, her mother-in-law may merely be anxious to help. On the other hand, help is often appreciated as long as there is not too much of it and the younger woman retains responsibility and control in her own home. There is, therefore, considerable importance attached to task divisions. For example, daughters-in-law like to prepare meals themselves because cooking marks out their status as wives and their culinary skills. Other tasks, which carry less status, are willingly delegated to their mother-in-law.

> She always wants to help me and I would prefer, when I'm cooking and catering, that she keeps out of the way. Lay the table, put the glasses out and pass things through to her but I get flustered if I think she's watching what I'm doing. I want to impress. I still want to impress and I want it to be nice but I'd rather do it myself. (Laura)

Much of the mother-in-law's conduct is prescribed by her own perception of the visit. If, for example, she sees it as a short vacation she may welcome a break from routine chores altogether, or merely do as much or as little as she chooses. Moreover, if this view is shared by her children, it provides a legitimate excuse to exclude her from the kitchen.

> It was a lovely visit. I couldn't have ever thought I would have enjoyed being so idle. We were shown the kitchen when we got there and Howard said, 'this is the kitchen and from now on you're barred'. And all I did was make a cup of tea the whole time we were there. It was great. We had a lovely time. (Mrs Richardson)

Mrs Richardson's comments usefully illustrate the dimensions of communication in family relationships. Here, her son Howard was involved in indirect communication between his mother and Georgina, the woman with whom he lived and was planning to marry. It would hardly have been an auspicious start to the mother-in-law and daughter-in-law relationship if Georgina had been the one to say, 'this is the kitchen and from now on you're barred' but Howard's intervention was a subtle and effective means of establishing the domestic boundaries between the two women.

Geographical distance between parents and married children allows for a greater degree of informal avoidance than is usual for people who live near to each other and because of this it does have functional importance. It reduces, for example, opportunities for 'interference' so much feared by daughters-in-law, regardless of the fact that there is limited evidence to suggest that mothers-in-law are inclined to interfere. Women believed that distance helped maintain a resemblance of peaceful relations, because conflict-producing events could be forgotten, at least until the next visit. They were equally convinced, however, that deprived of this safety-valve, overt antagonism would inevitably result.

> I think if she was closer it would be far worse for me because she would interfere, and where she is now she can't. She passes comments and you realize she disapproves of things that you do and the way you bring your children up but she's not here often enough... We can just smile and ignore her. (Elaine)

It seems, therefore, that geographical distance is of limited significance in affinal relationships between women and that, where negative feelings exist, absence does not necessarily make the heart grow fonder. Indeed, the element of formality in relations between mothers and daughters-in-law is often magnified by separation and prolonged visits only increase the strain. Women find it more difficult to get to know each other and frequently relations between them fail to develop further than the early stage where the daughter-in-law is a stranger but successor to her husband's mother.

Separation and divorce

Reconstituted families in which one or both parents have experienced divorce, an increase in the extent of step-relationships and the rise in single-parent families have confused traditional concepts of kin relations. Marital breakdown has considerable impact on in-law relationships, dividing loyalties and making obligations unclear. Frequently, in the realignment of friends and kin after separation and divorce, contact with in-laws declines and is eventually lost. Affinal bonds are not usually strong enough to survive marital breakdown and those who have not been close during the marriage are unlikely to be after the separation. Although studies of divorce suggest that women are more inclined than men to maintain links out of genuine affection (Spicer and Hampe, 1975; Weiss, 1975) evidence from mothers and daughters-in-law does not support this view. Even if relations between them are good, they are inevitably defined in terms of the marriage and the woman's relationship with the husband/son. There are no strong obligations to maintain contact when the marriage ends and divided loyalties often create difficulties in redefining affinal ties. Consequently, whilst some women said it should be possible to continue the relationship in the event of divorce, it was clear from those who had experienced marital breakdown that contact almost always declines.

> It was very, very difficult. She's a nice woman and we had a good relationship but it disintegrated very easily after the birth of my daughter and I split up with my husband. So perhaps it wasn't as wonderful as I'd thought. I mean, we were amicable, we didn't fight or anything, but there was no feeling there, where originally we had been very close. (Elaine)

> I didn't stay in contact with her. I went up once and she found it very difficult because it was her son and she must have thought that she would be seen to be taking sides. She didn't say so but it came across and so I didn't go again. I did mind because she was a very nice woman. I could always talk to her, we got on extremely well and she was very upset when we broke up. (Valerie)

Hostility towards the former mother-in-law is not common and tends to diminish over time. Much depends on perceptions and conduct during the breakdown of the marriage and whether the partner's family become involved. There is, for example, a fine line between perceptions of 'interference' and what is actually intervention by parents in an attempt to save the ailing marriage. This usually occurs when the couple are young and there are small children, factors which might justify parental intervention. In most cases, however, couples had decided to part before their parents were aware of the situation and admonishments to 'try again' were by now unwelcome. What is most needed at this stage is practical and emotional support. Other forms of intervention which attempt to influence the couple merely jeopardize future relations between in-laws.

> She was furious about it. More because we hadn't told her what the problems were. Because we said if we'd got any problems we'd tell her, like. We didn't because we thought we could sort them out on our own, but we couldn't and I just left. I think she was upset because I hadn't told her but I thought I could sort it out on my own. You know, everybody used to treat me as a kid. I'd got to ask everybody if this was right, or if this was right. And sometimes what they told me I knew was wrong for me. You know, when I had him back that wasn't my decision. It was mainly his mum's. (Tracey)

> She did try to save the marriage. She came to the house and sat us both down and wanted to know what was going on. But I wasn't really close

to her you see, and to me that was interfering. But she did try to save it – 'get back together for the kids' sake' . . . But I thought that was doing more harm than good anyway. (Clare)

Interestingly, the 'interfering' mother-in-law was not a common factor in separation and divorce. Only one woman attributed some of the blame to her mother-in-law, others cited the usual causes of marital breakdown such as physical and mental abuse, extramarital affairs and general incompatibility. The lack of association between divorce and in-law relationships suggests, therefore, that negative feelings between mothers and daughters-in-law are unlikely to seriously damage relations between husband and wife. However, the apportioning of blame does seem to be unavoidable in the general messiness surrounding divorce. Although the 1969 Divorce Reform Act dispensed with recriminating circumstances as a condition for legal separation, personal guilt and sometimes the disapproval of relatives and friends can linger in the aftermath of divorce. Whatever the circumstances, blood ties tend to take precedence and women believed it inevitable that a mother would side with her son. As a consequence, relations between mothers-in-law and daughters-in-law may be so troubled by divided loyalties that sustaining them beyond the end of the marriage becomes impossible. Therefore, when discussing the effects of divorce on in-law relationships, most women felt inevitable recriminations would sour relations and eventually sever the remaining links between them.

She was always interfering. So I do feel that she was partly to blame for us splitting up. (Rosemary)

Probably if she hadn't encouraged Ron to keep going back. He'd always got his mother to run back to and he'd done it a lot. But there again, I don't know, because at the end I'd got no feelings for him whatsoever. So I can't really blame it on her. (Marian)

I suppose she did blame me. Well, naturally, she wasn't going to blame her son was she? I think she thought there was something the matter with me. I think she thought, you know, 'Well, silly girl. Here she's got this wonderful husband and can't make it work'. (Valerie)

Although obligations between mothers and daughters-in-law are reduced by divorce, if there are children from the marriage contact may be continued out of a joint concern for them and the importance many people attach to a child's need for grandparents. Grandparents are disturbed by divorce and paternal grandparents may fear losing contact with the children. Access to young children is usually through the mother, and the majority of divorced mothers are custodial parents, so that paternal grandparents who wish to see their grandchildren have a vested interest in maintaining good relations with their former daughters-in-law. However, this may not be necessary if the father has rights of access as many divorced men find looking after small children difficult and, having nowhere to entertain them, often ask their own mothers to help out. This means that contact between grandparents and grandchildren is effectively maintained through one parent or the other to the reasonable satisfaction of all parties. The majority of daughters-in-law tend to distinguish between grandparental relationships and those between themselves and their mothers-in-law and have no wish to prevent them from seeing their grandchildren. Although divorce changes the focus of family interaction and involves the renegotiation of grandparental access, it sometimes happens that paternal grandmothers become more active in the lives of their grandchildren. They may see them for longer periods and at shorter intervals, often having them to stay at weekends. And they may also be an important source of material support.

> I see her sometimes. Sometimes she comes to pick up the children. We're all right. She asks me how I am and everything. And she sends the children money for birthdays, so I ring her up and thank her for that. I mean, I've got no argument with her. (Clare)

> She helps out with the children, not in vast amounts but she does help. She sends five pounds once a fortnight which is supposed to go towards their clothes but actually just goes into everyday living. But she knows this, she understands... (Helen)

The amount of support, both practical and emotional, which a divorced woman receives from her former in-laws is generally related to concern for the grandchildren and declines if she remarries. Having children is more significant than whether or not the parents-in-law approve of the separation and is linked to financial help and other practical services such as childcare. Whilst parents-in-law do not help as frequently as parents, those who provide one type of assistance are likely to help out in other ways, although providing moral support may be difficult given the conflict of loyalties between family members when a marriage ends. Often the only obligations between the mother and her former daughter-in-law stem from their joint interest in the children and without this contact may be severed. Children are a vital link which keeps the lines of communication open while both women come to terms with the separation, giving them time to reassess their personal feelings for each other. If, for example, the relationship between mother and daughter-in-law is based on friendship, then it is not exclusively through the son and both women have an emotional investment in it. Therefore, they both have to come to terms with the effects of separation on their own relationship and must realign their position vis-à-vis each other.

Moreover, because marital breakdown is usually perceived from the point of view of the couple, its impact on others in the kin network tends to be ignored. The difference is, when a marriage ends it is regarded as a loss for which both partners have a right to grieve, and grieving for the marriage encompasses other relationships which were part of it. It is questionable, however, whether the husband's mother has any 'right' to grieve at all, even if she feels that she too has experienced a loss. Therefore, the 'rules' by which people make sense of new experiences and changing roles sometimes fail to perform as anticipated and may break down altogether under abnormal stress.

The social and material disadvantages which are a consequence of divorce are particularly significant for women. The majority of divorced women experience a marked decline in their living standards and, having lost ground in the labour market, find it impossible to regain the financial security enjoyed when married. Lone mothers are also more socially isolated than other adults and, because of their domestic responsibilities, have few opportunities for social involvement. Their situation is not helped by the fact that much of adult social life excludes the unattached, so that without a partner women are stigmatized and out of place. It is hardly surprising, therefore, that a great many divorced women remarry, a practice which has led Delphy (1976) to suggest that divorce is not inconsistent with marriage. Material and social disadvantages draw women back into marriage because it offers most of them financial security and a fuller integration into adult social life. When the married and divorced states are compared, it is clear that divorce creates the conditions which favour remarriage for women. Therefore, in Delphy's view, divorce is both a continuation and discontinuation of marriage, for whilst individual contracts end, marriage as an institution thrives.

When a divorced woman remarries her children become part of a reconstituted family which is more complex than conventional, first-time families. Remarriage disturbs kin relationships, creating new ones and causing the loss of others. Issues concerning grandparents can be particularly contentious when there is a third set to accommodate, and often the role of paternal grandparents becomes ambiguous and is eventually lost. Evidence suggests that many non-custodial fathers tend to lose contact with their children if the mother remarries because access visits become problematic and are regarded as an intrusion by the remarried couple (Burgoyne and Clark, 1981). Since paternal grandparents tend to see their grandchildren via their son's access arrangements, if these are discontinued their personal involvement is also adversely affected. Even when friendly relations formerly existed, the sense of awkwardness between in-laws after divorce can prevent grandparents approaching the mother themselves.

> I'm convinced my first mother-in-law would like to see my daughter, but she hasn't got the guts to fetch her and her father just doesn't fetch her any more. So her grandmother doesn't see her any more because she hasn't got the courage to contact her direct. (Elaine)

Because the majority of mothers-in-law and daughters-in-law do not consider each other as intimates, it is difficult for them to maintain on-going relationships when the marriage ends. If, for example, the daughter-in-law remarries, her former mother-in-law can seem an unwelcome reminder of the past, whilst the older woman may feel disloyal sustaining a relationship with someone who has 'replaced' her son with another person. Communication may have broken down completely during the separation, so that both women can only guess how the other sees their relationship and whether it can be successfully realigned to fit the new situation. In the general uncertainty which this entails, it is frequently the children of the marriage who miss out.

> I would quite happily let Gemma see her because she was very nice with Gemma. But I have given her opportunities, you know, I let her know Gemma was in a ballet review but she made no attempt to come. So perhaps we weren't as close as I thought. Perhaps she just doesn't want any contact with me. (Elaine)

Friendly Relations?

Elaine provides an interesting example of how kin-keeping is sustained when kinship is challenged by divorce. It seems that kin-keeping between women breaks down because mother and daughters-in-law no longer relate to each other directly but through others – sons/ex-husbands; children/grandchildren – and these channels of communication are fragile and unreliable. Moreover, when it comes to sustaining relations, divorced women have reduced obligations towards their former in-laws and less if they remarry, because then their kin-keeping activities are directed towards their new kin group.

Separation and divorce inevitably change relations between mothers-in-law and daughters-in-law, affecting women's perception of the relationship and their conduct within it. Obligations and responsibilities are reduced by divorce and contact tends to decline, in some cases, completely. The relationship, which did not exist prior to the marriage but was achieved by it, may be so troubled by conflicting interests that it cannot be satisfactorily redefined afterwards. Although some women were able to maintain amicable, even affectionate, relations with their former in-laws, these usually revolved around their common interest in the grandchildren and often ended if the mother remarried. Others regretted the loss of affinal relationships after divorce but viewed them in terms of the marriage and did not expect them to continue after the separation.

The 'empty nest'

Many writers concerned with the ageing process have commented on losses associated with later life, referring to the 'empty-nest' transition when the last child leaves home, the effects of retirement from paid work and the gradual disengagement from social life which occurs in the final stages of the life-course (Troll *et al.*, 1979; Spence and Loner, 1971; Cumming and Henry, 1961). The first of these, the 'empty-nest' transition, now only rarely coincides with retirement, and certainly no longer signifies the onset of old age. Social and demographic changes in both childbearing and life-expectancy patterns have lengthened the post-childrearing period so that the 'empty nest' now occurs in middle age or, for some women, even earlier. The transition which takes place in women's lives when their children leave home has overwhelmingly been seen as problematic. Because the mothering role is expected to take priority over all others, the perceived loss of this is believed to cause a loss of identity and self-esteem and to be responsible for declining mental and physical health in middle-aged women (Brown and Harris, 1978; Bart, 1975, 1971). However, Roberts (1985) suggests that the 'empty-nest' syndrome is a common explanation for distress in older women, because it relies on stereotypes about the nature of motherhood and childcare. It is held that women are so bound up with, and fulfilled by, their domestic responsibilities that when their children leave depression and other loss-related symptoms are inevitable. More recent investigations have shown that for many women the post-parental period is not a time of crisis but a welcome opportunity for freedom and self-expression (Gambs, 1989; Roberts, 1985). These women are relieved that their childrearing work is over and find many compensations in freedom from this responsibility.

Criticisms of the 'empty-nest' concept are well-taken, although evidence from the mother-in-law group supports its validity because of meanings attached to it by the women involved. Reactions, of course, depend on individual differences and life-styles. Older women, for example, have been socialized to both depend on others and have others depend on them, and for many home-making is a full-time occupation. For these women, the 'empty-nest' period may indeed bring on depression in the face of their diminishing role. Studies suggest that women whose primary role is maternal have most difficulty adjusting to the departure of their children (Bart, 1975, 1971), whilst others link this to consistency in coping abilities throughout life (Troll et al., 1979). Therefore, women who cannot adjust to the events of middle age are likely to be those who had difficulty with critical life transitions in the past and will have with those to come such as widowhood and failing health. Bart, however, argues that the events of middle age are the most traumatic for women because 'at this point in the life course the inadequacy of the traditional female roles is apparent' (1975, p. 12). She points out that whilst role loss occurs at all stages in life, when women are young new roles replace old ones and rites of passage mark their importance. It is no coincidence, in Bart's view, that for many women, middle-aged depression, commonly associated with the menopause, occurs at the time their children depart. She suggests that this comes not from hormonal changes but from a change in the female life-course which is viewed negatively and for which there is no rite of passage.

Whilst there is no doubt that many women experience loss-related problems when their children depart, it is pessimistic and misleading to ignore the majority of middle-aged women for whom the post-parental transition is no more difficult than other life transitions. For example, only two mothers-in-law were experiencing difficulties associated with the 'empty nest' and for both there were other contributing factors including retirement from paid work and physical illness. It is also significant that both were mothers of an only son so there were no other children to cushion the blow when he left, and that neither woman had been able to establish close relations with her son's partner. The rest of the group had adjusted well, taking pleasure in their extended families whilst appreciating freedom from parental responsibilities. Even so, in various ways the majority of women referred to loss-related experiences and the inevitable changes when adult children move away.

> I do miss him. He's been married a long time now, of course, but I still miss him. And it's a great disappointment that things aren't better between us all. I don't think I can do anything now. If I could have done anything I would have done it long ago, and have tried to. But I just think, well it's just how it is. (Mrs Swann)

> I suppose what made it worse was the fact that I retired just before... And the fact that Glyn left home during that time... and suddenly he decided he was going to... and he'd gone. (Mrs Williams)

> He took a suitcase and all his stuff, you know. He left his books behind... odd bits that he used to come back for. But with his bedroom empty, yes, it was odd. But it's just a thing that you have to get used to. (Mrs Tagg)

> You do feel a loss. I've been through it so I know. It's a funny feeling as you can't explain actually. I don't know why. (Mrs Jones)

Friendly Relations?

> I didn't prepare myself. I don't see how you could. Because it's very difficult to imagine the emptiness it brings until it happens. And really, you can't imagine it before then I don't think. (Mrs Harris)

It is interesting that women expressed their emotional loss in relation to domestic labour and the practical tasks mothers perform on behalf of their sons. Domestic competence has close connotations with the mothering role and this may be particularly important for the mothers of sons. Although no able-bodied adult actually needs someone to cook and clean for them, women continue to service their sons as an expression of love and concern for their welfare. Many of the women interviewed admitted to reinforcing gender divisions in their children, encouraging the interest little girls have in housework yet simultaneously fostering dependence in their sons. As a consequence, boys seem more affectionate and more in need of their mothers' care. Overt expressions of affection between mother and son tend to decline as he grows, but her domestic work on his behalf reaffirms her self-worth and assures her she is still needed. It is not surprising, therefore, that when her son leaves home the emotional loss is difficult to separate from the void in her domestic role.

> I miss cooking for him very much. I still very often do buy three chops and three steaks and three of everything. I miss not having to do his washing. He'd have a clean shirt every day and sometimes in the morning there'd be a note on the table, 'can you wash my grey shirt for tonight?' And I'd quickly wash it out before I went on duty, you know, and spin dry it or hang it on the line. I miss that dreadful. (Mrs Williams)

Mrs Williams is a poignant reminder that for some women the transition to post-parenthood is an extremely painful process. Because they are family-oriented women most of their concerns have centred on their children and when the last (or only) child leaves, the physical and emotional impact can be desolating.

> Suddenly his room was empty and his wardrobe was empty. And one night, I don't know why, I went into his room and I thought, 'Glyn isn't coming home tonight'. It hadn't really struck home that he'd actually left. I went into his room and I don't know, for some reason I opened his wardrobe and it was empty. And it upset me something terrible... Suddenly, towards Christmas, it hit me.

And:

> At night we'd sit up late watching a film and my husband would look at his watch and say, 'Oh, our Glyn is late coming in'. But he was always coming in, even in the middle of the night if he stayed out late, I'd hear the 'click' of the door. Well now, since he's left my husband has been in the habit of bolting the front door and this may sound ridiculous but that does something to me. The thought that he might come home and not be able to get in... And he's had to stop doing it, I said, 'don't bolt that front door'. I can't abide that front door being bolted. (Mrs Williams)

What Mrs Williams so poignantly describes is, of course, a bereavement. Raphael states: 'Bereavement is the reaction to the loss of a close relationship and grief... the emotional response to loss, the complex amalgam of painful effects including sadness, anger, helplessness, guilt, despair' (1984, p. 33).

When her son left home, Mrs Williams not only experienced loss of a role but also loss of a person. This was how she felt but her feelings were not allowed legitimate expression because bereavement and loss are usually associated with death and, clearly, her son was not dead. Others, in similar circumstances, might feel that the reason for his departure (although not ideal since he left to cohabit, not to marry) was a cause for minor celebration rather than grief. Thus, individual factors are highly significant and suggest that generalizations about reactions to the 'empty nest' are often inappropriate and insensitive. Indeed, there is a danger that the term itself might trivialize what for some women is a complex and distressing experience.

The varying experiences of women confronting the 'empty nest' period signifies conflicting expectations mothers have for their children. Whilst on the one hand they value the present relationship for its immediate rewards, they want their child to move to independence and develop successful adult relationships of his own. Mothers anticipate and encourage the transition from child to independent, functioning adult, and prepare themselves as well as they can for the inevitable changes in their own lives. For some, however, adjusting to the physical and emotional separation required creates serious problems and, for these women, the 'empty nest' is indeed a crisis point of middle age.

Daughters-in-law were generally sympathetic to the losses associated with the 'empty nest' and understood why mothers might feel unhappy at this time. Because most of them had children of their own, they were able to visualize themselves in the same situation and recognized the changes that would occur. One of the coping strategies for confronting the 'empty nest' transition was their suggestion that women should discuss their feelings openly with their sons and if possible with their daughters-in-law. This advice is somewhat at odds with comments made by the same daughters-in-law expressing disappointment in the lack of communication skills between mothers and adult sons. It may be, however, that their comments reflect this disappointment and a desire for things to be different, since realistically they knew that 'talking about feelings' is not a significant feature of mother-son relationships.

> I suppose, ideally, to talk with the son, to be aware between themselves that there may be problems, that they are going to find it difficult. Say to the son, 'I'm going to find it difficult when you go', rather than actually say nothing and then have this awful feeling inside. (Wendy)

> I think the best thing she can do is to say, you know, just say, 'It feels very quiet, I don't have so much to do these days now I haven't got you to look after'. I think that helps a lot. That way the daughter-in-law won't think she's getting at her. And everybody knows what's the matter if she's feeling a bit tetchy. You know, at a loss what to do. (Valerie)

No mother-in-law had discussed the impact of her son's departure with him, not even Mrs Williams who had experienced quite serious problems. Mothers must conceal their feelings when the time comes for their children to leave, familiar behaviour for women who may have spent years avoiding self-disclosure so as not to burden their sons with unwelcome emotions.

> He didn't talk to me personally. He spoke to his father about it, but he didn't ever actually say to me, 'I'm moving out'. (Mrs Williams)

Some women agreed that earlier separations prepared them for their son's departure, making it easier when he married. However, marriage is a legitimate departure and has a note of finality lacking in other separations. When a son goes away to university, for example, it is acknowledged that the parental home is still his and his presence during vacations (accompanied by hold-alls full of dirty laundry) confirms this. Therefore, the 'empty nest' encompasses more than one's son leaving home. This is only the beginning of a prolonged transition which is completed when he marries and replaces his mother with a wife.

Generally, mothers-in-law had very positive views about their sons leaving to get married and were equally robust in their attitudes towards loss-related problems. Whilst acknowledging that the post-parental period calls for the reorganization of roles and relationships, they felt it was unwise and unnecessary to see this as a loss. Instead they emphasized the many compensations to be found both in extended family relationships and fewer domestic responsibilities.

> Women shouldn't feel a loss. They should count their blessings that they've got a daughter-in-law now. I mean, they've probably had a good family life and they should be glad that their son is going to have the same. (Mrs Orchard)

> I suppose it is a loss. But I don't know, if you keep in touch and they come and see you and you go to see them. I mean, it's nice to see them and I'm not glad to see them go, not really. But I'm pleased when they've gone because I can get tidied up again. (Mrs Tagg)

> Oh no, I felt no sense of loss. I just thought, 'Oh, the peace and the space'. But then again, they haven't gone far away from me. A friend of mine, her daughter went to Australia and that must be a terrible wrench. (Mrs York)

Some women said that mothers had plenty of opportunity to prepare themselves for their son's departure and 'should be preparing themselves almost from when he is born', although, of course, this is much easier said than done. Given that women are expected to be 'other-directed' (Spence and Loner, 1971) for most of their adult life and primarily in relation to their families, the change of situation when children marry cannot help but be abrupt. As we know, there is rarely pre-socialization for mothers prior to their children leaving home, no rite of passage for middle-aged women and no role for mothers-in-law in the marriage ceremony. In short, there is nothing to mark the years of mothering in the past or the changes now taking place.

I did try to prepare myself. I mean, I would never want to stop him enjoying his life because I've had mine but when he left home, well, it was still a shock. I think it is for any mother. (Mrs Williams)

It might be thought that the post-childrearing period is likely to be less traumatic for younger women. More are working outside the home during the childrearing years and have established roles and relationships which are separate from their domestic lives. They may also demand more in terms of marital satisfaction and share a greater number of interests and activities with their partners. Consequently, they are more likely to have developed resources and strategies for when their children depart and have less adjustments to make when the time comes. Indeed, several daughters-in-law compared themselves with middle-aged women in these terms, suggesting that their adherence to traditional gender roles made it difficult to fill the void left by departing children because being a mother had left little time for anything else.

However, it is important to avoid such a deterministic view of middle-aged women and certainly it would be inaccurate to describe the mothers-in-law as totally home-centred. For example, the majority worked during the childrearing period, some in part-time jobs which fitted in with their domestic responsibilities, whilst others continued to follow their careers or established new ones. One woman trained and qualified as a medical auxiliary, another ran a retailing concern, and both managed to combine their work commitments with childcare. Moreover, although employment and domestic responsibilities were time-consuming, all the women had some personal interests and hobbies which they had managed to sustain and the majority commented on interests shared with their partners. Consequently, they had a number of resources to help them and yet all experienced some of the feelings associated with the 'empty nest' transition.

For most mothers-in-law, however, loss-related feelings were only temporary and no doubt self-fulfilment in other areas apart from mothering helped some of them avoid more serious problems. On the other hand, they all operated within a set of traditional values in that their self-image as wives and mothers continued after their children left home. It is unwise, therefore, to generalize about middle-aged women or to see them as so bound up in domestic life that all else is excluded. Such an image is another example of the negative stereotypes which exist for this age group, a stereotype which is apparently true in its power to influence women and yet distorts reality at the same time.

Many women do not feel that their children leaving home is a crisis and those who do are exhorted to fill their lives with new possibilities. However, this is not always possible in a society preoccupied with youth culture and where there is little existing structure for the middle-aged. Lack of significant activities, therefore, is not necessarily from choice. For example, in her study of women and leisure, Deem (1986) states:

> this period between forty and sixty does seem to be one in which leisure, often for the first time since the early twenties, once more plays an important role for women. Yet the needs and interests of this group are often forgotten both by policy makers and by commercial providers, despite Featherstone and Hepworth's (1981) argument that for both sexes the later years of middle age are a major focus of consumerism. (p. 129)

Nevertheless, despite lack of provision, Deem found middle-aged women highly involved in leisure both with their partners and with female friends. Indeed, friendships are particularly important, for whilst most women have the potential for such involvement, for some lack of confidence can also restrict their opportunities for new social activities. Friendships in middle and later life are an important source of social integration and although friends are valued for the provision of emotional and practical support, companionship is often the defining characteristic (O'Connor, 1992; Jerome, 1981). The most important advantage of having friends at this age is the opportunity for shared activities and 'someone to do things with' (Jerome, 1981, p. 193).

One way of 'filling one's life' is to find other outlets for the nurturing role (Gambs, 1989; Uhlenberg, 1979). Indeed, for very many women it is unnecessary to seek outlets at all as their care-giving activities are expected to continue regardless of personal choice. It has been suggested that middle-aged women are 'the caught generation' (Marcus, 1978), the principal care-givers in the family who are expected to meet simultaneous demands from ageing parents, adult children and grandchildren, at a time when they might anticipate some freedom themselves (Rosenthal, 1983; Brody, 1981). Moreover, it is common for women's caring responsibilities to be generalized to people outside the immediate domestic setting. It is well documented, for example, that social policy which advocates community care 'solutions' for the needs of dependent people relies largely on the presumed goodwill and voluntarism of women (Finch and Groves, 1985; Land and Rose, 1985; Wilson, 1982). New emphasis on extending the nurturing role to unpaid work in the community implies that 'women are being granted a favour by being involved in social services' (Phillipson, 1981, p. 193). Uhlenberg (1979), for example, suggests that increasing numbers of elderly people provide ample opportunity for the constructive involvement of middle-aged women in their care, to the mutual benefit of both groups. However, as Phillipson points out, this assumes that, after years of providing family support, women would welcome an extension of their caring activities to others in the community. This deterministic view reflects ideas about women's 'natural' altruism and ignores their own interests and needs.

Becoming a grandmother

It has been suggested that grandparenthood provides an avenue for legitimate involvement in the lives of married children and strengthens ties which weaken at the 'empty nest' transition (Gambs, 1989; Yeandle, 1987; Crawford, 1981). The arrival of grandchildren is an important stage in the life-course and one generally welcomed by mothers-in-law. All the women in the mother-in-law group said the most positive aspect of being a mother-in-law was the potential for, and realization of, becoming a grandmother. This is seen as a positive transition and does not signify role loss or impending old age. The arrival of grandchildren no longer 'marks the assumption of a position as eldest of three generations within the family' (Crawford and Hooper, 1973, p. 476) as four-generation families are now commonplace. Therefore, grandchildren are warmly received both as a source of pleasure, and because they represent the continuation and connection of generations in the family.

Stevie is my first grandchild. Oh, it was great that was. We thought it was wonderful. The first grandchild is special. It's like your firstborn really. There's that... just that little extra. Just that little bond, I think, although you love them all, of course. (Mrs Jones)

They rang us up and said, 'How would you like to be grandparents next March?' And we said, 'Oh...', because we thought we'd never be grandparents. Once we were over 60, you know, we thought, 'We won't be grandparents'. But we are and it is nice. (Mrs Tagg)

I was pleased about having grandchildren, And I enjoy them. I love them, they're really nice. (Mrs Harris)

Mothers who had frequent contact with their married children were able to maintain this and extend it to include grandchildren when they arrived. Indeed, interaction with grandchildren depended on this since, to a large extent, it is the middle generation that conditions contacts in three-generation families. Therefore, parents can affect the behaviour of grandparents in that they only become involved as far as parents will allow. Evidence from daughters-in-law suggests that women encourage positive grandparenting involvement in their children's lives despite personal antagonisms with in-laws, but paternal grandmothers sometimes doubt this. For example, despite Mrs Swann's efforts to establish good relations with her daughter-in-law, the primary sentiment between the two women seems to be dislike and this was not improved by the arrival of grandchildren. Mrs Swann has little contact with her daughter-in-law and her son visits infrequently and usually alone. Therefore, she rarely sees her two grandsons and has been unable to establish the kind of grandmothering role she had hoped for. Instead, the traditional family values she held prior to her son's marriage have been seriously disturbed and her expectations of extended generational relationships unmet. Driven to despair over this, it is perhaps understandable that Mrs Swann felt her daughter-in-law was to blame.

We are grandparents but when the boys come here we don't feel like their grandparents because they have no close affinity with us at all. But I feel that's because we're not talked about in her household. So really, we've missed having grandchildren because I'd love them to run to me and say, 'Hello Granny' and love me, you know. I love them when they come and the little one is all right, but Ashley is like a piece of wood. But I'm quite sure it's because... she's probably said to them, 'Oh, Granny and I don't get on well together'. She might have said that to them, you know, and after all, it is their mother. But I am hoping that one day they'll say, 'Gran, can we come and stay with you?' Whether they will or not... To tell you the truth it's too upsetting. I could cry every day about it all and I try and put it out of my mind now. I have cried when I've thought about it all and the only thing I can do is to try and forget it, you know. (Mrs Swann)

Again, as Mrs Swann's comments show, the 'rules' by which people structure their relationships are not straightforward and frequently break down. Having

Friendly Relations?

'obeyed all the rules' as she understood them, Mrs Swann's relationship with her daughter-in-law, and thereby her grandsons, continued to be disappointing and unfulfilled. She believed, therefore, that there was nothing else but to learn to live with her disappointment and distress, and the emotional cost this involved is evident from the air of sadness in so many of her remarks.

However, the majority of women interviewed said that grandmotherhood is the most rewarding of the later life-transitions. Women look forward to being grandmothers, so much so that if they are denied this role there can be an acute sense of disappointment. It has been pointed out that many of women's life changes are contingent on their children becoming adults, and continuing the family course through a similar socialization pattern to their parents, (Caplan, 1981; Spence and Loner, 1971). Therefore, a woman's expectations of becoming a grandmother depend on the expectations she has for her daughter or daughter-in-law to have children. A decision made by the younger woman can affect her own life either by causing an anticipated change or delaying or preventing that change. Consequently, a daughter-in-law's refusal or failure to be a mother interferes with her mother-in-law's life expectations and her hopes of involvement with the next generation.

> We planned to have childen but we were married six and a half years before we did. They wanted grandchildren and that caused a lot of problems. I didn't want them, I'd got no interest at all. I didn't want a baby at the time and there was no way I was going to consider it. I was annoyed by the fact that they felt it was a duty. She used to do things like, 'I've brought a money-box for our baby. It's there, and I'm putting so much in once a week'. And I do believe she started buying baby clothes and I mean, this was years before I'd even started thinking about having a child. (Wendy)

Women often attach considerable importance to the genetic chain, a concern which, it is believed, stems from a lack of creative activities for women other than childrearing (Gittins, 1985; Caplan, 1981). Thus, in a very real sense, subsequent generations are a justification of their life's work, and daughters-in-law who are childless not only break the chain but, importantly, may be perceived as questioning the value of women's work as mothers (Caplan, 1981). Indeed, Caplan suggests that many women are waiting to be grandmothers from the beginning of the post-parental stage in order to resume mothering, although there is no evidence from this study that women want a repetition of the more demanding aspects of childcare. However, they do want a positive grandmothering role, so it is important for them not only to become grandmothers but to be 'on time' (Spence and Loner, 1971, p. 373), that is, before they reach an age they see as too old to enjoy it. Being 'on time' as a grandmother is contingent on married children also being 'on time' as parents, since failure in this respect affects the older generations in the family and delays their progress too. For example, two women who have been married several years but have no children each commented on the disappointment their mother-in-law feels not to be a grandmother. In both cases, the refusal or inability of the younger woman to play her part in meeting the older woman's expectations has led to some misunderstanding and regrets on all sides.

She would like me to have children. Once we got married, both mothers assumed we'd got married to have children and we hadn't necessarily. And so there was a bit of 'When are you having some kids?' And then when we were about 25, 26, both of them seemed to be saying, 'Are you going to have some kids? You've got to get going sometime'. And they've just started up again because we're 30 now. But they've both become a little more tactful. They're both desirous for us to have children but realize that it's our decision. They just give us helpful hints every so often. (Ruth)

I was talking to his mum about it, you know, saying 'I feel I'm not going to be a mum and I'm not going to be a grandma . . .' and she said, 'Well, how do you think I feel?' And I was so hurt then because, yes, she was expressing how she felt but at least she had her own children. But I don't think she was trying to put any pressure on, I think she just wanted to say how she felt and it just naturally happened. But I felt then, 'Oh, she must be so disappointed'. (Laura)

Being 'on time' also demonstrates the importance of the cohort effect on critical life transitions, because first-time grandmotherhood can occur at any time between the ages of, say, 36 and 65, depending on individual circumstances. Obviously, this has implications for the grandparenting style women feel able to adopt and also, because the age range is so wide, means that grandmothers as a group have no bedrock of shared experience on which to draw.

Living together

The failure to meet expectations is also demonstrated when children choose to cohabit rather than marry. Mothers are greatly disturbed when this happens and seem to be at a loss to know how to deal with it. Although normative attitudes towards sexual relations have changed during the past two decades, older people often find premarital sexuality difficult to accept. Women, especially, have considerable respect for the sanctity of marriage and are disturbed by the knowledge that their child is enjoying a sexual relationship outside the marriage institution. However, they are also bound by the ethic of privacy which governs sexual relationships and precludes expressions of disapproval. Providing the young couple are not openly living together, therefore, it is often easier for parents to turn a blind eye.

As long as she didn't know and Alec went out and maybe didn't come back until very early in the morning, she could assume other things. But when he didn't come home for a full night or stayed away for a weekend and made no secret of the fact that he was staying with me, then that was difficult for her to accept. (Pauline)

She firmly believed that Andrew and I were virgins until our wedding night, and I think really she didn't want to know. (Deborah)

Friendly Relations?

If, however, the couple decide to cohabit before marriage, the nature of their relationship is not easily ignored. Mothers may hesitate to interfere when the young people move in together particularly if they are well over marriageable age, but there are many anxieties and concerns. They worry about the success of the relationship and whether their son will end up alone, or what would happen if his partner became pregnant. Even if all goes well, it is often difficult to know how to treat the young woman or to see her as a future daughter-in-law if there are no moves in that direction. Older women attach a great deal of importance to traditional family forms and their understanding of kin relations is not fully restored until, or unless, the couple marry.

> They lived together for three years before they got married in a flat that she'd got. I remember Cheryl coming in and saying, 'Marcus is going to stay at my place, we've come for his clothes', and I said, 'OK, they're in his bedroom'... What can you do? He was thirty-odd and you can't tell a lad of that age he can't do it... (Mrs Tagg)

> They did live with each other before they got married. I don't know, maybe nine months, a year. It seems to be the thing to do nowadays. I'm not very keen on it myself but there's nothing you can do about it. He knew our stand on marriage so there was nothing more we could say. And, of course, he was thirty-something, he wasn't a young boy. (Mrs Harris)

> He's living with his girlfriend. It's something I didn't think I could have accepted, but I have. It's mixed feelings really, because marriage is important to me. But I don't think it would worry me any more about Howard because he's reached an age where... I know he thinks a lot of Georgina, it's not as if he's got a different girl there every week. That I wouldn't like. I would worry if they were going to have children and they weren't married. It is important to be married if you're going to have children, because I think the children suffer if you don't. (Mrs Richardson)

Besides altering concepts of 'normal' kin relations, cohabitation creates all sorts of practical problems from how to refer to the son's partner, to the sleeping arrangements when the couple and their parents visit each other. These issues, often requiring negotiation, can be plainly embarrassing to resolve and it is this as much as higher ideals which cause mothers to be relieved when the couple decide to marry.

> When they were coming for Christmas I said to Len [husband] 'What are we going to do?' He said, 'Well, you know they sleep together over there. It's a bit silly isn't it? Can't you accept that they sleep together?' I mean, that had been bothering Howard as well, because he phoned and said, 'What's the situation when we come? Do you think we'd better go in a hotel?' I said, 'No, certainly not. I've accepted it. I can see that it's a permanent relationship'. But, yes, I did think I was being very tolerant letting Howard bring somebody here and sleep with her and they weren't married. (Mrs Richardson)

> I tell you what was difficult and that was writing a birthday card or Christmas card. You never knew exactly how to address it. You couldn't put Mr and Mrs because they weren't married, and you couldn't put Mr ... and Miss ... well, I suppose you could but I wouldn't have liked to. So I just used to put Marcus and Cheryl. That was awkward. I'd say to his dad, 'How do I address their card?' 'Oh, just put Marcus and Cheryl...' You know, no bother at all with a man, but I thought about it. I thought, 'Well...' (Mrs Tagg)

A period of cohabitation before marriage is not generally encouraged by parents, although it may be accepted if initial fears regarding the impermanency of the relationship proved unfounded. But marriage signifies the maturity of the child and this is the reason why most parents cannot fully accept a less orthodox arrangement. To them, marriage is a meaningful rite of passage which signifies the 'normal' transition into adult life. Cohabitation not only delays marriage, it may be seen as replacing it in an unsatisfactory way. In the words of one mother-in-law, living together is 'play-acting'; affecting marriage without assuming its responsibilities, commitments and constraints.

Given that cohabiting couples are tolerated but hardly approved of, it is often easier for all concerned if young people organize their living arrangements at a distance. It is not insignificant, therefore, that of the couples who had cohabited prior to marriage, either one or both partners were born outside Stoke-on-Trent. Although deciding to live in the area was primarily linked to job considerations, it was also a convenient way for cohabiting couples to avoid the disapproving scrutiny of at least one set of parents. From the parents' viewpoint, distance allowed them to ignore the couple's unorthodox behaviour for much of the time and avoided having to explain it to other relatives and friends. Fewer locally-born people openly lived together before marriage (although the majority had established a sexual relationship with their partner). This no doubt reflects traditional concepts of kin relations in the area and, to some extent, parental influence on the younger generation although, of course, neither applies exclusively to Stoke-on-Trent.

> We knew it was a problem but we weren't going to stop sleeping together, this was our lives, but we knew we had to placate everybody around us. My parents weren't a problem, they were miles away, but we'd got Lily here and he had to maintain, and I wanted him to maintain, a friendly relationship with his mother. (Pauline)

> I don't know if she told the rest of the family. I mean, everyone knew that we weren't married, but I don't know that she explained that we were actually living together, because it's all at a distance so it's fairly easy. You can actually get away with a lot as long as you're not forcing it down everyone's throat. (Ruth)

Interestingly, women whose sons were cohabiting did not attach blame to their partners or reveal higher levels of tension than in conventional relationships between affinal women. Only one daughter-in-law said her mother-in-law had expressed disapproval directly by questioning the young woman's moral attitudes and behaviour. It is likely that this mother-in-law was acknowledging the dual standards of sexual morality which exist for men and women and the need for women to protect themselves from its inherent dangers. Society condones male promiscuity but women, whilst no longer expected to remain virgins until marriage, are expected to direct their sexual interests towards one person. Therefore, mothers are often anxious that cohabitation signifies an unstable sexual relationship and that their son will not take his partner seriously as a potential wife. They also know that there can be serious consequences for women who do not regulate their sexual behaviour, including premarital pregnancy and loss of reputation. It is more often these concerns than the flouting of convention or a personal dislike of the young woman which might press mothers-in-law to voice their objections.

There was no evidence from the mother-in-law group to suggest that women stricture their children's behaviour by raising a dissenting voice or that they see their son's partner as totally at fault. However, women in the daughter-in-law group believed there was some apportioning of blame by their partner's mother and that this was unfairly balanced in favour of her son. In all but one instance this belief was based on conjecture since older women, bound by the rule which prohibits 'interference' in the lives of young adults, did not broach the subject directly. Nevertheless, some daughters-in-law felt subjected to implicit criticism because their sexual behaviour was not confined within marriage. These opinions stemmed from the same concepts of sexual morality which concerned mothers-in-law. That is, convention dictates that women must attract a potential husband and, within traditional courtship patterns which hold out the promise of sexual and other services, achieve the ultimate goal of marriage. By entering this complex and somewhat demeaning ritual, women have the best hope of becoming wives. Therefore, in order to be taken seriously and so achieve this goal, they are required to control the sexual side of the relationship whilst simultaneously remaining attractive enough to sustain the man's interest.

> Oh yes, we're all fallen women aren't we? Scarlet women. So yes, she did direct her comments at me. I was the one who was supposed to keep us on the straight and narrow. It was only because of my lax morals if you like, that the situation was there. The fact that her son had slept with other women was neither here nor there, you know. He didn't seem to have any responsibility for what was going on. (Pauline)

> She never said it, but she was a bit hostile with me. I think she thought I was a bit 'loose'. Which I was quite upset about. Because Simon could never do anything wrong. Oh no, he'd be the innocent all along. Because he's her son, he's her little boy. So I led him astray. I led him into trouble. (Laura)

> I'd definitely led him astray. Oh definitely. Because I don't think her little boy would have gone and lived with someone had the opportunity not been there. Her impression was that her little boy would meet someone and do it properly, you know. White wedding and all that. (Ruth)

Cohabitation is not a sign that young people have rejected marriage, since all those who chose to cohabit did eventually marry. Furthermore, cohabitation and reproduction were entirely separate, for there were no births outside marriage and no evidence that the young woman becoming pregnant prompted a decision to 'legalize' the situation. In all cases, despite mothers' fears, cohabitation was a serious endeavour undertaken in the hope of eliminating some of the uncertainties of marriage and to avoid mistakes made by peers.

Decisions to marry ranged from a desire to make public a private commitment to the very pragmatic reason that it was easier to deal with bureaucratic form-filling if the couple shared the same name. Whatever the reasons, much to the relief of parents, cohabitation eventually became an unsatisfactory arrangement and initial aversion to marriage wore away. For the mothers' generation, marriage was 'normal'; not to get married was hardly an available option, let alone an attractive prospect. To these women, marriage is sanctified by tradition and for a child to reject it for no other reason than personal choice is incomprehensible and disturbing. From the mother's viewpoint, therefore, cohabitation is always a temporary and unsatisfactory alternative to a legal and binding commitment in marriage.

> And then we went at Christmas time and they made an announcement that we were all invited to a wedding... her mother and father were there and we were there, and we said, 'Ooh, whose wedding?', and they said, 'We've decided to get married'. And it was lovely, it was a real treat. And I must admit that life was a bit easier when they decided to get married. Well, not life, but the atmosphere was a bit easier... Because while they were living together there was always the thought that they might split up, and you wondered how it would affect them. Your son, obviously, but in this case Cheryl is such a nice girl that I wondered about her too. But you've got to be so careful that you don't put your foot in it. (Mrs Tagg)

Therefore, although mothers rarely press directly for marriage they are pleased and relieved when it happens. It resolves their doubts and fears about the stability of their child's relationship and the sexual fidelity of both partners. Moreover, it ratifies their understanding of kin relations and marks the continuation of family life by the legitimate expectation of grandchildren.

Conclusion

Social and demographic changes caused by geographical mobility, divorce and cohabitation, as well as important life-transitions including the post-parental period, grandparenthood and retirement, have important effects on in-law relationships between women. Whilst all these herald periods of change for women, and some associated losses, the transitions are not necessarily traumatic and attitudes towards them are mainly positive. However, this is not without qualification. There is much evidence to suggest, for example, that older women attach considerable importance to traditional family forms and that divorce and cohabitation seriously disturb their understanding of kin relations. Furthermore, although daughters-in-law are usually instrumental in these changes, they too find difficulty in defining or redefining conventional mother-in-law and daughter-in-law relationships.

Friendly Relations?

Many are also burdened by the knowledge that their actions have disappointed the older woman and, as a consequence, have a highly developed sense of responsibility, guilt and apportioned blame. Finally, it is clear that many of women's life expectations are contingent upon their adult children marrying and having children themselves. A decision by the younger generation to delay this process inevitably affects the mother's ability to develop a positive self-image in later life. Thus, it is important that younger women play their part in meeting the expectations of older women by affirming the value of family life and ensuring its continuation.

Chapter 6

Support Relationships between Women: Resistance to Care

This chapter examines ways in which relationships between mothers-in-law and daughters-in-law are influenced and changed by crises in the family life-course. These may be acute crises such as illness or bereavement, or more gradual processes of ageing and dependency, but all create complex problems which upset the routines of family life. Changes in circumstances brought about by such crises frequently lead to a reassessment of what might be expected from affinal relationships and renegotiation of responsibilities and obligations between family members. Much of the material presented here looks at caring in the sense of tending relationships. These are two-way relationships, that is, care by the younger generation of the older generation and vice versa, and it emerges that care of the older generation is much more fraught than the situation in reverse. For example, when daughters-in-law identify their own needs they do not refer to care in terms of personal tending but of being cared about. Moreover, they see their own needs as more manageable and dispensable than the needs of the elderly. Firstly, their own needs are usually immediate and fairly short-term, for example for help and support after childbirth, and secondly, they expect to have more resources at their disposal. Most daughters-in-law feel able to call upon their husbands and/or sisters and, importantly, on their mothers and when these people are available the mother-in-law is not expected or required to give much assistance. However, when daughters-in-law talk about caring for an elderly mother-in-law they refer to her needs as being those which require very personal tending and are worried that they will be solely responsible for providing this type of care. Again, this has to do with resources. The elderly are marginalized in our society; they are often infantilized and forced into 'structured dependency' (Marsden and Abrams, 1987) because of a lack of resources other than those provided by their families and this is reflected in the views expressed by women in both study groups. Indeed, visualizing the elderly as dependent is a form of determinism which tends to underestimate the autonomy many older people have and wish to retain. For example, attitudes towards ageing expressed by women in the mother-in-law group revealed their overwhelming concern with personal autonomy and freedom of choice. Thus, they expected to play an active role in decisions about how much support they might need in the future and from whom they would accept it.

Who cares?

There is no doubt that the obligation to care for dependent individuals has traditionally been imposed on the family. Indeed, this was a legal obligation enshrined in the Poor Law Act of 1601, although historically there have always been families who would not, or could not, assume their responsibilities. Therefore, there is no firm historical basis for assumptions that the elderly, sick and disabled were cared for by their kin and evidence suggests that, in the past, support was provided at least as much by the state (Laslett, 1983).

Much of contemporary social policy hinges on a false understanding of the past and an equally false understanding of the family as it exists today. This has been called 'the sentimental model of the family' (Oakley, 1976, p. 101) and is informed by Parsons' theory that the nuclear family is the most functional type in contemporary society not only for the socialization of the child but as 'the primary basis of security for the normal adult' (Parsons, 1965, p. 37). Whilst Parsons was concerned with a nucleus of an adult couple and their dependent offspring, living in a domestic unit separate from other relatives, functionalist theory underpins a number of assumptions about the family implicit in social legislation. According to Finch and Groves (1985) these are:

> that the family should be a private domain, where the state should interfere only in special circumstances; that the family is a fragile institution which needs to be protected; and that a range of social services has to be developed for people unfortunate enough to be without a 'normal' family. (Finch and Groves, 1985, p. 227)

The assumption contained in social policy is, therefore, that the 'normal' family not only socializes and cares for dependent children but, as 'the primary basis of security for adults', is also the main location where the elderly, widowed, sick and disabled are cared for.

An important observation regarding assumptions about the 'normal' family is that the influence of social and demographic change is largely ignored. In contemporary society the organization of domestic life is subject to processes which disturb and alter the structure of domiciliary units, and consequently the 'sentimental model of the family' – breadwinner, housewife and an average of two dependent children – is in fact a minority group. To begin with, increasing numbers of married women in the labour market suggest that very few will be full-time housewives for the duration of adult life, whilst the continuing rise in separation and divorce makes it highly likely that many of them will not remain married. As far as the dependent elderly are concerned, this latter point is significant, for where an elderly person needs care, social norms and expectations dictate that this should be provided by a daughter or daughter-in-law (Finch and Groves, 1985). However, recent evidence suggests that this expectation is qualified by actual behaviour. The General Household Survey on informal carers (Green, 1985) shows that women caring for parents-in-law outside the household receive more support from people in their own household than women caring for parents or relatives or friends. This suggests an expectation that daughters-in-law have less responsibility than daughters or women whose caring is generalized to others outside the domestic setting. Alternatively, daughters-in-law may be more successful in avoiding the responsibility of caring for parents-in-law because of their structural position in the kin network. There is some evidence that a hierarchy of obligations exists and that the nearest to fixed sets of obligations are those between husband and wife and parents and children. Thus, a woman may expect to put the needs of her parents before those of her parents-in-law, or to be involved in their care only if there is no available daughter. However, obligations and responsibilities towards in-laws are often reduced by divorce and decline still further if the woman remarries. Consequently, the previous structure of obligations becomes more complex and effectively excludes a number of women as potential carers of their former in-laws because on remarriage their obligations are directed towards a new family group. It is clear, therefore, that the sentimental model of the family, whilst prominent in political rhetoric and social policy, fails to address the reality of most people's lives. Consequently, the notion that women constitute a pool of carers, available in the home and ready for mobilization when needed, is at the very least unrealistic. Moreover, even supposing it were not, it leaves aside the important question about whether women would want to be used in this way.

This brings us to a second strand of functionalism which argues that the family stabilizes adults in their socially designated gender roles. Thus, 'instrumental' males, with their capacity for decision-making and responsible action, are primarily located in the public sphere as breadwinners. 'Expressive' females, on the other hand, are mainly occupied in the domestic sphere, where their nurturing abilities provide the physical and emotional support for a network of family relationships. Assumptions about female expressiveness are inextricably linked to the socially constructed roles of wife and mother and imply that women are particularly suited for caring since this has close connotations with the mothering role (Graham, 1984; Finch and Groves, 1982). The motherhood mandate affects all women whether they have children or not, since it extends beyond childcare to include practical and emotional support for others, kin and non-kin alike (Gittins, 1985). Thus, elderly widows have often nursed a sick husband and may themselves be cared for by a daughter or, to a lesser extent, a daughter-in-law (Finch and Groves, 1982; Hunt, 1978). Ungerson (1983) suggests that mothering and caring have much in common, involving skills which women practice every day via housework and childcare. These, combined with women's responsibilities for informal health work in the family, represent a form of expertise which, although rarely acknowledged, is uniquely female. Gilligan (1982), too, recognizes women's special ability to care and focuses on women's moral development derived from an understanding of responsibilities and concern for human relationships. She suggests, therefore, that 'women not only define themselves in a context of human relationships but also judge themselves in terms of their ability to care' (pp. 16–17). In short, the social construction of mothering, central to women's nurturant relationships, forms the basis of their moral obligation to assume caring responsibilities.

The difficulty is that both views seem to reinforce assumptions that there are distinctively male and female activities which are limited and constrained by socially defined gender roles. This suggests that caring is a gendered concept and, as such, is particularly resistant to an interchangeable sexual division of labour. Furthermore, as Ungerson (1983) makes clear, there are a number of taboos surrounding the sex of the carer and cared-for which may determine the boundaries of their relationship and thus make women appear the most obvious people to care. This is particularly important in relation to the care of the frail elderly and will be considered in detail later in the chapter. Suffice it to say at this point, however, that all theories about appropriate carers appear to trap women in their socialized gender role. Thus, women seem the obvious candidates (although they may not define themselves as such) and have few genuine alternatives given cultural assumptions about the function of the family and women's pivotal role within it.

Whilst there is much evidence to support women's key role as carers (Lewis and Meredith, 1988; Marsden and Abrams, 1987; Qureshi and Simons, 1987; Ungerson, 1987, 1983; Evers, 1985; Finch and Groves, 1985, 1982) the contribution made by male carers does appear to have been overlooked.[1] For example, there is a basis for arguing that a dimension of care exists which is neither family-based nor provided by women. David Clark (1988), in addressing the impact of AIDS on family relationships, has suggested that the family is not always the primary arena of care for those infected with the virus. Whilst recognizing that families will have an important role in caring for relatives with AIDS and that here the burden will devolve on women, Clark suggests that the particular taboos associated with AIDS have created the need for other forms of support. The physical, psychological and emotional dimensions of the illness are often so threatening to families of sufferers that some have refused to provide care, particularly families of gay men who, in a homophobic society, must cope with the stigmas of homosexuality and AIDS, as well as with the illness itself. Thus, there are exceptionally difficult circumstances in which caring for people with AIDS takes place and whilst some families are able to cope, others are not. A consequence of AIDS and HIV infections is that new models of care have evolved which involve neither the family nor women. According to Clark, it is gay men who have provided care and support for homosexuals and others with AIDS, and whilst people within and outside the gay community have become involved (including lesbians and heterosexual women) the fact that support was initiated by men suggests at least one dimension of care which questions normative concepts of family and gender.

There is, however, no escaping the fact that whilst men can and do care, the majority of support relationships involve women and it is they who are responsible for other people's health and well-being. Their role as providers of an informal health service within the home has led various commentators to suggest that the domestic domain is a workplace and, in particular, one where health work on behalf of others is carried out (Graham, 1985; Roberts, 1984). Graham argues that it is up to women to provide the material comforts such as a warm, clean home, good food and adequate clothing, seen as essential to protect against illness and also 'to orchestrate social relations within the home and to minimize the health damaging insecurities which can arise when these relations go astray' (Graham, 1985, p. 26). Moreover, it is women who are the link between health care provided within the family and formal health and welfare systems provided by the state.

A woman's responsibility for health is linked to her own well-being only so far as it affects her family. She is admonished to take care of herself so that she is able to take care of other people (Roberts, 1985). Paradoxically, a 'good' wife and mother does not take to her sick-bed unless the illness is literally one that immobilizes her, but continues to deal with the demands of her family even when she is unwell (Pill and Stott, 1982). This accords with the views of the women in this study who either were healthy or, more likely, carried on regardless when they were not. Most women said they were never ill or 'couldn't afford to be', although they also felt their husband could take over in a real emergency. Occasionally, female relatives might help out with childcare or shopping, but only in exceptional circumstances did mothers-in-law or daughters-in-law provide nursing care for each other.

Pregnancy and childbirth

When daughters-in-law talked about health and illness, they frequently mentioned pregnancy and childbirth, not because they saw these events as particularly problematic but rather because these are occasions of validated care. For a woman, the birth of her first child is a status passage involving a sequence of events which transforms her from non-mother to mother. Having a child changes couples into 'real' families and, importantly, elevates wives to a new status which is shared with their own mother and their mother-in-law. Oakley (1980) suggests that childbirth is assumed to represent a gain whereas other life-events such as bereavement or retirement represent loss. However, it is not unusual for first-time mothers to feel they have lost something in the process of having a child, the primary loss being loss of identity. Thus, becoming a mother is a 'mixed blessing' requiring adjustments not only in life-style but in one's sense of self. Breen's (1975) study of first-time mothers suggests that women who adjust well to motherhood give no evidence of conflict between the maternal role and personal identity. Furthermore, these women identify strongly with their own mothers and see themselves as more similar to them after the birth of the child. Importantly, they also see their mothers as 'good' mothers and, because of perceived similarities between the two women, describe themselves in the same way. Fischer (1983) has shown that women are more likely to increase contact with mothers than with mothers-in-law after the birth of a child, thus re-establishing with their mothers a maternity-oriented intimacy not shared with the mother-in-law. Not surprisingly, therefore, most daughters-in-law turned to their mothers as the next source of assistance after their husbands. This suggests a well-developed understanding of caring hierarchies and a lack of familiarity in in-law relationships which makes mothers-in-law inappropriate helpers at this time. The importance of the wife's mother was apparent from the beginning of the pregnancy when, in almost every case, she was the first relative to hear the good news.

> I told my mother straightaway, as soon as I knew. My husband told his mother and she was pleased. (Gaynor)

> We told my mum first. I think that's only natural really. We phoned them up. Well, we told my mum and then we phoned Kevin's mum right away and told her. (Vicky)

> We told my parents first and then very shortly afterwards we told Tom's. Oh, they were overjoyed. Both sets of parents were. (Wendy)

Friendly Relations?

Being 'overjoyed' was a common parental reaction to the prospect of having a grandchild, and the daughters-in-law who had planned to have children were also pleased when they knew they were pregnant. There were some women, however, for whom pregnancy was a traumatic and difficult event, either because they did not want a baby at the time or because they felt ill and unattractive throughout. Becoming a mother obviously involves changes in body image which may or may not be welcome, and often there are trying symptoms such as backache, nausea and constipation. None of these are guaranteed to make women feel sexually attractive in a culture which defines femininity in terms of a slim (thin?) body and glowing good health. On the other hand, having a baby is held out as women's greatest achievement, a positive and normal event and the most important affirmation of true femininity. As Oakley points out, given the contradiction between images of female sexuality and maternity, 'the disjunction between contravening the feminine standard (getting fat) and conforming to it (having a baby) would be expected to be a source of personal difficulty for some women' (1980, p. 211).

Even so, the majority of women do have relatively trouble-free pregnancies and many experience pregnancy and childbirth as enjoyable and emotionally satisfying. By contrast, those who find both events unpleasant are likely to see themselves, and be seen, as 'abnormal' and to be burdened by guilt because of it. This is particularly relevant if a woman's experience compares unfavourably with her mother-in-law's, albeit that the older woman's recollections may be unreliable. As previously stated, the mother-in-law, unlike the mother, has no intimate knowledge of her daughter-in-law's personal history and thus, if she is critical, seems to reject the younger woman entirely. Consequently, if the daughter-in-law is seen to be 'failing' in woman's 'natural' destiny when her mother-in-law apparently succeeded, there is little room for sympathy or understanding between them.

> I was ill when I was having Leanne. I had a urinary tract infection and wasn't well at all. I couldn't eat anything. But Jeff's mother thought that was all in the mind. You know, you were having a baby, there was nothing in that and you'd just got to pull yourself together. You know, women do it every day, she'd had three... (Frances)

> The main problem was that I was so enormous. I felt so unattractive, my hair was wrong, the coat I'd got was like a bell tent. Now, I must have spoken to his mother about it because pregnancy for her was when she felt the most beautiful. She loved being pregnant, having a baby was lovely, it was what you wanted. She would say that time and time and time again to me. She loved being pregnant whereas for me it was terrible. (Helen)

Although having a baby is not routinely associated with illness, the physical impact of childbirth and emotional adjustments to motherhood can leave women anxious and exhausted. Oakley (1980), for example, has commented on the state of anxiety experienced by new mothers on first being alone with, and responsible for, their baby and certainly in the first weeks after the birth women were grateful for outside help. Indeed those who turned to their husband as the first source of support quickly discovered that the transformation into a 'real' family is not a smooth one and often it is too fragile to stand the strain. Romantic images of a happy, competent and successful family soon gave way to the reality of an exhausted mother, bewildered father and a small, demanding intruder who never stopped crying.

> I didn't want anybody. I was so depressed I didn't honestly want anyone. I just felt so physically ill and I'd got this dreadful depression. And the plan was that Tom would take some time off but in the event he only took one day. Maybe I made it more difficult because I didn't really want my mother and I certainly didn't want his mother. I wanted him really and he had to go to work. That was it. I never saw him. But I felt a lot of anger and bitterness. And the same thing happened with the second baby. Exactly the same. I mean, I was OK, I was able to cope better but it wasn't just the physical support, it was the emotional support. It would have been nice to be a family. That was what I wanted. (Wendy)

Coming home with a new baby may be the time when daughters turn to their mothers for emotional support and practical help (Nice, 1992; Alibhai, 1989; Oakley, 1979). Mothers know about the anxieties and uncertainties which women feel when faced with the responsibilities of motherhood. Presumably mothers-in-law do too, but the element of formality in in-law relationships makes them unlikely confidantes when daughters-in-law are especially vulnerable. Mothers and daughters, however, have an intimate knowledge of each other; they may have similar perspectives and the lack of strong interpersonal boundaries enables them to communicate their feelings effectively.

Fischer (1983) suggests that after the birth of a child women need and receive more help from both 'sides' of the family both in terms of personal services and financial aid and gifts. She found, however, that mothers were more likely to do things, whilst mothers-in-law were more likely to give things. Evidence from this study suggests a clearer distinction between types of practical assistance from mothers and mothers-in-law and that, in both cases, daughters-in-law set limits on what they accept. For example, many women said they were possessive about their babies and wanted to care for them themselves. Therefore, they wanted help with cooking and household chores which enabled them to devote time to the baby. As long as there was no mother available or circumstances dictated how much she could be involved, women were grateful for help from their mother-in-law but there was a clear preference for their own mothers when both women were able to assist. This is nowhere more obvious than in the division of labour between the two women, for whilst the mother's role centred on her daughter and grandchild, the mother-in-law performed tasks which allowed her less contact with the baby.

> It worked out well because I could allow my mother to do things and say things. She was so concerned and wanted to help and it worked out. And Lily was able to take a role in that. She did the laundry you see. She came up and took the washing away. My mum did the cooking, I fed Sarah and poor Alec was shoved out the door. (Pauline)

We'd only got a little terraced house with an outside loo, so I went to my mum's with the baby when I came out. I stayed at my mum's for about two weeks and when I got back Adrian's mum had cleaned the house. She'd cleaned it all up and left me a little vase of flowers. I thought that was ever so nice, you know. And she did my washing every week, which was very good of her. (Jenny)

Well, we were still living with her so I brought the baby back to her house. But she was very good when I came out. I mean, Leanne was a bad feeder, she didn't feed very well and I just seemed to go from one feed to the next. You know, I was like a zombie for weeks. And she'd get up and feed her. She'd say, 'You go back to bed, I'll feed her'. I think that was really when I started to get on with her a bit better. (Frances)

Mothers and daughters-in-law are aware of the boundaries between them although individual perceptions differ and the boundary line might change at critical stages in the life-course. For example, daughters-in-law expressed considerable ambivalence about their mothers-in-law after the birth of a child. Some expected more support and were disappointed when none was offered, yet could not articulate their feelings. Paradoxically, mothers-in-law continued to restrict their involvement, often to a degree beyond what they and their daughter-in-law preferred simply because they were anxious not to intrude. Thus, both women perceived the same situation differently but were unable to express their feelings or reconcile their needs.

I'd washed the bedding for the cot, you know, the sheets and everything, the weekend before I'd gone into hospital. And when I came out with the baby they were still on the maiden [clothes horse] whereas I expected them to be aired and put on the cot and flowers and... you know. But it wasn't like that at all. Even, in fact... Martin stayed at his parents while I was in hospital and even his washing was sent back. You know, the practical side of things. There was many a time when I could have screamed, 'please do something', but like I say, I think on her part it was a case of not wanting to interfere. (Helen)

Clearly, then, the ambivalence between affinal women becomes more complex in the emotional aftermath of childbirth when mother-in-law and daughter-in-law are particularly vulnerable, both in relation to each other and their orientation around the child. It might be expected, given that maternal and paternal grandmothers have identical ties with the daughter-in-law's child, that her tendency to differentiate between them would create the conditions for misunderstanding and resentment. However, this does not comply with the sound common-sense attitudes expressed by women in the mother-in-law group. The consensus of opinion here was that women 'naturally' turn to their own mothers during pregnancy and childbirth and that this is a time when mothers-in-law should be prepared to stand back.

She had a little boy. I went and visited immediately. When she came out her mother looked after her but I think that's quite natural. (Mrs Harris)

Support Relationships between Women

I didn't go down. They are quite independent. I think her mother went down for a few days. It's normal, isn't it, for your own mother to do things like that. I don't think mothers-in-law should push too much. (Mrs Orchard)

No, I didn't mind. I think a girl's mum ... she's naturally more for her own mum. I mean, I was with my mum. (Mrs Richardson)

Yvonne turned to her own mum. It didn't bother me at all I don't think. Perhaps I was a bit hurt at first , but it didn't bother me because I knew she'd got her own mum and that was it. (Mrs Jones)

The strongly held conviction that a mother should support her daughter when she has a baby prompted some mothers-in-law to send for her when she was needed. Another who stepped in when personal difficulties prevented the mother from being there said how 'awkward' she felt about replacing her. Both responses demonstrate contradictions in the 'rules' which govern in-law relationships. Normative rules which prohibit 'interference' also allow for positive intervention when there is an obvious (or not so obvious) need. An essential requirement for mothers-in-law, therefore, is an extremely sensitive antenna which enables them to respond positively and at the right time.

His mother came up and saw what was going on. She could see that we weren't managing, so his mother rang my mother up. She said that we weren't managing but that we wouldn't let her help but she thought that we might let my mum come and help. She just felt that when a daughter has a baby she needs her mother there. Her mother had done the same for her and it was time my mother knew she was needed in that way. (Pauline)

When Lynne's baby was born he was very ill. He had to be christened straightaway and then he was rushed to Birmingham for a major operation. It was awful ... Her mother was away on holiday. On the Saturday night he was born ... Lynne's mum was ringing me, 'Come on, tell me, what do you think?' and I said, 'Well, Hilda, if I were you I'd want to be here'. She said, 'Right, I'm coming'. She could tell from my voice because I was so upset. (Mrs Richardson)

I felt a bit awkward because her own mother lived nearby. But she used to come here quite a bit and I did what I could, although I was working at the time. But you see, Tamsin's mother didn't help at all although she lived as close to them as I did. But I did feel a bit awkward because it should be the girl's mother, shouldn't it, who helps if she's there and if she's able. But Tamsin's mother just didn't get involved. She couldn't really because of her husband. I think she wanted to but she couldn't. Because, you see, Tamsin had never got on with her father. (Mrs Colclough)

It is clear, therefore, that although pregnancy and childbirth are not ordinarily associated with illness, these are times when a woman has a 'right' to a certain amount of care and, wherever possible, she prefers to receive it from her mother. Strong affective bonds between mothers and daughters make mothers the most appropriate helpers and mothers-in-law have a limited role unless the mother is absent. However, there is little evidence to suggest that mothers-in-law are deliberately excluded or that they perceive themselves as such. Moreover, the birth of a child does not significantly alter in-law relationships between women, since attitudes and behaviour established prior to the birth tend to continue afterwards.

Widowhood

Critical events in the later stages of the life-course are more likely to present women with a series of losses which have to be overcome and compensated for in some way. Perhaps the most significant loss is the death of a partner, which, even if expected, is shocking and distressing. Bereavement requires a series of adjustments for the widow in both role and status and these must be made largely through her own efforts. Murray-Parkes (1972) says that although marriage is an integral part of our social organization, there is nothing which ensures that the functions it performs will be carried out when it ends. Formal mourning is soon over so that the bereaved get little in the way of long-term support. Furthermore, bereavement deprives the widow of companionship and security and changes the basis of her identity both to herself and others. She may find it difficult to build new social relationships, yet finds the bereavement disturbs the structure of existing friendships so that these are lost until friends themselves become widowed.

Cumming and Henry (1961), comparing widowhood for women with retirement for men, suggest that whilst both experience the involuntary loss of a significant role, widowhood is an easier transition because 'widowhood is an honoured state' (p. 156). They go on to assert that widows have less trouble reintegrating themselves into social life than retired men because widows have 'a ready-made peer group' (p. 156) which they can join when their spouse dies. These somewhat sweeping evaluations of women's experiences are not supported in this study or others which suggest that many status transitions caused by bereavement are negative and that, in Western societies, widowhood, far from being an 'honoured state', is socially unfavourable and frequently stigmatized (Raphael, 1984; Troll et al., 1979). Moreover, opportunities to join a ready-made peer group depend on the proportion of the woman's friends who are also widowed. If she is among the first in her group to become widowed she may find difficulty in maintaining existing friendships which consist of married couples. Consequently, social interaction outside the family is likely to be reduced, sometimes to a degree which strains relations between the widow and her adult children.

Inevitably, widowhood leaves a void which children cannot fill. Contact increases when the death occurs and continues in the months after the funeral but eventually children want to pick up the threads of their former lives and the widow is encouraged to do the same. Thus, she is left to her own devices and loneliness and isolation may overwhelm her. Murray-Parkes (1972) has commented that after a death it is often unclear exactly what has been lost. The loss of a husband, for example, has secondary losses for the widow including loss of purpose and meaning to her life. Women whose identity was dependent on being married feel this acutely, as do those who nursed their husband through progressively failing health or terminal illness.

A widow does not recover from her loss; she makes an accommodation and it has been suggested that one year is the optimum period of acute bereavement (Gambs, 1989). During this time the widow is likely to feel emotionally out of control and overwhelmed by waves of unpleasant feelings which come from all directions and without warning. She may have difficulty coping with past and future orientations, focusing intently on her husband as if to hold him back from the finality of death. Thus, in the weeks and months following, the deceased is often referred to in the present tense and the widow may continue many of the routines of life as if he might yet return (Raphael, 1984). Others, overwhelmed by grief, may yearn for their own death or, paradoxically, fear death but believe survival is impossible now their husband is gone (Raphael, 1984; Bowling and Cartwright, 1982). Often this fear is transferred to others and the widow becomes overprotective towards those she depends on, for example by worrying excessively about her children's health. Some women turn to sons for support, often to the extent where the relationship changes and the man becomes a replacement for his father, whilst others develop compulsive care-seeking behaviour in relation to one particular child. Moreover, even when readjustment and recovery appear complete, there may be an upsurge of distress on the anniversary of the death or on special occasions once shared with the deceased.

> She became very clingy. There were a lot more phone calls and visits and 'when are you coming to see me?' And she'd ring for long chats if she was depressed. That must have been hard for her, a 60-year-old woman ringing a 25-year-old woman saying, 'what am I going to do? God, I'm depressed'. (Ruth)

> She was nearly living at our house. She came every night and she was on the phone every hour saying 'I can't live here on my own...' Really, she drove us all mad, ringing up all the time, 'Can I speak to Colin, he'll have to come and sit with me, I can't manage on my own...' It just drove us bananas in the end. (Janet)

Both in the initial stages of bereavement and afterwards, women are often closer to daughters than sons who sometimes find it difficult to share grief in a supportive way. Widows turn to daughters for emotional support and companionship whilst sons are responsible for practical matters such as finances and funeral arrangements. However, practical support by men is no less valid than emotional support by women and may be exceptionally difficult for a grieving son because it is consistent with his father's role. Indeed, practical support is emotionally involving for both the son and the widow because he is having to take over the responsibilities formerly held by the deceased. Daughters-in-law have a limited role if there is a daughter to support the widow, although contact may increase in the months after the funeral. In the absence of a daughter, daughters-in-law usually feel obliged to sustain the widow as much as possible even if the relationship is not close. This often means coping with a double burden since she must also support her grieving husband and may be considerably distressed herself.

> They did everything they could. One did one thing and one did another. Take Doreen, she just popped in. 'Get your coat on, we're going shopping'. Didn't take no for an answer. This was the first six weeks, then after the first six weeks they let me get on with it. But when he died I couldn't fault them, they were, they were marvellous and I shall always be grateful to them for that. (Mrs Jones)

> We weren't as close as we are now, I don't think, until Dad died. It was after Dad died that we became close. Because she was very good then. When I needed her, she was very good. (Mrs Brown)

> It was Adrian and his eldest sister because they're very close. Adrian went down quite a lot, at lunch time and at night and at weekends. They helped her more than anybody. Adrian helped her sort things out, took care of the funeral and everything. (Jenny)

> We did all the arranging for my father-in-law's funeral. Emotionally, I'm very bad. I mean, I could support my husband when I was all right but emotionally I am very bad at death. I go to pieces. It made a big difference to my life... Now, Gareth was very practical with his mum, got things going and everything and I did what I could to support him. (Ruth)

Clearly, the widow is not the only person who is bereaved for, in most cases, the loss of a husband means the loss of a father and father-in-law. Thus, each member of the family needs to mourn but the structure of family relationships may deny some members the 'right' to express their grief. This is particularly significant for daughters-in-law because affinal relationships are assumed to lack strong affective bonds. For example, one woman had loved her father-in-law dearly but had not spoken of this either to him or to other members of her family. Consequently, when the man died after a long and painful illness, she was desolate yet obliged to restrain her feelings.

> His dad was a very easy-going person, very nice. And I'd lost my dad when I was 12 and I think now that I probably took to him because he was replacing my dad in a way. I was absolutely heart-broken when he died. Absolutely. It was just as though I'd lost my father again. But whether any of them realized I looked upon him as a replacement for my own dad... well, I don't think so. (Jenny)

Sometimes, then, in-laws can feel excluded by bereavement. When Jenny's father-in-law died his children seemed to 'close ranks' around the widow and did not share their grief outside the immediate family. Jenny, who was extremely upset, felt her distress was both inappropriate and unwelcome. There were problems too, because her husband mourned differently from herself, so that for both of them the loss was isolating and, outwardly at least, their grief curtailed.

The death of a spouse leaves the widow in emotional turmoil, disrupting her life and the lives of the children. Therefore, daughters-in-law, whether motivated by affection or simply an obligation to help close kin in a crisis, sustained their

Support Relationships between Women

mother-in-law as much and as long as they were able. In some cases, however, the widow did not resume 'normal' life as quickly as her daughter-in-law expected and eventually supportive relationships were strained. Individual perceptions of the grieving process differed but where this seemed prolonged the widow was sometimes accused of attention-seeking behaviour. Others felt demands on their husband had been excessive and resented perceived threats to their own position and the disruption of family life.

> I think she's played on it all these years. I think she did and still does. Like, 'I've just lost my husband...', she's still getting over that one. 'You don't know what it's like to lose your husband'. 'You don't know what it's like to be 85'... Well, true I don't. But there's no answer to that kind of thing is there? (Joyce)

> She was sort of saying she was so depressed she was suicidal and things like that. But I always thought she was trying to put more demands on her boys, you know, trying to get as much out of the situation as possible. I can't help thinking she went over the top a bit, trying to pull a few more strings. She thought, 'Here's a good reason, I can get my boys to stay with me. I can't be left'. She was nothing like my mother. My mother was totally the opposite to that. (Gaynor)

> Well, I did try to go very, very carefully. But I wouldn't let her use my husband as her substitute husband which she tried to do with Jeff. And that was when we did have a row because she wanted him to be his father and he wasn't, he was my husband. (Frances)

The pain of bereavement is acute and the widow's behaviour unfamiliar and unpredictable to herself and others. When sympathy and support bring no signs of improvement relatives feel helpless and patience wears thin. Negative, sometimes harsh, responses to another's grief rarely signify an uncaring attitude, but they are often a reflection of inexperience. In the absence of a social script to guide them, people draw upon their own fears of death and dying, so that inappropriate responses tell us more about others than the bereaved person. Murray-Parkes (1972) states that bereavement, 'while rare in life to each of us, will be experienced by most sooner or later' (p. 4) but until such time and, especially for the young, the pain of grief is not easily understood. For example, a woman commented that her widowed mother-in-law did not require much emotional support because she had nursed her husband through a distressing illness and had been well-prepared for his death. This woman was not insensitive but neither do her views comply with theoretical concepts of bereavement or empirical evidence of the individual experience. Responses to bereavement suggest that grief may be no less intense when a death is expected than among those who experience a sudden loss of a spouse (Raphael, 1984; Bowling and Cartwright, 1982; Gambs, 1989).

> Supporting her, we did support work but I don't think we could give comfort support, emotional support. But she didn't need it because she was well-prepared, she'd known for nine months. So I suppose she had

> time to sort it out in her own way before he died. You know, she had six or nine months. I mean, like, 'I didn't have time to tell him how much I loved him...' Well, she had time to do those things and to show him when she was nursing him. (Ruth)

> He was ill for about twelve months. He didn't know he'd got cancer and I wouldn't let them tell him. He knew he was poorly but he'd got that hope that he was going to get better. So I don't know. Perhaps I should have been more prepared. But nothing can prepare you, I don't think. (Mrs Jones)

> We'd been out and I'd gone through to make a cup of tea. He sat down on the settee... I can see him now, winding his watch up. I came back and... I mean, that was it. I looked at him and I knew. (Mrs Brown)

When the intensity of grief fades, the widow is faced with the difficulty of forming a positive understanding of herself as a single person. This is easier if she has friends who are also widowed and can help her reintegrate into social life. The support of contemporaries is a valuable resource when relatives start taking up the threads of their own lives (Bankoff, 1981; Jerome, 1981). Male friendships are also important for some women, not because they are actively seeking remarriage but because many more social outlets are available for couples. However, married children sometimes discourage male friendships. They may consider their mother's behaviour unseemly, believing her to be beyond an age when relationships with the opposite sex are appropriate. In some cases they resent the idea that she may be replacing their father with another man. On the other hand, children may see the friendship as a source of companionship and support which reduces their obligations for their mother's welfare.

> She's got a friend now. He's a nice chap. He's got a car so he can take her out and they have a good time together. He's good for her. I mean, he comes and goes as he pleases, she can't boss him about. (Frances)

> I've got a friend now as I go out with. We just go out for a drink or I go to his house for a meal and he'll come here. It's just company, nothing else... But I'd never get married again. No, I honestly wouldn't, because it wouldn't be fair on whoever it was because I should always be comparing. But it's very nice to have a friend to go out with. (Mrs Jones)

Widowhood is a critical life event which increases obligations between close kin and has the power both to unite and divide family members. During the bereavement process the widow must modify her self-image both to encompass her husband's memory and to adjust to her single status. To do this she needs regular and reliable family support from her children and, in the absence of daughters, from daughters-in-law. Therefore, whilst some women did turn to sons for emotional support, the majority in the study expressed their deepest grief to a close female relative. Indeed, there was more evidence of conflict where sons assumed sole responsibility for their mother's welfare or where mothers turned to sons for a lot of support. Daughters-in-law who were involved in sharing the bereavement supported the widow immediately after the death and in the months that followed, encouraging her, as far as possible, to establish an independent life of her own. Widows were equally anxious to manage alone despite the loneliness and isolation experienced, to varying degrees, by all of them. They were grateful for family support but acknowledged that, in the long term, children must be allowed to lead their own lives whilst the widow rebuilt hers. Here, they relied largely on their own efforts and resources, since any feelings of confidence or positive self-regard seemed to come more from the widows themselves than from support from family, friends or social networks.

Caring relationships in later life

Although widowhood can happen at any stage in married life it commonly occurs among older women and its incidence increases with advancing age. Thus, widowhood frequently corresponds with various changes in dependency and support which occur in old age and which may be gradual or abrupt. Whilst old age is not inevitably problematic, the growing numbers of people over 75 indicates an increase in the frail, dependent elderly now and in the future. This age group is the most vulnerable to disability and most likely to need primary care and medical and social services. The great majority are very old women whose health has deteriorated to an extent which makes them dependent on others for their day-to-day care. And, as previously mentioned, it is more often a close female relative who takes on the primary caring role.

The impact of social and demographic change on the family suggests that many women caring for elderly relatives today will be in a disadvantaged position when they become old and frail. Increases in survival rates for the elderly have corresponded with a reduction in family size since the beginning of this century (Parker, 1985; Wicks, 1982). Families no longer include large numbers of children and there has been a steady rise in the proportion of childless marriages in the post-war years. As a consequence, there are fewer potential carers for future generations of elderly people and increasing numbers with no immediate kin. Moreover, the current age structure of the population means that many old people are cared for by other old people. Thus, there are particular stresses on late middle-aged or 'young' elderly women who have an aged mother or mother-in-law needing constant care. And because generations of women have been considered suitable for caring, many of those being cared for now will have cared themselves for an aged husband or parent.

Only one daughter-in-law, Sonia, had experienced a major caring role. Sonia had provided full-time primary care for her dependent mother-in-law in the same household, during the two years prior to the woman's death. She had received some informal, but very little statutory support. Equally, none of the mothers-in-law were receiving care from relatives and although some had experience of caring for elderly parents in the past, at the time of the interviews, none were involved in support relationships as carers. Therefore, the majority of women were talking about support relationships which might occur in the future, and whilst they referred to notions of love, duty and obligation, they also demonstrated considerable resistance to family care. By asking women to rehearse the future in this way, it became clear that notions of the family as an arena of informal care which is central to community care policies is one which women themselves might wish to resist.

Although none of the mother-in-law group had reached an age they considered 'old', they were, understandably, uncomfortable with a topic which required consideration of impending infirmity. Most felt fortunate that their health was good or, if not, that it did not prevent them from being independent. Income and health permitting, the preference was to maintain separate households but to live close enough to enable at least one child to have regular contact. Some women said they would move in with married children only if separate accommodation could be arranged, thereby allowing two or three generations to live together but with less intimacy. Indeed, two women in the daughter-in-law group had done this, extending their property to include a so-called 'granny flat' where their mother-in-law lived semi-independently from the rest of the household. However, social inequalities between families determines choice since the provision of separate accommodation requires cash resources. These are usually obtained by the elderly relative selling her house or, alternatively, mother and children, both having houses to sell, making a joint purchase of one large property. Clearly, as both options depend on property ownership there is a greater degree of choice for some families than others.

The least favoured option for dependent elderly was institutionalized care. Many women perceived residential homes as places of abuse and neglect and some recalled images of the workhouse but although there was pessimism about geriatric institutions they were not entirely rejected. Whilst women acknowledged the need for support in old age, they were determined not to be a burden to their children and said that rather than live with them, they would opt for the best residential care available. Thus, women anticipated being instrumental in defining future support relationships, although these were expressed views and, interestingly, the belief that 'children owe you nothing' did not appear to hold for past behaviour towards their own parents. A number of women had shared their homes with an elderly, dependent relative and, undoubtedly, personal experience influenced their attitudes towards giving and receiving primary home care.

> Oh no, I'd never agree with that. I've always thought that rather than be a trouble to my children I would say that I would go into a home. But I don't think you should inflict yourself on your children. It isn't fair, is it? (Mrs York)

> Now, I'm going on how I'd feel if I was old. I'd sooner stay in my own house. And if it came to the fact that I couldn't look after myself, I'd sooner them put me in a home. I think so but there again you don't know until you come to be in that position. (Mrs Jones)

> Yes, I have thought about that. But I feel that I would like to be independent of my children... if possible, not to be a burden to them. Because I have had that experience. I looked after my mother until she died. She lived here and I've had my father-in-law living with us too. It's very difficult. You've really got to think about it before committing yourself. (Mrs Orchard)

No, never. I had my mother living with me and that was awful. She was very hard to look after, very hard. She could be very cruel and nothing I did was right, ever. But I don't see why you should, I honestly don't. It's your life to lead after all and I don't see why you should have to look after elderly parents. I don't want my sons to have to look after me. I think if it happened to me I'd rather go into a home. I think a home is the place. It might sound selfish, but I have experienced it first hand and I do think a home is the place. (Mrs Tagg)

Women in the mother-in-law group expressed the preference to live independently for as long as they were able and research has shown that for most people this desire is realized (Arber and Ginn, 1991; Bond, 1990; Shanas, 1979; Brody, 1978). The majority of older people are not mentally or physically frail, although health tends to decline in those aged over 85. It has been estimated that one in five might suffer from dementia (Bond, 1987) and three in five a long-term disabling illness (OPCS, 1982). Thus the option to live independently is exercised by the vast majority of older people until or unless they reach an age where they need constant care. At this point, there is unlikely to be a clear choice between entering an institution or living with one's family. Residential care is seen as inappropriate in the majority of cases since it is assumed to create dependency and significantly reduce autonomy and choice for the individuals concerned. This philosophy is at the heart of the Griffiths Report (1988) and enshrined in the National Health Service and Community Care Act (1990), and has provided the justification for the closure of long-stay geriatric hospitals and the running-down of local authority residential homes for the elderly. At the same time a flourishing private sector has developed, expanding by 27.5 per cent between 1982 and 1984 (Larder et al., 1986). It has been suggested that three times as many severely impaired old people live at home than in institutions of any kind and the care they receive is from a household member – a spouse or another relative (Bond and Carstairs, 1982). Moreover, three-quarters of women over 85 who are not living with their husbands but with other people are being cared for by married children (Rimmer, 1981) and here the majority of support relationships are with daughters or daughters-in-law. Frailty, therefore, is not the first or only predictor for residential care. The significant difference between frail elderly receiving residential support and those living in the community is the availability of the family. Those who have no informal carers to support them are cared for in public or private residential homes. Consequently, most community care policies incorporate the private residential sector into their arrangements, to meet the needs of the unsupported elderly who require high levels of care.

With a daughter-in-law as a potential carer, mothers-in-law have a poor prospect of exercising other options unless they have economic resources to buy private care. Most people turn to close kin for support in old age because it seems either 'natural' or inevitable. Furthermore, as Evers (1985) points out, the beginnings of support relationships often develop gradually as physical and mental health decline. Thus, there is often an almost imperceptible process of dependency leading to total reliance on the support relationship. Beyond this, patterns of responsibility and dependency between family women are informed by an assumed public consensus that caring for one's relatives is 'the right thing to do'. This underpins social policy concerned to keep people in the community and provides a frame of reference for social and health workers who may exhort relatives to give or receive primary care. Thus, the 'sentimental model of the family' is the basis for social caring relationships and simultaneously ignores the actual quality of those relationships. This is particularly significant for mothers and daughters-in-law who may have spent years practising self-imposed avoidance, only to find themselves in an intimate, supportive relationship because there is no other alternative.

The obligation to care for dependants is part of a structure of widely recognized norms and values which provide guidelines for appropriate behaviour between family members. However, it is important to understand this as a flexible structure which operates differently in particular societies and historical periods. Anderson (1971) has argued that the basis for kin assistance in the past was calculative. He suggests that kin helped each other only if there was the possibility of obtaining a fairly immediate return, although in the long term parents might help children with some expectation of receiving assistance in old age. However, this calculative aspect of kin relations may have been a direct response to the social and economic conditions of the time. This study, for example, found little evidence that mutual advantage prompted kin assistance. Similarly, the history of past relationships was not a significant factor in honouring short-term obligations, although it was more important when women considered long-term care. It appears, therefore, that there are some aspects of family support which cannot be fully explained by debts owing or incurred, or by referring to simplistic notions of reciprocity.

Various commentators have pointed out the difficulty in separating concepts of altruism and reciprocity in kin relations (Bulmer, 1987; Finch, 1987a; Marsden and Abrams, 1987; Qureshi and Simons, 1987). It is assumed that altruism exists in close personal relationships founded on love, for example, those between husband and wife and parents and children. But if love is the only motivation for altruistic behaviour it does not explain acts of goodwill between others, including some involving in-laws, and between unrelated people such as friends or neighbours. Moreover, reciprocity as evidence of sentiment is at the heart of even the most intimate relationships and is reinforced by strong moral norms which underpin family obligations. Thus, one partner might care for the other not purely out of love but in return for services received in the past and a daughter might care for her elderly mother because her mother once cared for her. However, the concepts of reciprocity and altruism are even more complex in support relationships between mothers-in-law and daughters-in-law. Unlike mothers and daughters, the women have no intimate knowledge of each other derived from a shared past and some may never form positive affective bonds. Consequently, although the quality of relationships seems largely irrelevant when honouring short-term obligations, it has much more significance in attitudes towards coping with long-term dependency needs.

Land and Rose (1985) have commented that 'whereas altruistic practices are structured into women's lives, they are structured out of men's' (p. 93). The assumption that women will fill caring roles derives from the family setting where power relationships between the sexes are reinforced by an external framework of beliefs about gender-related obligations. Identifiable patterns of dependency and support within the private sphere suggest that women's 'natural' altruism is an unconvincing explanation for their burden of care. Land and Rose have used the term 'compulsory altruism' to describe other-regarding behaviour which does not involve free choice and argue that the taken-for-granted 'naturalness' of female caring masks what is often involuntary action in the absence of viable alternatives.

A different view links caring to reciprocity in kin relationships, influenced by calculating mechanisms which balance long-term and short-term returns. It is useful, at this point, to return to Sahlins' (1965) concept of generalized reciprocity where the obligation to return can be deferred for long periods. A good example of generalized reciprocity is a person who provides primary care for a dependent relative with minimal expectation of reward. Because reciprocal transactions in kin relations may involve very long periods of time, assistance being given now is often in return for obligations previously fulfilled. (Bulmer, 1987; Finch, 1987a). Therefore, what appears to the outsider as purely altruistic may, in fact, be related to debts incurred in the past. Importantly, in later life-course transactions, the donor may not necessarily be directly indebted to the recipient. One person may very well assist another because of their obligation to a third party. For example, a daughter-in-law might care for her elderly mother-in-law because of an overriding obligation she feels towards her husband. A further, incomplete, explanation for seemingly altruistic behaviour is internalized belief and the avoidance of guilt. This stems from a range of commonly-held norms which have been referred to collectively as the 'public morality' (Voysey, 1975). In critical life situations the individual's understanding of public morality is made use of to construct meaningful action and enables people to explain their conduct in a way which is plausible to themselves and others. This also accords with Cornwell's (1984) useful concept of 'public' and 'private' sentiments, where at one level people feel morally obliged to assist their relatives, yet at another they resent it.

> I've got a thing about looking after your parents. You know, I think they deserve looking after and I can't do with people who just leave their old folks and let them rot or whatever. I feel very strongly about this because if it was my mother I'd have to have her here and look after her. So in a way, I think what a shame for Terry, because he wouldn't want my mother but he would probably want to do it for his. And I don't know if I could cope with it, because I'd be the one looking after her. (Rachel)

> I would hate to think of anybody going into an institution, anybody that didn't want to. So we'd have her here. I wouldn't like it although I wouldn't admit to that. But there wouldn't be any pressure about her going into a home because I would be made to feel guilty. Tom would want us to have her, there's no doubt about that, although I wouldn't be very happy because basically we don't get on together. (Wendy)

> I would never, never put any person into a home. No matter what adjustments were in my own life, my mother-in-law will never end up in a home. When she gets to the stage when she's having difficulty living with herself or living on her own all she's got to do is come. Because nothing, in my opinion, is worth putting an old person in a home. (Nancy)

Friendly Relations?

Evidence that some people within the family network are more responsible for caring than others suggests the existence of hierarchical rules for discharging kinship obligations (Qureshi and Simons, 1987). Also important, where long-term assistance is concerned, is the quality of particular relationships and to what extent it is felt that obligations have been honoured in the past. Patterns of social relations earlier in the life-course are particularly important for mothers and daughters-in-law as reference points for ascertaining legitimate expectations later on. Consequently, there is more pessimism about the prospect of giving and receiving care in those relationships where one woman has been perceived as consistently hostile to the other.

> In weaker moments I've thought, 'Oh, if anything happened to Henry perhaps I could sort of live near them and things will be better' but when she comes I know that would be absolutely impossible. And so now I've come to terms with that even, and I never think of that because I just wouldn't... I couldn't live with her or near her. I feel that she wouldn't want to do anything for me. (Mrs Swann)

> How I feel now towards Stuart's mum I just wouldn't want to do it. I can't communicate with Stuart's mum in any way, she's just totally rude. So I couldn't care for her. Because she is so rude and nasty to me that I would not have the patience to do it. I would end up really wanting to hit her. (Annette)

It appears that no straightforward answers exist to questions of who cares for whom in the kinship network, and why. Concepts of obligation, altruism and reciprocity overlap in such a way that one cannot be easily explained without reference to the other two. Nor do any of them fully explain why some people more than others are considered appropriate and available to take on the caring role. Nevertheless, it is clear that kinship groupings are the arena for most caring relationships and that, effectively, family care means care by family women. Because of its taken-for-granted aspect few women are in a position to make dispassionate decisions about caring since refusal to care risks public disapproval and serious problems of self-perception. Commonly held norms about social care which underpin public policy are also strong moral imperatives for actual and anticipated conduct towards dependent kin. It is important to stress, therefore, that the caring issues referred to here are ones which the women interviewed had already considered for their own lives. They had all given thought to the emotional and physical costs of support relationships and expressed considerable conflict about the prospect of giving and receiving primary care.

Even so, women found it difficult to 'rehearse the future' by considering the prospects of ageing and dependency, because both seemed so bleak they preferred not to think about them. This tells us something about images of ageing in our society and, importantly, suggests a rejection of the 'sentimental model of the family'. For example, although women did not want to address these issues, when they did they talked in terms of independence and autonomy for older people rather than dependency and support relationships. This was particularly important for the mothers-in-law and, indeed, their resistance to questions about ageing may have stemmed from a recognition that in our society older people are marginalized and their views largely ignored.

> I think about it very often. I hope and pray that I wouldn't need any such care ever. It's something you start thinking about as you get older but I think, personally ... I think about it and then I dismiss it. I don't like to think about it. (Mrs Williams)

> It's difficult for me to say what will happen. It would depend on the circumstances wouldn't it? I mean, I haven't come to that yet. Perhaps if I was twenty or thirty years older, I'd have more thoughts on it. (Mrs Orchard)

> It's very difficult isn't it? I think it's one of those situations I dread happening. Yes, I think I wouldn't want it at all really. (Susan)

> I could not do it. I'm sure I couldn't do it for my own mother. I couldn't, I really couldn't. I don't even know if I could do it for my husband at this stage. I don't know if I've got that caring ability. So I just hope it doesn't happen. I know I couldn't do it but I know I'll feel guilty. I'll go through as much turmoil not doing it as probably I would if I was doing it. (Laura)

> I've thought about it. I mean, I've had the experience of living with her and I know how difficult it can be for us to actually get on living in the same house. So how would I cope? I don't know really, maybe it's an ostrich reaction. I just hope it won't happen, and yet at the same time I know that one day we'll have to face looking after her either in her own home or having her to stay. (Pauline)

Although ambivalent images of ageing can provide a formula for some women to avoid support relationships, the assumption that it is women who routinely take on caring roles is pervasive. Three daughters-in-law said they 'knew' that eventually they would be responsible for their mother-in-law's care, despite the fact that in at least one case the relationship was fraught with conflict. This expectation was not a matter of choice but reflects a moral obligation combined with an absence of genuine alternatives. As Finch and Groves (1982) point out, 'Even when it appears that a female relative has "chosen" to provide care at home, she herself may not experience that as a real choice' (p. 432).

As already stated, caring relationships can develop gradually, often over a period of many years. In most cases initial support for the elderly relates to the provision of practical services family members give to each other as a matter of course. There are obvious distinctions between assistance with shopping or transportation and regular tasks such as food preparation, house cleaning or laundering, and these, in turn, are very different from dressing, bathing or toileting. However, because women are responsible for caring, it is likely that daughters or daughters-in-law will be involved from the outset in providing many routine services for elderly parents. As support becomes more extensive with increasing age it is only a short step for the younger woman to undertake full-time tending of the most personal kind. This is important, because whilst many women gave their in-laws some practical assistance, they did not see it as a part of a sequence of events which might result in a dependency relationship. Rather, they envisaged that a crisis of some sort would precipitate a family conference and the negotiation of appropriate courses of action. Families do mobilize in response to crises although one adult child (usually a female) tends to become responsible for providing day-to-day care.

> My brother-in-law from Oxford suggested that we had someone from social services to be paid a wage... you know, a housekeeper to look after her. And I said that just wouldn't work, right from the outset. And another offer was for her to have three months with everybody but we felt that she would have no base of her own. And two of the family live away, it would have meant taking her up and down the country. So I said we should have her here. It was a unanimous decision and all sorted out financially between her children. (Sonia)

Some women said that rather than make a hasty decision in response to a crisis situation, it was better to have contingency plans. This meant opening up family discussion well before parents reached the stage of dependency, to allow them an active role in decision-making about their own future.

> You can choose a nice home before you get to the stage where you're not thinking properly. You can plan ahead for what you want to do and let your children know what you want to do. I'm a great believer in talking about what's going to happen. Oh yes. And before you get too old as you can't be reasonable about it. I think it should be discussed with your children so that they all know what your feelings are. (Mrs Richardson)

> Both mothers have said they don't want to come and live with us because they don't think we'd get on. Which I can only be thankful for. If the time comes I don't know if they'd stick to that but financially we would be able to cope by helping them to get into a good nursing home. (Ruth)

However, contemplating the future when one's mother is still healthy and active is one thing. Forward planning can take on a different complexion when she begins to show signs of age.

> You know, sometimes I've expressed a worry that she's getting old. Which she is. And he says, 'Oh, sometime we're going to have to think about what we're going to do'. And I'll say, 'Well, we've already thought that out'. 'Yes, yes, we have thought it out but...' But he obviously isn't... I mean, it's not as cut and dried as we try to make it. (Ruth)

In reality, there is not always an acute episode calling for an immediate response or, indeed, long-term family talks resulting in concrete plans for the future. Rather, the elderly person displays a gradual degree of incapacity and, over the same period of time, it becomes increasingly 'obvious' to the rest of the family that one person is the appropriate carer (Finch, 1987a). That such care tends to devolve on a woman suggests an implicit selection process in families which effectively rules out the need for more formal negotiations. So pervasive is the taken-for-granted aspect of female support relationships that families often make the same assumptions about women and care as those found in social policies and maintained by social and welfare workers. Moreover, similar assumptions influenced attitudes expressed in the study. For example, reference to a hierarchy of obligations led some women to suggest that, all things being equal, a daughter rather than a daughter-in-law is the expected relative to care.

> Hopefully, I'll never have to come across this one with him having two sisters. If they didn't obviously I would step in. But it always ends up on just one's shoulders then doesn't it? (Rachel)

> It's something Simon and I have talked about and we don't think either of us could cope with her living with us. It would be easier if his sister had her. They're closer but why should she, why should the burden fall on her? Perhaps she could because it's her mother and she loves her but look what she'd give up. (Laura)

With very few exceptions, women were reluctant to both give and receive primary care if this necessitated co-residence. The consensus of opinion was that if the mother-in-law reached a stage where she required 24-hour care by her daughter-in-law in the same household, institutionalization was essential.[2] It was co-residence rather than providing care of a very personal kind which determined the limits of support relationships, since the majority of daughters-in-law seemed prepared to attempt to meet tending needs providing they could be carried out in their mother-in-law's home. Broadly speaking, there were two schools of thought which saw residential care as the last, or next to the last resort. Some people rejected outright the possibility of caring in a joint household because of the intolerable strain placed on marriage and family. Others, acknowledging problems of conscience, felt compelled to at least try but said that the physical and emotional costs would gradually erode the support relationship.

> I certainly could not have my mother-in-law under any circumstances. I find it hard to think of myself in that way because it seems harsh and cruel but I would be so miserable. In fact, I don't think Nick would ask me because it's too important to us that our marriage works and she would put an incredible strain on it. (Elaine)

> I wouldn't like to have her here to care for her. If I've got to do it I'd rather care for her in her own home. I couldn't have her here. So if she definitely couldn't cope in her own home I suppose she'd have to go into a home. I suppose it is possible with a lot of support to keep them in their own home and I think in my case I'd rather give that support and visit every day or whatever and keep her in her own home. But if that was impossible, she'd have to go into a home. (Gaynor)

I think I'd see how Douglas felt because it's his mother and if he felt that he didn't want to put her in a home I would try my best to look after her. I don't know how I'd be and I don't think I'd be that willing but I think I would try. Because I don't like to think of her going into a home unless it's absolutely necessary. (Susan)

I think as they get older they get a little bit clingy. You know, if they know that they can't get around or do anything for themselves. I think they need to be near the people they know and who love them. It is difficult but I don't think I could put anybody in a home if they wanted to stay with me. (Sylvia)

These attitudes suggest that women make a conscious effort to hold a different view of the family than the 'sentimental model of family life'. Supporting someone in their own home maintains the boundaries between both households and allows a higher degree of domestic privacy for both carer and cared-for. This also has links with the issues of autonomy and independence mentioned earlier, as a person living in her own home may have more opportunity to decide herself how much and what type of support she needs. It fits well with the philosophy of community care, although it is debatable how much 'choice' of provision service-users actually have. However, for old people unable to continue living alone but who do not wish to live with their families, there may be less opportunity to exercise other choices, for example, to opt for residential care.

The clear assumption in the rhetoric about care provision is that women will routinely shoulder the burden of supporting the frail elderly. This assumption is evident in the organization of both community and institutionalized care which rely heavily on the unpaid or low-paid work of women. For example, community care policy involves care plans and 'packages of care' designed by social workers but delivered by the combined efforts of the informal, voluntary and commercial sectors with some statutory input. The personnel responsible for the delivery of care packages are usually women who accept little or no payment for what is 'hard caring work' (Baldock and Ungerson, 1991, p. 153). As far as informal carers are concerned, there is no reference to equal opportunities within the NHS and Community Care Act or, indeed, any value placed on the financial contribution of unpaid carers (Walker, 1991). Equally, Finch and Groves (1982) point out that the typical institutional carer is a part-time, female worker whose lack of qualifications and status are seen to justify the low wage levels in this sector. The majority are married women whose family commitments restrict their employment opportunities. Their caring work effectively keeps down the costs of public provision for the elderly, although the costs for individual workers in terms of physical and mental stress are often unacceptably high.

Central to policies on care of the elderly in the public and private arenas are crude definitions of women's roles and responsibilities. Many arise from a model of caring which extends motherhood to all other forms of care by women whether or not they are appropriate. Whilst there are prescriptions for the care of children, there are none for the care of dependent adults, although both are perceived as having valid claims for care. The difference is, of course, that a child's decreasing levels of dependency are fairly predictable, whilst an elderly person may deteriorate in a much less systematic and foreseeable way (Land and

Rose, 1985). This uncertainty creates tensions in support systems for the elderly and makes adequate care difficult to define and carry out. Tensions also arise from the problem of role reversal where carers must adopt the parenting role and may be particularly inappropriate for daughters-in-law and mothers-in-law in support relationships.

Various studies have looked at what happens when a previously independent and respected parent becomes reliant on a child for basic care (Hicks, 1988; Lewis and Meredith, 1988; Marsden and Abrams, 1987; Fischer, 1986). It has been suggested that a reversal of the young-parent/small-child situation is an inappropriate response. What should happen is the development of what Blenkner (1965) has termed 'filial maturity' in the adult child. This, she argues, occurs in middle age and involves seeing oneself as dependable as a consequence of being depended upon. Achieving filial maturity means accepting responsibility for an elderly parent in a way which allows parent and child to interact as two individual and mature adults. However, whilst this is a useful way of looking at dependency relationships it may be incompatible with the motherhood model of care and, therefore, difficult to practise. Whilst not wishing to suggest that role reversal is a desirable approach to the dependent elderly, it may be unavoidable when very personal tending is required. The motherhood model was often referred to when daughters-in-law reflected on differences between caring for their mothers and caring for their mothers-in-law. Many women felt that it would be easier to care for the mother because she would be less resistant to a reversal of the parent/child relationship.

> You know, when I helped to nurse her before when she was poorly... she'll refuse to take tablets. She will be very argumentative. You see, if I said to my mum, 'Right, I'm getting your breakfast now', she'd say, 'I don't want any', and I'd say, 'You do need it, I'm going to make you a little bit of something and we'll see what you can eat', and get on with it. Now, Stuart's mum is totally different. She wouldn't have it, she would be very, very difficult. (Annette)

> I would find it easier to care for my mum I think. Probably because I could tell her what she'd got to do. You know, if they're ill or they're old and they won't eat properly... I could turn round and say, 'Look, you've got to do this...' I don't know whether I could do that with my mother-in-law. Probably because of the type of person she is. You know, she can be quite... I won't say bossy but she knows what she wants and she knows how to get it and that's it, you know. (Jenny)

> I think you could say things to your mum that you perhaps wouldn't say... I mean, having you running up and down stairs every few minutes... You could say to your mother, 'Look, Mother, I'm not having this, there's no need for it...' whereas with your mother-in-law you'd perhaps put up with it for a while and not say anything. (Frances)

For some daughters caring for their elderly mothers, role reversal may be the only way of coping with the situation. At first sight, this seems to involve a shift in power to the daughter, although as Nice (1992) points out 'power' in this situation may actually mean responsibility, whereas for the mother it may mean a very real loss of personal power to determine her own life. It is debatable, therefore, whether a mother would be any more willing to be treated as an infant than a mother-in-law. Certainly the authoritative attitudes expressed by some women were taken up by mothers-in-law, leading at least one to suggest that daughters-in-law are often more suitable to care. On the other hand, it may be that passivity stems from personality characteristics rather than simply being a consequence of reversed relationships.

> I should think you'd be better cared for by your daughter-in-law than your daughter. Your daughter knows you too well and would be more impatient with you. Where a daughter-in-law, she would draw back, where a daughter would go in as it were. I think you find that with mothers and daughters... I mean, although we get on like a house on fire, if we were under each other's feet we'd blow up. (Mrs York)

> I think it would be harder with my mum because she's the type of person that's very independent. If she thought she could get up she would, you know, it would be difficult to try and keep her down. Whereas Russell's mum, not so much because she... If she's ill, she's ill and she'll just sit there. I mean, I can tell her what to do more than I could with my own mum. She'll take directions from me. (Sylvia)

Other reasons for preferring to care for mothers rather than mothers-in-law reflected the strong affective bonds believed to exist between mothers and daughters. Many women felt that the emotional warmth which these relationships allow creates an intimacy which might relieve some of the stresses of caring.

> I did care for my mother-in-law and I think I did it reasonably well. But with my own mother things would be more natural. I can't say that it was unnatural with my mother-in-law but it would be different, on a different footing. I think if it was my own mother I could discuss it with her and say, 'I hope it does work out but if it doesn't shall we look for an alternative?' I could say that to my mother but with my mother-in-law I don't think I could have done. But fortunately, it did work out. (Sonia)

> It would be easier to care for my mother because the feelings go a lot deeper obviously. Because she is my mother. And I would feel it was my duty and I wouldn't have to think about doing it for my mother. (Wendy)

> It would be easier to care for your mother because it would be the blood tie. I think I could look after my mother-in-law or my mother. I could do it for either but it would probably be easier for my mother. (Vicky)

> My mum, I could probably care for her because there is that emotional bond. But I wouldn't want to. I don't want to, I don't see that as my role in life... (Laura)

Clearly, then, ideas about loving relationships which underpin social policy can be found in attitudes towards elderly mothers, although intimacy was also perceived as allowing free expression of negative as well as positive feelings.

> I may be able to cope better with my mother in a sense of being able to say what I think. You see, I don't have to wrap things up so much with my mother, whereas with Lily I have to be more tactful. And in a difficult situation where you're actually caring for somebody, you really have to have a very open relationship where you can actually say what you feel. Now with my mum I can do that, with Lily I can't. (Pauline)

> It's got to be your mother. You couldn't say exactly what you wanted to your mother-in-law, whereas if it was your mum you could say 'You're getting on my nerves a bit . . .' I think it would be easier, but not easy. It's never easy, but of the two I'd have to say my mother. (Gaynor)

If the motherhood model of caring is inappropriately applied to the needs of the elderly, support relationships between mothers and daughters-in-law may be more acceptable than between mothers and daughters. This type of caring has two important aspects. Firstly, many of the 'rules' which frame mother-in-law and daughter-in-law relationships define interpersonal boundaries between the two women. Some allow for affective behaviour but others refer to formality and social distance and it is these which commonly distinguish ties of blood from ties by marriage. Consequently, caring between mothers and daughters-in-law may be particularly resistant to the motherhood model but might provide opportunities for more equitable and autonomous relationships.

> She was very naughty when her own daughters came. She wouldn't let them bath her, she'd keep throwing the soap out of the bath. And she was difficult if they tried to dress her. I thinking probably she allowed me to do things for her because I was her daughter-in-law. It's a special relationship isn't it? Always a bit formal because it starts off that way. Also, she was in my home so perhaps she felt she ought to behave herself. I mean, I was looking after her willingly and I hope patiently. It would have been stupid to play me up. So although she used to have tantrums with her daughters, she would take it from me. And we never, ever, in all that time, had a cross word. (Sonia)

Secondly, the mother's personal biography and her past as an independent adult may be less significant for a daughter-in-law. Unlike a daughter, a daughter-in-law's relationship with her mother-in-law is established by marriage and each has important periods in her life the other has not shared. Therefore, the emotional effects of witnessing the woman's decline are likely to be fewer than those felt by her daughter, since the latter must mourn the loss of her mother's past and become reconciled to the indignities inflicted by age. Consequently, whilst the costs of care on daughters-in-law are undoubtedly high, in emotional terms at least, they may be less than those on a daughter.

In some senses it may be easier for me to deal with the pain and suffering of my mother-in-law than it would my mother. Because I do find it difficult to deal with my mother being in pain because it's almost like I'm feeling it myself. I think I could detach myself a bit from my mother-in-law because in a sense I haven't shared her hurts in the same way. I'd sympathize, I wouldn't like to see her suffering or being really, really stressed, but I don't think I would identify in the same way as I would with my mum. (Pauline)

I think it would be easier to care for my mother-in-law. Because emotionally, caring for my mother would be dramatic. She would be ill and going senile and that I would find very difficult to adapt to. Me and my mother-in-law, we're not close, there isn't any love and I could care for her more in a clinical way. My own mother I would have to kind of grieve for the loss of what she was, you know, when she was in her prime. Now I would care for both of them if they were ill and my mother-in-law I would try and be kind and considerate but it would be more like... I wouldn't have that emotional thought about it, you know? I'm still my mother's child whereas I think I could care for my mother-in-law without any emotion. (Joyce)

Although the motherhood model seems an inappropriate response to the elderly, it is too often assumed to be an adequate prescription for their care. Moreover, Ungerson (1983) states: 'it seems the motherhood model is so convenient as a guide to the techniques of tending that it may act to exclude men from many caring tasks' (p. 68). She supports the view that caring is gendered by identifying two important taboo systems applicable to caring relationships. First, the very strong incest taboo in our society which many carers have to overcome; secondly, the taboo about the removal of human dirt. This has a central place in the mothering of babies and young children and is extended to the frail elderly through the motherhood model of care. Ungerson suggests that women are seen as the obvious candidates for the management of human dirt because they are already polluted by menstruation and childbirth, and that because the work is so unpleasant men have refused to do it. However, for many of the daughters-in-law much of the resistance to caring for elderly relatives stemmed from a very real fear of dealing with incontinence. Although some women felt that a strong affectional bond between the carer and the cared-for might facilitate personal tending, they recognized that, except possibly in relation to young children, it can be extremely distressing. This points to a contradiction between the ideological which associates tending with mothering and the personal which suggests that dealing with incontinence is no less polluting for women than for men. Women undertake these tasks not because they are particularly suited to carrying them out but because, as Ungerson suggests, normative expectations and gender inequalities have made it difficult for them to resist. However, we know that there are circumstances when men provide care and evidence suggests that some of it involves personal care activities such as help with washing, dressing and toileting (OPCS, 1988). On the other hand, there is a higher proportion of women than men who have sole responsibility for a dependant irrespective of whether care is provided in the same or a separate houshold (OPCS, 1988). This is supported by

Marsden and Abrams (1987) whose study of married daughters caring for their mothers in the same dwelling found that virtually all care was provided by women. Husbands gave some help with practical tasks but did very little which involved even being with the elderly person.[3] Thus, as long as there are women available to care, men seem unlikely to become responsible for personal tending. Women are culturally-designated carers and it is they who must *routinely* overcome powerful fears in order to deal with incontinence and other intimate tasks.

In the debate on residential and community care for the elderly, some authors have argued that inadequacies in provision have increased demands on family women. Research has shown, for example, that few public policies account for carers' needs and that, typically, health and welfare professionals see the elderly person, not the carer, as their client (Parker, 1985). Therefore, although primary home carers may receive some support from welfare agencies, it is too often secondary and incidental to the needs of the person being cared for. It is also questionable how much realistic support they provide since these resources tend to be allocated to the elderly who live alone. Moreover, an elderly person living with others is less likely to receive statutory services such as a home help, meals on wheels or day care. It has been argued, therefore, that 'social services substitute for families rather than support them' (Walker, 1991, p. 55).

Lack of support for families caring for elderly dependants can have serious consequences for women providing primary home care. Studies have shown that when intensive care is required this can have severe effects on the carer's health, thus making family support systems fragile and vulnerable to breakdown (Lewis and Meredith, 1988; Wicks, 1982). When this happens there is a need for immediate support from other sources, but restrictions on public spending and social policy which places care of the elderly firmly in the family mean that alternative resources are frequently unavailable. However, potential carers may hope to avoid severe physical and mental stress by access to conventional support services and respite care and, indeed, there may be misconceptions about how much formal support might be available. Such expectations are not supported by those who have experience of providing care. Sonia, for example, had no formal support other than visits from her mother-in-law's general practitioner and a community nurse, and her accounts of the realities of caring contrast vividly with some of the expressed views.

> I think it would depend on whether it was a mental or physical condition. I mean, some people go a bit senile. I don't know whether I could cope with that as well as I could cope with a physical condition. I mean, when it's bedpans and things like that you usually have a nurse, don't you, to help. (Susan)

> If she became very frail, you know, incontinent or whatever, I don't think I could manage that. I think when they get to that stage they need... Well, you know, she'd have to be looked after by somebody professional. (Frances)

> I think I could have my mother-in-law at a push. But I do think then, you'd need several holidays a year if only for a few days. So she would have to be prepared to go into a home when that happened to give me

Friendly Relations?

> some relief. I mean, there are some homes that do that, don't they? They take old people in to give their relatives a break. (Deborah)

> She was incapacitated, you know. She couldn't walk. She was doubly incontinent as well. She never had to be fed but she used to be greedy to eat, which was very humiliating for the children to watch her, you know. It was terribly sad. She was very childlike ... She used to say 'As long as you're near, Sonia, I'm safe'. She just relied on me entirely and she didn't really want anybody else. And she used to cry bitterly about how she was and how we had to do everything for her and she could do nothing for us. But we had our fun with her as well. She was very fun-loving and very intelligent. I don't want to say she was senile. But she was very possessive and, yes, I admit there were times when I could have shaken the living daylights out of her. (Sonia)

The notion of shared care or 'care packages' appears to offer some relief to carers at least until the extent of formal provision is examined. Levels of support are low for those living with others even though they are most likely to be severely impaired older people who need 24-hour care. Scarce resources are not provided to families who care because it is assumed that they will meet all the needs of the person being cared for. For example, Parker states:

> Very severely disabled people living with married children (ie with a daughter or daughter-in-law) were much less likely to receive any services than any other group. This is despite there being no evidence to suggest that the needs of severely disabled people living with their married children were less than those of others. (1985, p. 70)

It was also been noted that shared care rarely represents a genuine division of caring between the informal and formal sectors. Rather, it constitutes a crisis response when family support systems break down and caring is taken over by statutory agencies. This tends to be respite care which affords carers some relief but prevents the permanent admission of dependants into residential homes (Bulmer, 1987; Parker, 1985).

A case for residential care?

Women were reluctant both to give and receive primary care; they viewed the prospect of caring with dismay, believing that it requires special skills they might not possess, and expected to become involved only because there are no genuine alternatives. The overriding preference for women in both study groups was to maintain their independence by living in separate households, or if this was not possible, access to good quality residential care. It would appear, therefore, that there is a clear case for more imaginative public policies for the elderly in both the community and residential sectors. For example, the objective of allowing older people to live independently in the community for as long as possible requires a strong commitment by government at the level of provision. Particular emphasis has been placed on housing policies for the elderly, including improvements to existing homes and a massive increase in purpose-built accommodation (Wicks, 1982). Certainly, the need for more and better housing is borne out by the study since the consensus of opinion in both groups was that sheltered housing is the ideal combination of independence and support for the more active elderly. Women also favoured community-based care provision which would enable them to remain in their own homes. They were particularly concerned about access to domiciliary services such as home helps and backup support from health and welfare professionals if necessary. The right mix of formal care and family support was seen as a viable means of maintaining a level of independence and reflected an unwillingness to allocate major caring responsibilities to female relatives.

This, of course, is entirely consistent with the avowed aims of official community care policy. The intention is to keep people independent in their own homes and to give service-users the power to decide what sort of help they need and from whom. However, for the frail elderly this choice may be largely illusory. It is debatable whether reliance on the state for personal care at home allows for more autonomy than reliance on relatives, and raises the question of whether the home is the best environment for highly dependent people. Some writers have commented that many of the conditions observed by Goffman (1961) in 'total institutions' apply to the housebound elderly (Victor et al., 1992). As ill-health and immobility increase, the person may be confined to one room within the home and have decreasing contact with the outside world. Care plans may impose the same sort of routines found in institutions. Everything takes place within the same space and by the same series of people who arrive throughout the day to carry out specialized tasks. It is difficult to see how this is more 'normalized' than the living conditions in institutions. Furthermore, when strangers are relied upon for personal care, the cared-for may have little control over their own space or belongings and this does little to preserve autonomy and independence.

Finch (1984a) has argued that residential care can provide a solution to the gendered and sexist dimensions of community care policy. Although this has been criticized by Harris (1985) as 'utopian' and by those who argue that Finch polarized community and residential care and that her view of community care is too bleak (Baldwin and Twigg, 1991), clearly there is a need for residential care for some elderly people. Whilst some daughters-in-law declared themselves willing to try to support their dependent mothers-in-law, most were alarmed by the prospect of giving care. They felt that even with unrivalled support they would still opt for good residential care if given the choice. These views were echoed by mothers-in-law although they were more pessimistic that such care is available in either the private or public sectors.

Moving into residential care is distressful if it is unwanted. However, if it offers attractive living arrangements and services which provide a way for the frail elderly to live securely in their community, it can be a positive choice. Finch and Groves (1982) have speculated on what might be good quality residential provision and their suggestions were echoed in various ways by the women in this study. The main criterion is residential care of a type which the frail elderly themselves, and their families, would find attractive. This includes living arrangements where residents are afforded privacy, treated with respect and provided with those services which help them maintain, as far as possible, the normal rhythm of life. This would, in turn, minimize the less attractive aspects of communal living whilst providing the frail and vulnerable with a secure environment within which to live out the last years of their lives.

Evidence from this study supports those who advocate residential care as the best option for women (Finch and Groves, 1982). An important advantage is the opportunity it provides for a flexible approach to families, many of whom will want to be involved with the welfare of their elderly relatives without the burden of full-time care and responsibility. Here, the concept of shared care written into community care policy but which at present seems to offer comparatively little support to family carers might be adopted more successfully. Shared care, designed as a means of keeping people in the community, is also a way of forging a positive relationship between formal and informal carers within the residential sector. This approach would require a reassessment of roles within the residential sector, as well as an improvement in the status, pay and conditions of its employees. As Foster (1991) points out, an enchanced role for relatives inevitably means a loss of control exercised by care assistants and nursing staff, and this is unlikely to be achieved under their present conditions of work. A reassessment seems essential since the women in this study have made it clear that families have no wish to abandon their elderly relatives nor any intention of leaving them to languish, unwanted, in institutions. What they want is a supportive environment for their dependants and themselves, to enable them to retain their normal lives whilst taking on some, but not all, of the responsibilities of care.

Conclusion

This chapter has been concerned with patterns of dependency and support between mothers and daughters-in-law during the family life-course. It has focused on the negotiation and renegotiation of obligations at critical life-transitions, and has revealed how these are shaped and influenced by reference to public morality and concepts of altruism and reciprocity. By looking at situations likely to be experienced at some time by the majority of women, the analysis has been concerned to assess what is expected of them in family terms throughout the life-course. Therefore, three areas have been examined: childbirth, bereavement and ageing. In all three situations a hierarchy of obligations can be seen to exist which dictates that mothers and daughters are the expected relatives to care for each other. The strong affective bonds which exist between them suggest that theirs is the most appropriate female support relationship and when it is activated the involvement of in-laws tends to be peripheral. If, however, a support relationship between mother and daughter is not possible, mothers-in-law and daughters-in-law usually feel obliged to help each other even if their relationship is not close. When the crisis is acute, after childbirth or during a bereavement, there is usually a good prospect of recovery and the quality of the relationship is largely insignificant when honouring obligations. However, patterns of relationships in the past are more important when prolonged, intensive assistance is required, although there are other reasons which also affect attitudes to care. We have seen, for example, that issues surrounding care question attitudes of responsibility and obligation which daughters-in-law feel towards their mothers-in-law and how these are informed by perceptions of socially acceptable behaviour between kin. Consequently, a woman who resists caring for her dependent mother-in-law may risk public disapproval, pressure from formal agents and serious problems of self-perception.

It is suggested that women are highly resistant to primary home care provided for, and by, female relatives. Women in both groups commented on the strains of family life, invasion of privacy, lack of autonomy and independence and the sheer hard work which caring involves. It seems, therefore, that the ideal of altruistic care which underpins social policy is distorted in reality and that even where it exists it does so at considerable costs to carers and the cared-for. Importantly, it emerged that tensions in support relationships between mothers and daughters-in-law were expected to be no worse than those between mothers and daughters. This is highly significant, for it suggests that in the later stages of the life-course the differences between affective bonds and formal boundaries become blurred. Alternatively, it may be that the mixture of emotions in tending relationships allows for all possibilities, including love, duty, aversion and bitterness. Therefore, although some women felt that caring for their elderly mother might be slightly easier and more acceptable, the crux of the matter is that, given a free choice, very few women expressed a willingness to give or receive primary care in relation to any of their female kin.

Notes

1 Evidence from the General Household Survey, 1985, shows that men make a greater contribution to caring than is often assumed. It shows that women were more likely to be carers than men but the difference was not very marked, 15 per cent compared with 12 per cent. However, since there are more women than men in the total adult population of Great Britain, it is true that the number of women caring was considerably greater than that of men, 3.5 million compared with 2.5 million (Green, 1985).
2 It must be emphasized that these were expressed views. Studies of informal carers show that, in reality, most people reject the idea of a permanent residential solution and continue to shoulder total responsibility until the elderly person dies or their own health breaks down (Lewis and Meredith, 1988; Ungerson, 1987).
3 Arber and Gilbert (1989), using evidence derived from the General Household Survey, 1980, have examined the gender balance of care in relation to co-resident carers. They state:

> the gender balance of co-resident caring for the elderly differs according to four types of kin relationships: (a) caring as part of a marital relationship – men and women are equally likely to care for an elderly spouse, (b) a filial relationship involving an unmarried carer – slightly fewer unmarried sons than unmarried daughters care for an elderly parent, (c) a sibling relationship – elderly sisters are much more likely to be carers than brothers, and (d) a filial relationship involving a married carer – we assume that men are unlikely to be carers. (p. 113)

Conclusion

This study has focused on family relations in Stoke-on-Trent in the mid-1980s, concentrating on maternal relationships between women established by marriage. In order to examine social and material relationships between gender and generations within the private domain of the family, a career approach tracing developments in the individual and family life courses has been adopted. Using both social and demographic changes and critical life-events as a framework, it has been possible to examine women's perceptions and experiences of their relationships and patterns of meaning and interaction in family life.

There are a number of problems encountered in researching into fundamental and taken-for-granted dimensions of society. The family is an institution familiar to us all because kinship and marriage structure most people's domestic arrangements for most of their lives. Its 'taken-for-granted' nature is reflected in sociological research which sees the family as a basic unit requiring little exploration. The family tends to be questioned in the context of 'abnormal' disruptions caused, for example, by marital breakdown and divorce and, whilst recent perspectives have critically examined 'successful' families (Morgan, 1975) and relations between women and men in the domestic domain (Barrett and McIntosh, 1982; Comer, 1974; Oakley, 1974), other important dimensions of family life have not been addressed.

Stacey (1981) has argued that problems with analyzing the family arise from classical sociological theories which originated in the public domain. Male sociologists concerned primarily with the market place, industry and the state gave scant attention to the domestic sphere. When they did consider the family it was from the male point of view using theories developed in the public arena. For example, having systematically ignored women for decades, sociological concern with the family during the 1950s made it difficult to exclude women completely. According to Evans (1982) women were 'in the family like jam in a doughnut – invisible but essential' (p. 64) for whilst men's changing relationship to the family was of interest to sociologists, women's role and its consequences were not. It was left to feminists to challenge traditional concepts about the family by pointing out the dependent relationship between the public domain and women's unpaid work in the domestic sphere.

Although Stacey has explored links between the public and private areas of social life, she points out that the legacy of social theories developed in the past constitute a 'conceptual straitjacket' (1981, p. 189) still perpetuated by some

Conclusion

sociologists today. There is not yet a theory which encompasses both the domestic and public spheres and difficulties arise from applying theories relating to the market place to studies of family life. For example, conflict models used to study formal organizations are not appropriate for family research because the experience of conflict is different. Gittins (1985) has made clear the need to differentiate between ideals and ideology about family life and the realities. Family ideology which emphasizes relationships founded on love between individuals with shared aims and interests masks tensions which arise because the same individuals often have conflicting needs. Relations of power between the sexes and generations exist within families and the forces creating affection can also engender antagonisms. However, because the family is a sentimental order and a community of feeling, people experience guilt about conflict and attribute it to individual rather than structural failings. Furthermore, a disproportionate amount of guilt devolves on women because they take a heavier responsibility than men for the happiness and emotional well-being of family members.

Since the sociology of the public domain has provided no theory which can fully encompass the private, sociologists studying the family have drawn on work produced in other disciplines. Anthropologists, for example, have improved on functionalist theories of the family by providing definitions of kinship which encompass both social and biological dimensions but many of the issues from other cultures, where kinship is the major organizing principle, are less socially significant in advanced, industrial societies. Psychological concepts, such as role-theory, provide valuable information about how individuals interact in groups but reflect a micro focus on the family which further isolates it from wider structures of which it is a part. Various feminist perspectives have alerted us to power relationships which exist in the private domain and to questions of gender in relations between individuals in the family and between families and the state (Hartmann, 1987; Land, 1976). It has been argued, for example, that values concerning the fundamental 'naturalness' and inevitability of the family which are implicit in social and welfare policy distract attention from the economic basis of the marriage relationship. Many feminists insist that the family and the market place are both founded on economic relations and labour contracts, and that the politics of the public domain cannot be understood without reference to the politics of the family (Delphy and Leonard, 1992; Gittins, 1985; Stacey, 1981; Leonard, 1980).

Although many feminist writers have shown how the view of the family from the public domain has ignored women's concerns and rendered them 'invisible', there remain aspects of family life and women's relationships which have not been fully explored. Much of the recent literature does not adequately address what it means to be a member of a family. Not only is it necessary to differentiate between the family as an ideal and the reality, it is vital to understand how people interact in families and between households. There is a need to move away from focusing exclusively on relationships between husbands and wives and parents and children in the nuclear family and to reconsider, in the light of social change since the early 1960s, the importance of extended family relationships between genders and generations.

This book has attempted to do so by focusing on a particular relationship between family women which has hitherto been ignored in the sociology of the family. Thus, there are connections between the 'invisibility' of mother-in-law and daughter-in-law relationships in family research and the 'invisibility' of dimensions of family life which have been overlooked in the view from the public domain. What this study has aimed to provide is a new perspective on the family and on women's lives by examining themes and concepts which underpin patterns of meaning and interaction between individuals in the extended domestic setting. These form the core of the book and have allowed for the exploration of issues which are relevant to women's understanding, perceptions and experiences of family life.

The imbalance between the ideal and reality of family life is a recurring theme. Ideals about love, companionship and sexual relations create an expectation that everyone will marry, obtain an independent home and raise a family of their own. This obscures the reality of gender inequalities in marriage and, importantly, the fact that getting married creates not one relationship but several. It brings together two, previously unrelated, groups and requires people to establish close links with others whom they have had no part in selecting. Entering another family as an in-law is a unique experience because it involves the creation of family relationships with a group of people related to each other but with whom the new member has no previous connections. There are no guidelines for appropriate behaviour between in-laws but because all families are different it is usually inappropriate to pattern behaviour on one's own family and new ways have to be learned. Thus the extended family is an agent of adult socialization which is wholly different from the socialization of the child. Socialization of children occurs from birth within a familiar setting via a process of interaction with parents and siblings, whilst socialization beyond childhood is assumed to take place outside the home. However, marriage involves a unique form of socialization in an ambivalent setting. Although the understanding of the family as an institution and an experience is familiar to most people, the social relations in family units which individuals enter on marriage are not.

Integrating into the new family occurs during the courtship period which allows prospective in-laws time to establish their relationships. Because women are responsible for orchestrating social relations in the private realm, it is the mother who must welcome the newcomer and contribute to the formation of attachment. It has been suggested here that the first meeting between the mother and her son's future partner can be a daunting experience for both women and that impressions formed at this stage often have a lasting effect. Many women referred to the expectations mothers had for their son's choice of partner and some felt they had been judged unfavourably. Yet, contrary to these beliefs, most mothers-in-law held very positive views about their daughters-in-law and were not disappointed. Moreover, those who did regret their son's marriage were influenced by the dictum not to interfere in the lives of adult children and this, combined with a desire to avoid family estrangements, precluded maternal expressions of concern or dislike.

As marriage rituals have no formal roles for mothers, women mark what is for them a personal status passage by their own forms of ceremonial. Food plays a significant part here since formal meals in the informal family setting have associations with special events. A private meal to which the prospective daughter-in-law is invited has a public dimension which contains messages about women's roles and shifting power relationships between gender and generation. Although the meal is special it reinforces the usual about family life and, importantly,

Conclusion

is a vehicle by which mothers welcome daughters-in-law and 'give away' their sons.

The idealism which surrounds the family was evident not only in the expectations mothers and daughters-in-law held for each other but for relationships between the couple's respective parents. These are comparable to in-law attachments both in the sense of ambiguity and lack of personal choice. Whilst the parents' failure to get on was unlikely to adversely affect the marriage, most women said it was better if they established good relations. Thus, the ideology of the family as a cohesive unit influenced people's expectations, coerced their conduct and was a source of concern if it was not realized.

It is possible to draw strands from the narrative which illustrate how family ideology influences the understanding of family life. Family ideology has increasingly defined marriage as a private relationship, resistant to intrusions from kin and non-kin alike, and this was evident in concepts of boundary maintenance between individuals and households. These relate to physical boundaries which influence interaction and also interpersonal boundaries which exist between affinal kin. Neither are mutually exclusive; sentiment and feeling, obligation and duty are entwined in family life and contribute to the frequency and type of involvement people expect. It was clear that relationships between parents and children persisted after children married and even when affective ties were weak, some form of contact was maintained. In the majority of cases regular visiting patterns and other forms of interaction were well-established and, in estranged relations between mothers and daughters-in-law, wives continued to support links between mothers, sons and grandchildren. However, an understanding of boundaries was explicit in interaction between extended kin. Perceptions of insufficient or excessive contact reflected divisions between idealism and reality and different interpretations by generations of what the family should be. There were, for example, differences in ideas about appropriate visiting behaviour in relation to parents and to married children. Visits to the parental home contained a strong element of informality which made invitations and prior arrangements unnecessary. However, normative rules prescribing marital privacy meant that visits in the opposite direction were subject to regulation by mothers and wives who, respectively, avoided and discouraged unexpected calls.

Women's preoccupation with 'fairness' and 'balance' was a significant feature in patterns of interaction in family life. This was explicit in their attitudes to those occasions in the year when family obligations take precedence. The Christmas festival, for example, had particular associations with family values and imposed certain obligations which were almost impossible to resist. People were compelled to make complicated annual arrangements in order to meet expectations that at least some of the festive season would be spent with their parents and parents-in-law. Women were at the centre of negotiations, concerned to balance competing claims from parents in a way which avoided favouring one set more than the other. In reality this meant either a continuous round of visiting or a great deal of cooking and entertaining in their own homes, so that for many women Christmas was a stressful event. Family ideology was perhaps most explicit at Christmas when attempts to achieve an unrealistic ideal emphasized the conflicts and tensions which were part of women's experiences of family life.

Obligations and sentiment were important factors in prescriptions for mutual aid between generations although, again, these were circumscribed to some extent by differing ideas and conflicts of interest. Generally, where the assistance required related to a perceived short-term, fairly immediate need, women responded positively to each other although daughters-in-law expressed resentment when they saw mothers' demands as excessive. However, negative feelings did not restrict action and indeed, as far as short-term transactions were concerned, moral obligations towards family overrode personal feelings. Reciprocity was more important for the older generation as mothers-in-law expressed reluctance to accept assistance unless they could return it. Daughters-in-law took a more pragmatic view and many were in receipt of childcare and other services where the obligation to return, although acknowledged, had been deferred for long periods. Reciprocity in kind was acceptable, if not expected, but the sentiments individuals held about family relations precluded an economic dimension to all forms of practical assistance. Women expressed strongly-held views that performing services for financial gain was inappropriate behaviour and there was no evidence that motives for assisting kin were calculative in any sense.

Although some working mothers were receiving childcare support from their mothers-in-law, women expressed varied views about grandmother care. Short-term assistance, either on a regular basis or in response to a specific request, was rarely refused although some had clear ideas about what constituted a legitimate claim. However, none of the mothers-in-law were providing long-term support for working mothers and, significantly, they were not prepared to do so unless there was exceptional hardship in the parental family. This questions social policy which, in the post-war period, has consistently cut back on state provision for pre-school children on the assumption that grandmothers are an available family resource. Even when they are, not all middle-aged family women are in the same position. Although older women did not refer to the quality of the mother and daughter-in-law relationship as a factor which influenced decisions about childcare support, daughters-in-law tended to express a preference for help with childcare from their own mothers. Thus, maternal grandmothers may be no more willing to become mother substitutes than paternal grandmothers, but feel compelled to accept forms of responsibility they would prefer not to have.

An area which requires more research than has been possible here is the flow of financial assistance between generations and households in extended families. This study has shown that, contrary to the limited evidence in the literature (Bell, 1968, 1970), working-class extended family aid exists in comparable proportions to that found between generations in middle-class families. Little is known about the distribution of money between generations and households because this is considered a private matter and not the proper concern of strangers. Consequently, the economy of extended kinship, particularly among the working class, has been overlooked by sociologists either because it is difficult to research or because of its irrelevance in view of assumptions about working-class resources. These assumptions have beens questioned here and whilst it has not been possible to develop the debate, it provides a basis for further research and speculation.

Negotiations relating to economic support occurred between women and between other family members including in-laws and sometimes operated in quasi-secrecy which excluded some people and involved others. Interpersonal boundaries were effective not just with regard to financial negotiations but in the discriminative practices employed by some women. For example, the values

Conclusion

involved in gift-giving were quite significant in mother and daughter-in-law relationships as a means of expressing dislike as well as affection.

The ambiguous position of the mother-in-law in the kin network is illuminated by the mother-daughter bond, for although the mother-in-law relationship is quasi-maternal it is experienced as something different. The mother/daughter relationship has no equivalent although in rare circumstances when the mother is missing it may be replaced by another. Therefore, though mothers and daughters-in-law hoped to achieve something similar or even become friends, very often their relationships were neither. Strong interpersonal boundaries which characterize in-law relationships connote a formal dimension missing in mother-daughter or friendship bonds. Mothers and daughters-in-law have no bedrock of shared experience to draw on and, in some cases, one may have personality characteristics the other finds unattractive. Nevertheless, although investment in family relationships contains an element of choice, some interactive involvement is expected even when affective bonds are weak. Moreover, social boundaries, unlike affective bonds, rarely remain fixed over the life-course so that mothers and daughters-in-law must continually reassess their relationship and their feelings for each other.

It has been argued here and elsewhere (Hareven, 1982; Yanagisako, 1977) that women are the 'kin-keepers' in the kin network, responsible for their own relationships and those between others. Women orchestrate social relations between mothers and adult sons and between mothers and sons-in-law but there is no-one in the kin network to undertake kin-keeping on behalf of mothers and daughters-in-law. The women must establish and sustain their relationships without the support of others and in the best way they can. Furthermore, if one seeks a nurturant relationship on the basis of mother or friend which is not reciprocated, the potential for conflict is increased.

A discussion of communication and mediating patterns between extended kin endeavoured to expand analysis of kin-keeping by questioning normative expectations of female affectiveness. For example, although feminism has generated valuable research on power relationships between husbands and wives, little attention has been given to shifting dimensions of power in asymmetrical relationships between family women. This was explicit in women's mediating role between mothers and sons where daughters-in-law made choices about the relational work they would do on the mother's behalf. Differing interpretations of mediation had significance for how situations were perceived in this connection. Since both women had intimate bonds with the husband/son, some mothers sought intimacy with their daughters-in-law on the basis of mediation but often daughters-in-law experienced this as manipulation. Not only was this easier to reject than intimacy, it was made legitimate by stereotypes of the 'interfering mother-in-law' to which people referred when describing their own actions and those of others. The regulating aspect of such stereotypes had a disabling effect on mothers-in-law because the dictum not to 'interfere' sometimes imposed constraints on their involvement with married children to a greater degree than they preferred. Consequently, daughters-in-law were relatively more powerful because they were able to make choices about kin-keeping not available to mothers-in-law, including decisions not to mediate if they so wished.

In all intimate relationships the potential for conflict exists but it is intensified between in-laws because of their ambiguous positions in the kin network. It is also more destructive and therefore rarely expressed or openly acknowledged. Women were concerned to avoid conflict, even if it meant suppressing personal feelings, because of repercussions on other family members and because peaceful coexistence seemed the most effective means of conducting their own relationships. Even where negative feelings ran high, formal boundaries between mothers and daughters-in-law prevented overt hostilities. Between mothers and daughters, however, an intimate knowledge of each other allows for expressions of anger without fear of rejection. In in-law relationships anger has to be avoided because too often there is no emotional intimacy to sustain them and, consequently, the risks are too high.

Many of the feelings which generated conflict were influenced by negative mother-in-law imagery. For example, the image of the 'possessive mother' had meaning for both mothers and daughters-in-law in their understanding of their relationships. Mothers-in-law were particularly concerned about the dangers of possessiveness and certainly did not appear to want to hold onto their sons. Indeed, if successful mothering means raising children to be autonomous adults able to form relationships of their own, most mothers (including all those in this book) are 'successful' and therefore 'possessiveness' as an ideological construct makes very little sense. However, 'possessiveness' as an experience did have meaning for those daughters-in-law who felt that their mother-in-law's attachment to her son was exaggerated. It is important not to overstate this point of view given women's insecurities in the marriage relationship but it is worth making because of its validity for the women concerned.

Mothers-in-law occupy an ambiguous position and many of their anxieties stem from a sense of relegation to the periphery of the family when once they were at the centre. As wives and mothers they have a vested interest in their families and expect to retain an involvement with their children when they marry. However, women have few rights to their adult children and some, as a consequence of their changed role and status, experience a sense of loss and insecurity which may be interpreted as 'possessiveness' by others. Social processes have marginalized middle-aged women who have had few resources outside the private domain and little opportunity to develop positive self-images beyond those of wife and mother. Indeed, it is the lack of power and influence in other spheres which create the conditions for conflict between women of different generations in the family. The considerable expertise they derive from their work in the home has little status outside although it has a validity and importance for the women themselves. Much of it involves servicing others and what Stacey (1981) has called 'people work' (p. 182). However, the acquisition of skills regarded as necessary to carry out these tasks is a cause of tension between women, reinforced by notions of the 'interfering mother-in-law'. Some mothers-in-law might have wished to share their knowledge with their sons' wives but seemed constrained by fears of being thought 'interfering'. Again, they were in a relatively powerless position compared to daughters-in-law who, as recipients of advice, were able to define its status and could, if it was unwelcome, reject it on the basis of 'interference'.

It has been argued that humour plays a fundamental role in in-law relationships because the unique position of the mother-in-law is culturally recognized and expressed through the medium of mother-in-law jokes. No other domestic relationship is acknowledged in the same way and the overwhelmingly negative representations of mothers-in-law in popular culture act as a control

Conclusion

resource which regulates the behaviour of family women. The regulation of individuals is an explicit dimension of social life and, in both formal and informal settings, humour is an indicator of power differentials which are rarely challenged. For example, Powell (1988) states: 'Formalised humour will generally fulfil an ideological function in supporting and maintaining existing social relations and dominant ways of perceiving social reality' (p. 100) and this is also reflected in informal humour where subordinates feel compelled to respond to jokes even if they themselves are the target. Humour takes many forms and can be a coping strategy as well as a regulating device but when expressed in jokes and joking behaviour which disparage the mother-in-law it appears to be gender-specific. That is, it is used by men rather than women and is specifically related to power relationships and social control.

Cultural recognition of the mother-in-law as a legitimate subject for jokes allows for informal joking behaviour between sons and mothers-in-law in the private setting. Unlike that found in the joking relationships referred to by anthropologists (Radcliffe-Brown, 1952) it is not based on friendly equality but is a controlling device which asserts the man's status. Relations between a man and his mother-in-law are not expected to go well because it is assumed that the marital bond will conflict with the ties the wife has with her mother. This is the only socially recognized tie between women which has the potential to undermine the marriage relationship and therefore may be perceived by some men as threatening and invasive. Humour, in these circumstances, operates as a control mechanism, discrediting mother-daughter bonds and regulating the behaviour of both mother-in-law and wife.

It has been argued here that, apart from the conjugal relationship, many men interact with kin at a superficial level because cultural expectations of masculinity make it difficult for them to do otherwise. However, mother/son relationships contain a paradox which is made explicit by the form taken in mother-in-law jokes. Although emotional ties between mothers and adult sons are expected to diminish, jokes which single out the wife's mother demonstrate the continuing importance of mother/son ties. There are no jokes about the man's mother, suggesting that, whilst overt expressions of affection between them are inappropriate, she at least has a right to more respect from her son than he accords his mother-in-law. This was also confirmed by the marked absence of abuse in the reciprocal joking and horseplay which characterized some mother/son relationships. It seems, therefore, that men are not compelled to regulate their mothers' behaviour because the mother does not threaten to undermine her son's interests. However, she does not escape regulation in relations with her daughter-in-law or, indeed, the self-imposed regulation mothers-in-law practice themselves.

Humour, then, plays a fundamental role in the negotiation and renegotiation of the mother-in-law's conduct. It makes explicit those forms of control which reinforce power differentials in relationships of gender and generation by supporting some and discrediting others. Humour also demonstrates the connections between the public and private spheres. Formalized humour expressed in popular culture reinforces family ideology by confirming the stability of family life and the permanency of marital ties. It also contributes to the devaluation of older women in both spheres in its distortion of the mother-in-law as a subject for mockery and rejection.

Ideology which represents the family as a stable unit diverts attention from the fact that families do not remain constant but are subject to change over time. Some changes are related to an alleged crisis in the family such as increases in divorce, cohabitation and illegitimacy, whilst others are anticipated as part of the normal pattern of family life. However, change of any kind has the potential to disrupt existing family networks and alter the structure of relationships established by marriage. Whether anticipated or not, people must make accommodations in their lives and develop strategies in order to cope with changes in their roles and relationships.

Although there is no such thing as the 'ideal' family, contemporary media images of a young married couple with two bright, immaculate offspring would have us believe that this is the type of family to which most people belong. And because it is similar to most people's experience of the family at some stage in their lives, it is meaningful to us all. Reality is suspended in this image and the ageing process which alters the organization of families and households is ignored. However, personal nostalgia, although usually distorted in memory, promotes the feeling that this stage of family life is the 'ideal'. This contrasts with the family situations of older women because there is no 'ideal' time to be a mother-in-law. So many of the changes which occur in later life are associated with loss and those which have positive connotations are often contingent on decisions made by other people.

It has been argued that the family life-course is a valid concept because individual and family transitions are reference points which give meaning to people's lives. Women anticipated important events through their understanding of the life-course and were disturbed if their expectations of future roles and relationships were unfulfilled. For example, all the mothers-in-law operated within a set of traditional values about the family and, for many, the development of a positive self-image in later life depended on the continuation of the family by the next generation. Relationships between family women were made possible by the roles they played and young women who postponed their own life-transitions prevented older women from having a meaningful role and delayed their progress too.

The changes which occur when women are young have mainly positive connotations and rites of passage mark their importance. However, there are no rites of passage for middle-aged women when their children leave home and no forms of pre-socialization to prepare them for this event. Most mothers continue to service adolescent and adult children for as long as they share the same household. This is particularly significant with regard to sons because, despite optimistic views about egalitarianism in families, there is still more expected from daughters in domestic terms. Thus the emotional loss which most women experienced when their sons married was difficult to separate from the void in their servicing role. It would appear that women who attach most importance to their identities as mothers have most difficulty adjusting to the changes imposed by the post-parental stage but the causes of their problems are social. Like the ideology of the family, there is an ideology of motherhood which does not represent the reality of being a mother and diverts attention from the fact that the process and skills of mothering are socially devalued. Consequently, when childrearing is complete there is no social recognition of the mother's achievements and nothing to mark past years of mothering. It is hardly surprising, therefore, that some women experienced their son's departure in bereavement terms, given that much

Conclusion

of social life excludes this age group and offers few opportunities for other positive roles.

However, it would be misleading to describe all the mothers-in-law studied as having suffered loss-related problems when their sons married. Whilst they all referred to some emotional upheaval at this stage in their lives, most women said it was a temporary state and expressed positive attitudes about the future. They seemed to have adjusted well to their sons leaving home and said that this should not be seen as a loss. Most had various resources to support them and found that the post-parental period brought many compensations. As might be expected, women who had good relations with their daughters-in-law and continued involvement in extended family life seemed the most content, especially those who derived pleasure from their 'active' grandmothering role.

Many of the social and demographic changes in contemporary society have altered the structure of family households and kin relationships. Now the family is more often fractured by divorce than death and lone mothers are likely to be divorced rather than widowed. Equally, couples often choose to cohabit for a period before they marry and both cohabitation and divorce disturb concepts of kin relations and family life. The implications for mothers and daughters-in-law have been examined within the context of 'rules' which frame social relations and provide prescriptions for appropriate behaviour between kin. Both divorce and cohabitation could be said to constitute 'abnormal' situations where the rules usually applied to family life are inadequate and where there are no others to draw on. Both have considerable impact on family women creating ambiguity in the ties between them, dividing loyalties and making obligations unclear.

Whether or not mother and daughter-in-law relations can continue after divorce depends on how they were perceived during the marriage. Very few of the divorced women studied had sustained relations with their former mother-in-law because they had viewed them in terms of the marriage and joint ties with the husband/son. Therefore, when the marriage ended, in-law relationships declined in most cases completely. Sometimes limited contact was maintained out of a common interest in the grandchildren, but those daughters-in-law who had remarried found it almost impossible to integrate former in-laws into their new family group and eventually the role of the paternal grandmother was lost. On the other hand, if the mother-in-law and daughter-in-law had perceived each other as friends during the marriage, the relationship was difficult to realign afterwards because family loyalty was considered more important than friendship and the mother was usually compelled to support her son. However, relationships based on friendship were not exclusively through the son and, therefore, when the marriage ended there were other losses too. Women had to come to terms with their own separations and some found that their friendship could not be sustained as they had hoped. Therefore the rules which performed as anticipated in 'normal' situations did not always perform well in 'abnormal' ones and sometimes broke down altogether.

Normative rules are also inadequate when young couples live together before marriage because cohabitation disturbs traditional concepts of what the family should be. Older women attached a great deal of importance to be the sanctity of marriage; for them it is a meaningful rite of passage which confirms adult status through the undertaking of a legal and binding commitment. There was no evidence that the young women studied did not take the same view but contemporary attitudes towards sexual relations allowed them more choice than couples in the past. Cohabitation had not been an available option for the mothers-in-law and when their sons chose it they felt anxious and insecure. Many of the rules framing in-law relationships were inappropriate because it was difficult for mothers to see their son's partner as a daughter-in-law if the couple were not married, thus making relationships between the women even more complex and ambiguous. However, prohibitive rules retained their importance precluding, in most cases, maternal expressions of disapproval for fear of being accused of 'interference'.

Those in the study who chose to cohabit did so as a serious endeavour and, to the relief of their parents, they all eventually married. Again, this questions the idea of 'possessive mothering', for although mothers rarely forced the issue they wanted marriage for the sons. It resolved their anxieties about the permanency of the relationship and restored their faith in 'normal' relations and the continuation of family life.

An examination of support relationships between affinal women demonstrated the connectedness of the family both between individuals and between the public and private spheres of activity. Ideology has imposed a view of the family as somehow detached from the rest of society yet its social functions are an explicit part of the experience of family life. Indeed, the notion of divisions between the public and private world is unsustainable because work and social relations permeate all social institutions. The home is the primary workplace for women; their occupation is domestic and the orchestration of emotional relations is their concern. Women provide support services for their dependent relatives and are the link beween formal welfare provision and primary home care. Ideology systematically ignores the complex pattern of dependency and responsibility that exists in the family setting by suggesting that families are egalitarian, complementary units founded on love and devotion between individuals. It is this 'sentimental model of the family' which informs social policy and upon which legislators and state agencies base their administrative arrangements. Many of these arrangements impinge on ideas about the 'normal' family and fairly traditional views of domestic life. They also assume a general consensus about the nature of kinship obligations and the affective element of all family relationships.

In this study care has been examined in terms of tending relationships and the differing concepts of being cared for and cared about. In two-way support relationships between family women of different generations, concern was expressed about the management of care and available resources. For example, daughters-in-law identified their own dependency needs as being fairly short-term and requiring emotional and practical support rather than very personal care, and most women had personal support networks at their disposal. However, care of the elderly was seen as much more problematic, involving an unpredictable process of decline with corresponding increases in support. Therefore, when daughters-in-law talked about the needs of a frail and elderly mother-in-law, they spoke in terms of personal tending and were concerned that, as carers, they would be isolated and expected to cope alone.

Dependency situations likely to be experienced by most women at some time during the life-course provided a framework within which to explore attitudes towards short-term and long-term care. In all three situations a hierarchy of obligations was identified which determined that mothers and daughters were

Conclusion

the expected relatives to care for each other but if this was not possible, mothers and daughters-in-law felt bound to provide support even if they had poor interactive relationships. When the crisis was acute and prospects for full recovery were good, the obligation to care took priority over personal feelings and the quality of relations in the past. Fairly immediate, short-term support in response to childbirth or bereavement stemmed from personal concepts of duty and altruism combined with external beliefs governing obligations between kin. However, where long-term, intensive care was concerned, personal biographies and patterns of social relations were highly significant for prospective support relationships between mothers and daughters-in-law. Consequently, the 'sentimental model of the family' is often inappropriate for women who have little affection for each other, yet in the later stages of the life-course may be expected to form intimate, caring bonds.

Assumptions regarding support relationships between mothers and daughters suggested that, as daughters-in-law, women are able to resist some aspects of care-giving. Evidence from the study shows that where there is a daughter to care, daughters-in-law do not expect to be involved at the level of personal tending although they are prepared to give back-up assistance if required. It appears, therefore, that daughters-in-law may be able to avoid caring for parents-in-law because of their position in the kin network although, as daughters, responsibility for their own parents is likely to devolve on them. This is important because the women studied expressed opinions about caring for elderly mothers which did not differ significantly from those referring to mothers-in-law. Crucial factors in attitudes towards caring relationships concerned the necessity for joint households and the attendant strains on family life and, importantly, fears associated with personal tending. Indeed, much of the resistance to caring stemmed from anxieties about dealing with incontinence in an adult, suggesting that this is a task no less distasteful and polluting for women than for men.

Resistance to care was not the prerogative of daughters-in-law for mothers-in-law too had strong reservations about receiving support from their female relatives. They anticipated being instrumental in defining future support relationships and opposed the view of the elderly as a passive group by their determination to have an active role in decision-making about how much care they might need. Ambivalent images of ageing provided a formula for mothers-in-law to avoid support relationships for whilst none had reached an age she considered 'old', they all vowed to retain their autonomy and independence for as long as they could. A few had gone so far as to make contingency plans for the possibility of disabling old age but most preferred not to look too far into the future and merely expressed a desire to live independently and avoid burdening their children. Indeed, in the case of very frail and dependent people, there was strong support for residential care as an alternative to family care in the same household, even though residential care was not considered an attractive option.

Certainly the attitudes expressed by mothers-in-law and daughters-in-law reflected an overwhelming concern with personal autonomy and freedom of choice, as well as a desire to avoid, as far as possible, the 'structured dependency' of older people. References to independent households, domestic privacy and the priority of marital relationships, together with concern about the availability of domiciliary and welfare services, reflected attitudes which suggest that women make a conscious effort to hold a different view than the 'sentimental model of the family'. Nevertheless, it is difficult for women to resist caring responsibilities given that support from female relatives often seems inevitable in the last resort. Although the women studied advocated various professional and service inputs to support the elderly, other research has shown that informal carers will continue to care in whatever circumstances for as long as they are able (Lewis and Meredith, 1988; Ungerson, 1987). In the current political climate, both a lack of imaginative public policy for the elderly and viable alternatives for carers and the cared-for in terms of community and residential provision seem to force some elderly people to seek support from their families when they would not otherwise need to. The declared intention of government is to reduce the welfare role of the state and to limit spending on public services whilst simultaneously advocating familial responsibility and a resurgence of private philanthropy through charitable organizations. It seems, therefore, that the pressures on family women to provide care are set to increase. This being the case, strains indirectly imposed on families by government policies may undermine the effective welfare role of the family.

The ambivalence of the mother-in-law relationship mirrors the ambivalence of the family itself. It has been argued that the family, idealized in our social and political systems as the most desirable, indeed the only possible way of life, is an arena of conflict and division as well as pleasurable experience. Therefore, at the level of interpersonal relationships and interaction, nothing can be taken for granted about its nature, structure and meaning. Equally, the family cannot be analyzed as an isolated unit or a fundamental institution discrete from other forms of social organization. The public domain impinges on the family and, crucially, on family women, through the organization of domestic activity to meet the demands of bureaucracies and formal institutions. Thus, women are the bulwark between the public and private spheres, responsible for the health and emotional well-being of family members and providing informal care services to augment and support professional organizations.

The book has explored the ambivalence of the family within the social structure by focusing on what could arguably be called the most ambivalent of family relationships – that between mothers and daughters-in-law. The ambivalence of the mother-in-law relationship in the kin network, as quasi-mother or friend but often neither, is brought into focus when contrasted with other relationships – between husband and wife, parents and dependent children and mothers and adult daughters – which are largely taken-for-granted. Thus, mothers-in-law are 'inside' and 'outside' the family much as older women are marginalized by society. When a woman's son marries she surrenders her role to another who may have a different conception of what it should be. Consequently, the mother finds herself on the fringes of extended family life, where her conduct is a matter of negotiation and subject to the regulation of others.

Although there are structural factors which frame in-law relationships, the structure itself is complex. Many of the elements involved in relations between women are also taken-for-granted and thus the highly varied nature of their relationships is overlooked. The family is increasingly presented as a privatized, nuclear unit and boundaries are maintained between individuals and households, but extended family relations with primary kin are still important. It is women as 'kin-keepers' who support and maintain these relationships and through this mainly 'invisible' activity opportunities for affection as well as conflict exist between mothers and daughters-in-law.

Conclusion

It was argued earlier that notions of the family as a 'natural' and fundamental unit in society have informed much of sociological research. This means that, apart from sociologically interesting exceptions identified as 'abnormal' families, many dimensions of family life (and by definition women's lives) have remained unexplored. Indeed, at one level, all families are exceptional because of the diversity in domiciliary units, extended households and, importantly, interpersonal relationships between kin. Therefore, family sociology requires a new theoretical agenda which can encompass the diversity and variation of family life. These issues have already been addressed to some extent in research which has challenged family ideology (Gittins, 1985) and that which has sought to locate the family within the social structure (Allan, 1985). This book represents an endeavour to generate further debate by exploring the meaning and experience of interpersonal roles and relationships and how these are structured by positions in the family.

Bibliography

ABBOTT, P. (1987) 'Women's Social Class Identification: Does Husband's Occupation Make a Difference?', *Sociology*, vol. 21, no. 1, pp. 91–103.
ABERLE, D.F. (1961) 'Navaho', in SCHNEIDER, D.M. and GOUGH, K. (Eds) *Matrilineal Kinship*, University of California Press.
ALIBHAI, Y. (1989) 'Burning in the Cold', in GIEVE, K. (Ed.) *Balancing Acts: On Being a Mother*, London, Virago.
ALLAN, G. (1979) *Sociology of Friendship and Kinship*, London, Allen and Unwin.
ALLAN, G. (1985) *Family Life: Domestic Roles and Social Organisation*, Oxford, Basil Blackwell.
ANDERSON, M. (1971) *Family Structure in Nineteenth Century Lancashire*, Cambridge, Cambridge University Press.
APTER, T. (1990) *Altered Loves: Mothers and Daughters during Adolescence*, Hemel Hempstead, Harvester Wheatsheaf.
ARBER, S. and GILBERT, N. (1989) 'Men: The Forgotten Carers', *Sociology*, vol. 23, no. 1, pp. 111–18.
ARBER, S. and GINN, J. (1991) *Gender and Later Life*, London, Sage.
ARCANA, J. (1981) *Our Mothers' Daughters*, London, The Women's Press.
ARGYLE, M. and HENDERSON, M. (1985) *The Anatomy of Relationships*, London, Heinemann.
BADINTER, E. (1981) *The Myth of Motherhood: A Historical View of the Maternal Instinct*, London, Souvenir Press.
BAKER, H.D.R. (1979) *Chinese Family and Kinship*, London, Macmillan.
BALDOCK, J. and UNGERSON, C. (1991) ' "What d'ya want if you don' want money?": A Feminist Critique of "Paid Volunteering"', in MACLEAN, M. and GROVES, D. (Eds) *Women's Issues in Social Policy*, London, Routledge.
BALDWIN, S. and TWIGG, J. (1991) 'Women and Community Care: Reflections on a Debate', in MACLEAN, M. and GROVES, D. (Eds) *Women's Issues in Social Policy*, London, Routledge.
BALSWICK, J.O. and PEEK, C.W. (1971) 'The Inexpressive Male: A Tragedy of American Society', *The Family Co-ordinator*, vol. 20, pp. 363–8.
BANKOFF, E.A. (1981) 'Effects of Friendship Support on the Psychological Well-Being of Widows', in LOPATA, H.Z. and MAINES, D. (Eds) *Research in the Interweave of Social Roles: Friendship*, vol. 2, Greenwich, CT, JAI Press.
BARRETT, M. and MCINTOSH, M. (1982) *The Anti-Social Family*, London, Verso.

BART, P.B. (1971) 'Depression in Middle-Aged Women', in GORNICK, V. and MORAN, B.K. (Eds) *Woman in Sexist Society*, New York, Basic Books.
BART, P.B. (1973) 'Emotional and Social Status of the Older Woman', in *No Longer Young: The Older Woman in America*, Institute of Gerontology, University of Michigan.
BATES, A. (1964) 'Privacy: A Useful Concept', *Social Forces*, vol. 42, pp. 429–34.
BELL, C. (1968) *Middle Class Families*, London, Routledge and Kegan Paul.
BELL, C. (1970) 'Mobility of the Middle Class Extended Family', in HARRIS, C.C. (Ed.) *Readings in Kinship in Urban Society*, Oxford, Pergamon.
BERGER, P.L. and KELLNER, H. (1980) 'Marriage and the Construction of Reality', in ANDERSON, M. (Ed.), *Sociology of the Family*, 2nd ed., Harmondsworth, Penguin.
BERNARD, J. (1975) *Women, Wives, Mothers*, Chicago: Aldine Publishing.
BLAXTER, M. and PATERSON, E., with MURRAY, S. (1982) *Mothers and Daughters: A Three-Generational Study of Health Attitudes and Behaviour*, London, Heinemann.
BLAXTER, M. and PATERSON, E. (1983) 'The Goodness is Out of It: The Meaning of Food to Two Generations', in MURCOTT, A. (Ed.) *The Sociology of Food and Eating*, Aldershot, Gower.
BLENKNER, M. (1965) 'Social Work and Family Relationships in Later Life With Some Thoughts on Filial Maturity', in SHANAS, E. and STREIB, G. (Eds.) *Social Structure and The Family: Generational Relations*, New Jersey, Prentice-Hall.
BOND, J. (1987) 'Psychiatric Illness in Later Life: A Study of Prevalance in a Scottish Population', *International Journal of Geriatric Psychiatry*, vol. 2, pp. 39–58.
BOND, J. (1990) 'Living Arrangements of Elderly People', in BOND, J. and COLEMAN, P. (Eds) *Aging in Society: An Introduction to Social Gerontology*, London, Sage.
BOND, J. and CARSTAIRS, V. (1982) 'Services for the Elderly: A Survey of the Characteristics and Needs of a Population of 5,000 Old People', *Scottish Health Service Studies*, no. 42, Edinburgh, Scottish Home and Health Department.
BORCHORST, A. (1990) 'Political Motherhood and Child Care Policies: A Comparative Approach to Britain and Scandinavia', in UNGERSON, C. (Ed.) *Gender and Caring: Work and Welfare in Britain and Scandinavia*, Hemel Hempstead, Harvester Wheatsheaf.
BOTT, E. (1964) *The Family and Social Networks*, 2nd ed., London, Tavistock.
BOWLING, A. and CARTWRIGHT, A. (1982) *Life After A Death: A Study of the Elderly Widowed*, London, Tavistock.
BRACKEN, P. (1963) *Instant Etiquette Book*, London, Arlington Books.
BREEN, D. (1975) *The Birth of a First Child: Towards an Understanding of Femininity*, London, Tavistock.
BRODY, E.M. (1978) 'The Ageing of the Family', *Annals of the American Academy of Political and Social Science*, vol. 438, pp. 13–27.
BRODY, E.M. (1981) 'Women in the Middle and Family Help to Older People', *Gerontologist*, vol. 21, part 5, pp. 471–8.
BROWN, G.W. and HARRIS, T. (1978) *Social Origins of Depression: A Study of Psychiatric Disorder in Women*, London, Tavistock.
BULMER, M. (1987) *The Social Basis of Community Care*, London, Allen and Unwin.

Bibliography

BURCHIVEIL, L.G. and SUSSMAN, M.B. (1962) 'Parental Aid to Married Children: Implications for Family Functioning', *Marriage and Family Living*, vol. 24, pp. 320-32.
BURGESS, R.G. (1984) *In the Field: An Introduction to Field Research*, London, Allen and Unwin.
BURGOYNE, J. and CLARK, D. (1981) 'Starting Again? Problems and Expectations in Remarriage', *Marriage Guidance*, vol. 19, part 7, pp. 334-6.
BURGOYNE, J. and CLARK, D. (1984) *Making a Go of it: A Study of Stepfamilies in Sheffield*, London, Routledge and Kegan Paul.
CAPLAN, P.J. (1981) *Between Women: Lowering the Barriers*, Toronto, Personal Library.
CAVENDISH, R. (1982) *Women on the Line*, London, Routledge and Kegan Paul.
CHODOROW, N. (1978) *The Reproduction of Mothering: Psychoanalysis and The Sociology of Gender*, University of California Press.
CHRISTENSEN, J.B. (1963) 'Utari: Joking, Sexual License and Social Obligations Among the Luguru', *American Anthropologist*, vol. 15, pp. 1314-27.
CICOUREL, A. (1974) *Method and Measurement in Sociology*, New York, Collier-Macmillan.
CLARK, D. (1988) 'AIDS and the Family', *New Society*, 27 May, pp. 20-2.
COMER, L. (1974) *Wedlocked Women*, Leeds, Feminist Books.
CORNWELL, J. (1984) *Hard Earned Lives: Accounts of Health and Illness from East London*, London, Tavistock.
COSER, R.L. (1959) 'Some Social Functions of Laughter: A Study of Humor in a Hospital Setting', *Human Relations*, vol. 12, part 2, pp. 171-82.
COTTERILL, P. and LETHERBY, G. (1993) 'Weaving Stories: Personal Auto/Biographies in Feminist Research', *Sociology*, March.
COULSON, M., MAGAS, B. and WAINWRIGHT, H. (1975) 'The Housewife and Her Labour under Capitalism', *New Left Review*, no. 89, pp. 59-71.
CRAWFORD, M. (1981) 'Not Disengaged: Grandparents in Literature and Reality: An Empirical Study in Role Satisfaction', *Sociological Review*, vol. 29, no. 3, pp. 499-519.
CRAWFORD, M. and HOOPER, D.T. (1973) 'Menopause, Family and Ageing', *Social Science and Medicine*, vol. 17, pp. 469-82.
CUMMING, E. and HENRY, W.E. (1961) *Growing Old: The Process of Disengagement*, New York, Basic Books.
CUNNINGHAM-BURLEY, S. (1985) 'Constructing Grandparenthood: Anticipating Appropriate Action', *Sociology*, vol. 19, no. 3, pp. 421-36.
DAHL, I.S. and SNARE, A. (1978) 'The Coercion of Privacy: A Feminist Perspective', in SMART, C. and SMART, B. (Eds) *Women, Sexuality and Social Control*, London, Routledge and Kegan Paul.
DALE, A., GILBERT, N. and ARBER, S. (1985) 'Integrating Women into Class Theory', *Sociology*, vol. 19, no. 3, pp. 384-409.
DALLY, A. (1982) *Inventing Motherhood: The Consequences of an Ideal*, London, Burnett Books.
DAVID, M. (1991) 'Putting on an Act for Children', in MACLEAN, M. and GROVES, D. (Eds) *Women's Issues in Social Policy*, London, Routledge.
DEEM, R. (1986) *All Work and No Play? The Sociology of Women and Leisure*, Milton Keynes, Open University Press.
DELPHY, C. (1976) 'Continuities and Discontinuties in Marriage and Divorce', in

LEONARD-BARKER, D. and ALLEN, S. (Eds) *Sexual Divisions and Society: Process and Change*, London, Tavistock.
DELPHY, C. (1977) *The Main Enemy*, London, Women's Research and Resources Centre Publications (Explorations in Feminism 3).
DELPHY, C. (1981) 'Women in Stratification Studies', in ROBERTS, H. (Ed.) *Doing Feminist Research*, London, Routledge and Kegan Paul.
DELPHY, C. (1984) *Close to Home: A Materialist Analysis of Women's Oppression*, London, Hutchinson.
DELPHY, C. and LEONARD, D. (1992) *Familiar Exploitation: A New Analysis of Marriage in Contemporary Western Societies*, London, Polity Press.
DINES-LEVY, G. and SMITH, G.W.H. (1988) 'Representations of Women and Men in Playboy Sex Cartoons', in POWELL, C. and PATON, G.E.C. (Eds) *Humour in Society: Resistance and Control*, London, Macmillan.
DISHER, M.W. (1974) *Winkles and Champagne*, Bath, Cedric Chives Ltd (as a New Portway Special Reprint).
DOUGLAS, M. (1968) 'The Social Control of Cognition: Some Factors in Joke Perception', *Man*, vol. 3, part 3, pp. 361–76.
DOUGLAS, M. (1975) *Implicit Meanings*, London, Routledge and Kegan Paul.
DUPREE, M.W. (1981) 'Family Structure in the Staffordshire Potteries 1840–1880', unpublished PhD thesis, Cambridge University.
EDGELL, S. (1980) *Middle Class Couples: A Study of Segregation, Domination and Inequality in Marriage*, London, Allen and Unwin.
EICHENBAUM, L. and ORBACH, S. (1984) *What Do Women Want?*, London, Fontana.
EICHENBAUM, L. and ORBACH, S. (1985) *Understanding Women*, Harmondsworth, Penguin.
EVANS, M. (1982) 'In Praise of Theory: the Case for Women's Studies', *Feminist Review*, no. 10, pp. 61–74.
EVANS-PRITCHARD, E.E. (1951) *Kinship and Marriage among the Nuer*, Oxford, Oxford University Press.
EVERS, H. (1985) 'The Frail Elderly Woman: Emergent Questions in Aging and Women's Health', LEWIN, E. and OLESON, V. (Eds) *Women, Health and Healing: Toward a New Perspective*, London, Tavistock.
FAGIN, L. and LITTLE, M. (1984) *The Forsaken Families: The Effects of Unemployment on Family Life*, Harmondsworth, Penguin.
FEATHERSTONE, M. and HEPWORTH, I. (1981) 'Ageing and Inequality: Consumer Culture and the New Middle Age', paper given to BSA conference, University of Aberystwyth.
FINCH, J. (1983) *Married to the Job*, London, Allen and Unwin.
FINCH, J. (1984a) 'Community Care: Developing Non-Sexist Alternatives', *Critical Social Policy*, no. 9, pp. 6–18.
FINCH, J. (1984b) '"It's Great to Have Someone to Talk to": The Ethics and Politics of Interviewing Women', in BELL, C. and ROBERTS, H. (Eds) *Social Researching: Politics, Problems, Practice*, London, Routledge and Kegan Paul.
FINCH, J. (1987a) 'Family Obligations and the Life Course', in BRYMAN, A., BYTHEWAY, B., ALLATT, P. and KEIL, T. (Eds) *Rethinking the Life Course*, London, Macmillan.
FINCH, J. (1987b) 'The Vignette Technique in Survey Research', *Sociology*, vol. 21, no. 1, pp. 105–14.
FINCH, J. (1989) *Family Obligations and Social Change*, London, Polity Press.

FINCH, J. and GROVES, D. (1982) 'By Women, for Women: Caring for the Frail Elderly', *Women's Studies International Forum*, vol. 5, part 5, pp. 427–38.
FINCH, J. and GROVES, D. (1985) 'Community Care and the Family: A Case for Equal Opportunities', in UNGERSON, C. (Ed.) *Women and Social Policy*, London, Macmillan.
FIRTH, R., HUBERT, J. and FORGE, A. (1970) *Families and their Relatives*, London, Routledge and Kegan Paul.
FISCHER, L.R. (1983) 'Mothers and Mothers-in-Law', *Journal of Marriage and the Family*, vol. 45, pp. 187–92.
FISCHER, L.R. (1986) *Linked Lives: Adult Daughters and their Mothers*, New York, Harper and Row.
FLAX, J. (1981) 'The Conflict Between Nurturance and Autonomy in Mother-Daughter Relationships and within Feminism', in E. HOWELL, E. and BAYES, M. (Eds) *Women and Mental Health*, New York, Basic Books.
FORCEY, L.R. (1987) *Mothers of Sons: Towards an Understanding of Responsibility*, New York, Praeger.
FOSTER, P. (1991) 'Residential Care of Frail Elderly People: A Positive Reassessment', *Social Policy and Administration*, vol. 25, no. 2, pp. 108–20.
FREUD, S. (1953) *Totem and Taboo*, translated by James Strachey, London, Hogarth Press.
FREUD, S. (1960) *Jokes and their Relation to the Unconscious*, translated by James Strachey, London, Routledge and Kegan Paul.
GAMBS, J.D. (1989) *Women Over 40: Visions and Realities*, New York, Springer Publishing.
GILLIGAN, C. (1982) *In a Different Voice: Psychological Theory and Women's Development*, Cambridge, MA, Harvard University Press.
GINSBERG, S. (1976) 'Women, Work and Conflict', in FONDA, N. and MOSS, P. (Eds) *Mothers in Employment*, Uxbridge and London, Brunel University Management Programme in association with Thos Coran Research Unit.
GITTINS, D. (1985) *The Family in Question: Changing Households and Familiar Ideologies*, London, Macmillan.
GLASER, B.G. and STRAUSS, A.L. (1967) *The Discovery of Grounded Theory: Strategies for Qualitative Research*, Chicago, Aldine Atherton.
GOFFMAN, E. (1961) *Asylums: Essays on the Social Situations of Mental Patients and Other Inmates*, New York, Anchor.
GOFFMAN, E. (1967) *Interaction Ritual: Essays on Face-to-Face Behaviour*, New York, Anchor Books.
GOLDTHORPE, J. (1980) *Social Mobility and Class Structure in Modern Britain*, London, Clarendon Press.
GOODE, W.J. (1964) *The Family*, New Jersey, Prentice Hall.
GOODY, J. (1976) *Production and Reproduction: A Comparative Study of the Domestic Domain*, Cambridge, Cambridge University Press.
GRAHAM, H. (1984) *Women, Health and the Family*, Brighton, Harvester Press.
GRAHAM, H. (1985) 'Providers, Negotiators and Mediators: Women as the Hidden Carers', in LEWIN, E. and OLESEN, V. (Eds) *Women, Health and Healing: Towards a New Perspective*, London, Tavistock.
GREEN, H. (1985) *Informal Carers*, London, HMSO (General Household Survey, Series GH5, No. 15, Supplement A, OPCS).

GRIFFITHS, R. (1988) *Community Care: Agenda for Action. A Report to the Secretary of State for Social Services*, London, HMSO.
HAREVEN, T.K. (1982) *Family Time and Industrial Time: The Relationship Between the Family and Work in a New England Industrial Community*, Cambridge, Cambridge University Press.
HARRIS, R. (1985) 'End Points and Starting Points', *Critical Social Policy*, no. 12, pp. 115–22.
HARTMANN, H. (1987) 'The Family as the Focus of Gender, Class and Political Struggle: The Example of Housework', in HARDING, S. (Ed.) *Feminism and Methodology*, Milton Keynes, Open University Press.
HICKS, C. (1988) *Who Cares: Looking After People at Home*, London, Virago.
HOLME, A. (1985) *Housing and Young Families in East London*, London, Routledge and Kegan Paul.
HUMPREY, C. (1978) 'Women, Taboo and the Suppression of Attention', in ARDENER, S. (Ed.) *Defining Females: The Nature of Women in Society*, London, Croom Helm.
HUNT, A. (1978) *The Elderly at Home*, London, HMSO.
HUNT, P. (1980) *Gender and Class Consciousness*, London, Macmillan.
JEFFERY, P. (1979) *Frogs in a Well: Indian Women in Purdah*, London, Zed Press.
JEROME, D. (1981) 'The Significance of Friendship for Women in Later Life', *Ageing and Society*, vol. 1, no. 2, pp. 175–97.
JOHNSON, F.L. and ARIES, E.J. (1983) 'The Talk of Women Friends', *Women's Studies International Forum*, vol. 6, pp. 353–61.
KAHANA, B. and KAHANA, E. (1971) 'Theoretical and Research Perspectives on Grandparenthood', *Aging and Human Development*, vol. 2, part 4, pp. 261–8.
KOMAROVSKY, M. (1967) *Blue-Collar Marriage*, New York, Vintage Books.
LAND, H. (1976) 'Women: Supporters or Supported?', in LEONARD-BARKER, D. and ALLEN, S. (Eds) *Sexual Divisions and Society: Progress and Change*, London, Tavistock.
LAND, H. and ROSE, H. (1985) 'Compulsory Altruism for Some or an Altruistic Society for All' in BEAN, P., FERRIS, J. and WHYNES, D. (Eds) *In Defence of Welfare*, London, Tavistock.
LARDER, D., DAY, P. and KLEIN, R. (Eds) (1986) Institutional Care for the Elderly: the Geographical Distribution of the Public/Private Mix in England, Bath, Centre for the Analysis of Social Policy, University of Bath (Social Policy Papers, no. 10).
LASLETT, P. (1965) *The World We Have Lost*, London, Methuen.
LASLETT, P. (1983) *The World We Have Lost – Further Explored*, (3rd ed.) London, Methuen.
LEECH, E. (1979) 'The Official Irish Jokesters', *New Society*, 20/27 December, pp. 7–9.
LEIRA, A. (1987) 'Time for Work, Time for Care: Childcare Strategies in a Norwegian Setting', in BRANNEN, J. and WILSON, G. (Eds) *Give and Take in Families: Studies in Resource Distribution*, London, Allen and Unwin.
LEONARD, D. (1980) *Sex and Generation: A Study of Courtship and Weddings*, London, Tavistock.
LEONARD-Barker, D. (1978) 'The Regulation of Marriage: Repressive Benevolence', in LITTLEJOHN, G., SMART, B., WAKEFORD, J. and YUVAL-DAVIS, N. (Eds) *Power and the State*, London, Croom Helm.

Bibliography

Lévi-Strauss, C. (1971) 'The Family', in Shapiro, H.L. (Ed.) *Man, Culture and Society*, New York, Oxford University Press.

Levine, J.B. (1976) 'The Feminine Routine', *Journal of Communication*, vol. 26, no. 3, pp. 173–5.

Lewis, J. and Meredith, B. (1988) *Daughters who Care: Daughters Caring for Mothers at Home*, London, Routledge.

Lienhardt, G. (1966) *Social Anthropology*, 2nd ed., London, Oxford University Press.

McKee, L. and O'Brien, M. (1983) 'Interviewing Men: "Taking Gender Seriously"', in Gamarnikow, E., Morgan, D., Purvis, J. and Taylorson, D. *The Public and the Private*, London, Heinemann.

McRobbie, A. (1982) 'The Politics of Feminist Research: Between Talk, Text and Action', *Feminist Review*, no. 12, pp. 46–57.

Marcus, L. (1978) 'The Situation of the Elderly and their Families: Problems and Solutions' (report prepared for the National Symposium on Aging in Ottawa), Ottawa, National Bureau on Aging.

Marsden, D. and Abrams, S. (1987) '"Liberators", "Companions", "Intruders" and "Cuckoos in the Nest": A Sociology of Caring Relationships over the Life Cycle', in Allatt, P., Keil, T., Bryman, A. and Bytheway, B. (Eds) *Women and the Life Cycle: Transitions and Turning-Points*, London, Macmillan.

Meacham, S. (1977) *A Life Apart: The English Working Class 1890–1914*, London, Thames and Hudson.

Miller, J. Baker (1978) *Toward a New Psychology of Women*, Harmondsworth, Pelican.

Morgan, D. (1975) *Social Theory and the Family*, London, Routledge and Kegan Paul.

Moss, P. (1982) 'Community Care and Young Children', in Walker, A. (Ed.) *Community Care: The Family, the State and Social Policy*, Oxford, Basil Blackwell.

Murcott, A. (1983) '"It's a pleasure to cook for him": Food, Mealtimes and Gender in some South Wales Households', in Gamarnikow, E., Morgan, D., Purvis, J. and Taylorson, D. (Eds) *The Public and the Private*, London, Heinemann.

Murphy, M. (1987) 'Measuring the Family Life Cycle: Concepts, Data and Methods', in Bryman, A., Bytheway, B., Allatt, P. and Keil, T. (Eds) *Rethinking the Life Course*, London, Macmillan.

Murray-Parkes, C. (1972) *Bereavement: Studies of Grief in Adult Life*, London, Tavistock.

Nice, V. (1992) *Mothers and Daughters: The Distortion of a Relationship*, London, Macmillan.

Norman, W.S. (1958) *Etiquette and Good Manners*, London: The English Universities.

Oakley, A. (1974) *The Sociology of Housework*, Oxford, Martin Robertson.

Oakley, A. (1976) 'The Family, Marriage, and Its Relationship to Illness', in Tuckett, D. (Ed.) *An Introduction to Medical Sociology*, London, Tavistock.

Oakley, A. (1979) *From Here to Maternity: Becoming a Mother*, Harmondsworth, Penguin.

OAKLEY, A. (1980) *Women Confined: Towards a Sociology of Childbirth*, Oxford, Martin Robertson.
OAKLEY, A. (1981) 'Interviewing Women: A Contradiction in Terms', in ROBERTS, H. (Ed.) *Doing Feminist Research*, London, Routledge and Kegan Paul.
O'CONNOR, P. (1992) *Friendships between Women: A Critical Review*, Hemel Hempstead, Harvester Wheatsheaf.
OFFICE OF POPULATION CENSUSES AND SURVEYS (1982) *General Household Survey 1980*, London, HMSO.
OFFICE OF POPULATION CENSUSES AND SURVEYS (1988) *General Household Survey 1985*, London, HMSO.
PAHL, J. (1983) 'The Allocation of Money and the Structuring of Inequality Within Marriage', *Sociological Review*, vol. 31, no. 2, pp. 237–62.
PARKER, G. (1985) *With Due Care and Attention: A Review of Research on Informal Care*, London, The Family Policy Studies Centre.
PARKIN, F. (1971) *Class, Inequality and Political Order*, London, McGibbon and Kee.
PARSONS, T. (1964) *The Social System*, London, Routledge and Kegan Paul.
PARSONS, T. (1965) 'The Normal American Family', in FARBER, S., MUSTACCHI, P. and WILSON, R.H. (Eds) *Man and Civilisation: The Family's Search for Survival*, New York, McGraw-Hill.
PATON, G.E.C. (1988) 'The Comedian as Portrayer of Social Morality', in POWELL, C. and PATON, G.E.C. (Eds) *Humour in Society: Resistance and Control*, London, Macmillan.
PERKINS, T.E. (1979) 'Rethinking Stereotypes', in BARRETT, M., CORRIGAN, P., KUHN, A. and WOLFF, J. (Eds) *Ideology and Cultural Production*, London, Croom Helm.
PHILLIPS, G.D.M. (1986) 'Men Talking to Men about their Relationships', *American Behavioral Scientist*, vol. 29, no. 3, pp. 321–41.
PHILLIPSON, C. (1981) 'Women in Later Life: Patterns of Control and Subordination', in HUTTER, B. and WILLIAMS, G. (Eds) *Controlling Women: The Normal and the Deviant*, London, Croom Helm.
PHILLIPSON, C. (1987) 'The Transition To Retirement', in COHEN, G. (Ed.) *Social Change and the Life Course*, London, Tavistock.
PILL, R.M. and STOTT, N.C.H. (1982) 'Concepts of Illness Causation and Responsibility: Some Preliminary Data from a Sample of Working Class Mothers', *Social Science and Medicine*, vol. 16, pp. 43–52.
PLANT, M. (1975) *Drug Takers in an English Town*, London, Tavistock.
POLLERT, A. (1981) *Girls, Wives, Factory Lives*, London, Macmillan.
POWELL, C. (1988) 'A Phenomenological Analysis of Humour in Society', in POWELL, C. and PATON, G.E.C. (Eds) *Humour in Society*, London, Macmillan.
POWELL, C. and PATON, G.E.C. (Eds) (1988) *Humour in Society: Resistance and Control*, London, Macmillan.
QURESHI, M. and SIMONS, K. (1987) 'Resources within Families: Caring for Elderly People', in BRANNEN, J. and WILSON, G. (Eds) *Give and Take in Families: Studies in Resource Distribution*, London, Allen and Unwin.
RADCLIFFE-BROWN, A.R. (1950) 'Introduction', in RADCLIFFE-BROWN, A.R. and FORDE, D. (Eds) *African Systems of Kinship and Marriage*, London, Oxford University Press.

RADCLIFFE-BROWN, A.R. (1952) *Structure and Function in Primitive Society*, London, Cohen and West.
RAPHAEL, B. (1984) *The Anatomy of Bereavement: A Handbook for the Caring Professions*, London, Hutchinson.
RICH, A. (1977) *Of Woman Born: Motherhood as Experience and Institution*, London, Virago.
RIGBY, P. (1968) 'Joking Relationships, Kin Categories and Clanship Among the Gogo', *Africa*, vol. 3, pp. 133-55.
RIMMER, L. (1981) *Families in Focus*, London, Study Commission on the Family.
ROBERTS, E. (1984) *A Woman's Place: An Oral History of Working Class Women 1890-1940*, Oxford, Basil Blackwell.
ROBERTS, H. (1985) *The Patient Patients: Women and their Doctors*, London, Pandora Press.
ROBERTSON, J.F. (1977) 'Grandmotherhood: A Study of Role Conceptions', *Journal of Marriage and the Family*, vol. 39, pp. 165-74.
ROGERS, S. (1981) 'Women's Space in a Men's House: The British House of Commons', in ARDENER, S. (Ed.) *Women and Space: Ground Rules and Social Maps*, London, Croom Helm.
ROSENTHAL, C.J. (1983) 'Family Responsibilities and Concerns: A Perspective on the Lives of Middle-Aged Women', *Resources for Feminist Research*, vol. 11, part 2, pp. 211-12.
ROSSER, C. and HARRIS, C.C. (1965) *The Family and Social Change*, London, Routledge and Kegan Paul.
RUBIN, L.B. (1976) *Worlds of Pain*, New York, Basic Books.
RUBIN, L.B. (1983) *Intimate Strangers*, New York, Harper and Row.
SAHLINS, M. (1965) 'On the Sociology of Primitive Exchange', in BANTON, M. (Ed.) *The Relevance of Models in Social Anthropology*, London, Tavistock.
SEGALEN, M. (1986) *Historical Anthropology of the Family*, Cambridge, Cambridge University Press.
SEITER, E. (1986) 'Feminism and Ideology: The *Terms* of Women's Stereotypes', *Feminist Review*, no. 22, pp. 59-80.
SHANAS, E. (1979) 'Social Myth, as Hypothesis: The Case of the Family Relations of Old People', *Gerontologist*, vol. 19, pp. 3-9.
SHARMA, U. (1980) *Women, Work and Property in North West India*, London, Tavistock.
SIMMEL, G. (1955) *Conflict and The Web of Group Affiliations*, translated by K. WOLFF and R. BENDIX, New York, The Free Press.
SPENCE, P. and LONER, R. (1971) 'The Empty Nest', *The Family Co-ordinator*, vol. 20, October, pp. 369-75.
SPENDER, D. (1980) *Man-Made Language*, London, Routledge and Kegan Paul.
SPICER, J.W. and HAMPE, G.D. (1975) 'Kinship Interaction after Divorce', *Journal of Marriage and the Family*, vol. 37, pp. 113-19.
STACEY, M. (1981) 'The Division of Labour Revisited or Overcoming the Two Adams', in ABRAMS, P., DEEM, R., FINCH, J. and ROCK, P. (Eds) *Practice and Progress: British Sociology 1950-1980*, London, Allen and Unwin.
STAMP, P. (1985) 'Balance of Financial Power in Marriage: An Exploratory Study of Bread-Winning Wives', *Sociological-Review*, vol. 33, pp. 546-57.
STANLEY, L. and WISE, S. (1993) *Breaking Out Again: Feminist Ontology and Epistemology*, London, Routledge.

SYKES, A.J.M. (1966) 'Joking Relationships in an Industrial Setting', *American Anthropology*, vol. 68, pp. 188–93.
TOLSON, A. (1977) *The Limits of Masculinity*, London, Tavistock.
TOWNSEND, P. (1957) *The Family Life of Old People*, London, Routledge and Kegan Paul.
TROLL, L.E. (1971) 'The Family in Later Life: a Decade Review', *Journal of Marriage and the Family*, vol. 33, pp. 263–90.
TROLL, L.E., MILLAR, S.J. and ARCHLEY, R.C. (1979) *Families in Later Life*, California, Wadsworth.
UHLENBERG, P. (1979) 'Older Females: The Growing Challenge to Design Constructive Roles', *The Gerontologist*, vol. 19, part 3, pp. 236–41.
UNGERSON, C. (1983) 'Women and Caring: Skills, Tasks and Taboos', in GAMARNIKOW, E., MORGAN, D., PURVIS, J. and TAYLORSON, D. (Eds) *The Public and the Private*, London, Heinemann.
UNGERSON, C. (1987) *Policy is Personal: Sex, Gender and Informal Care*, London, Tavistock.
VICTOR, C., HIGGS, P. and WARD, M. (1992) 'An Option to Keep Open', *Health Service Journal*, vol. 102, no. 5289, pp. 22–3.
VOYSEY, M. (1975) *A Constant Burden: The Reconstruction of Family Life*, London, Routledge and Kegan Paul.
WALKER, A. (1991) 'The Social Construction of Dependency in Old Age', in LONEY, M., BOCOCK, R., CLARKE, J., COCHRANE, A., GRAHAM, P. and WILSON, M. (Eds) *The State or the Market: Politics and Welfare in Contemporary Britain*, London, Sage.
WALL, R. (1977) 'The Responsibilities of Kin', *Local Population Studies*, no. 19, pp. 58–60.
WEISS, R.S. (1975) *Marital Separation*, New York, Basic Books.
WESTWOOD, S. (1984) *All Day, Every Day: Factory and Family in the Making of Women's Lives*, London, Pluto.
WHITEHEAD, A. (1976) 'Sexual Antagonism in Herefordshire', in LEONARD-BARKER, D. and ALLEN, S. (Eds) *Dependence and Exploitation in Work and Marriage*, Harlow, Longman.
WICKS, M. (1982) 'Community Care and Elderly People', in WALKER, A. (Ed.) *Community Care: The Family, the State and Social Policy*, Oxford, Basil Blackwell.
WILLMOTT, P. (1987) *Friendship Networks and Social Support*, London, Policy Studies Unit.
WILSON, E. (1982) 'Women, the "Community" and the "Family"', in WALKER, A. (Eds) *Community Care: The Family, the State and Social Policy*, Oxford, Basil Blackwell.
WOLFRAM, S. (1987) *In-Laws and Out-Laws: Kinship and Marriage in England*, London, Croom Helm.
YANAGISAKO, S.J. (1977) 'Women Centered Kin Networks in Urban Bilateral Kinship', *American Ethnologist*, vol. 4, pp. 207–26.
YEANDLE, S. (1987) 'Married Women at Midlife: Past Experience and Present Change', in ALLATT, P., KEIL, T., BRYMAN, A. and BYTHEWAY, B. (Eds) *Women and the Life Course: Transitions and Turning-Points*, London, Macmillan.
YOUNG, M. and WILLMOTT, P. (1957) *Family and Kinship in East London*, Harmondsworth, Penguin Books.

Bibliography

YOUNG, M. and WILLMOTT, P. (1973) *The Symmetrical Family: a Study of Work and Leisure in the London Region*, London, Routledge and Kegan Paul.

YUDKIN, S. and HOLME, A. (1963) *Working Mothers and their Children*, London, Michael Joseph.

ZIJDERVELD, A.C. (1968) 'Jokes and their Relation to Social Reality', *Social Research*, vol. 35, pp. 286–311.

ZILLMAN, D. and STOCKING, S.H. (1976) 'Putdown Humour', *Journal of Communication*, vol. 26, no. 3, pp. 154–63.

Index

address, terms of 4
  mothers-in-law 16–18
  sons' girlfriends 133
affection 85–90
  and caring 162
ageing, attitudes to 156–7
AIDS, caring for people with 140
'alternative' comedy 101
altruism 154–5
  compulsory 48, 155
anger 74
  joking behaviour 96
arguments 73–4
assertiveness 67
assistance
  for carers 165–6
  childbirth 143–4
  divorced parents 120
  financial 52–61, 120
  reciprocal 43–6
avoidance relationships 91–2, 93

babysitting 46–8
banter 92–4, 97
bereavement 146–51
birthday presents 59, 60

care 137–41
  child 48–52
  community 128, 153, 160, 167–8
  in later life 151–66
  pregnancy and childbirth 141–6
  residential 166–8
  respite 166
  widowhood 146–51
childbirth 141–6
childcare services 46–52
childless couples 130–1

children
  and grandparents 128–31
  divorced parents 119–20, 121
  'interference' 82–3
  joking relationship 92
  'spoiling' 82–3
  interview problems 9
China 32n.1
Christian names as terms of address 17–18
Christmas
  presents 59, 60
  visiting 42–3
class, social
  differences 13, 14–15
  financial aid 52, 53–6
  middle 52, 53, 56, 113
  working 52, 53–6, 99
co-residence
  permanent
    childcare 49–50
    dependent mothers-in-law 159, 169n.3
  temporary 115–16
coercive nature of jokes 98
cohabitation 131–5
cohort effect 112–13, 131
comedians 98–107
communication patterns
  jokes 103–4
  mother-son 65–70
community care 128, 153, 160, 167–8
companionship and 'empty nest' 128
complaints, jokes as 97, 104
compulsory altruism 48, 155
confidence 87–9
conflict in generational relationships 72–6

195

Index

'conservative' comedians 99
control, social
    joking behaviour 91–8
    mother-in-law jokes 98–107
conversations
    descriptions of women's 100
    mother-son kin-keeping 65–9
    between mothers-in-law and
        daughters-in-law 86–90
cooking, formal meals 20–2
courtship 13–32
criticism, jokes as 97, 104

death 146–51
    insurance 55
dependent mothers-in-law 151–69
disloyalty 105–6
divorce 117–22
    care 139
domestic cultures 18–20
    'empty nest' 124
    visits 39–40, 116–17
dominant groups, stereotypes 109–10

employment
    Stoke-on-Trent 5
    working mothers
        childcare 48–52
        financial control 54
'empty nest' 122–8
endowment policies 55
engagement 25–31
estrangement 76
extended family 11

fairness, financial assistance 57
family life-course 112–13, 130
fathers-in-law
    death 146–51
    joking relationships 110–11n.2
female comedians 100–1
filial maturity 161
financial aid 52–61
    divorced parents 120
first impressions
    mothers-in-law and daughters-in-law
        13–16
    mothers-in-law and mothers 24
first names as terms of address
    17–18
food 18, 19–20
    formal meals 20–2
    'spoiling' of grandchildren 82–3
formal meals 20–2

friendship
    and 'empty nest' 128
    and widows 150

geographical distance 113–17
    cohabiting couples 133
gifts 56–8, 60–1
    indirect 59–60
girlfriends
    cohabiting 131–5
    previous 15–16
governments, childcare policy 49, 52
grandparental terms of address 17
grandparenthood 128–31
    divorced parents 119–20
    remarriage 121
    'interference' 82
    joking relationship 92
'granny flats' 152
grounded theory 10

health
    anxieties 88
    responsibilities 140–1
help
    for carers 165–6
    childbirth 143–4
    divorced parents 120
    financial 52–61, 120
    reciprocal 43–6
'helpmeet' model 70
holidays, visits as substitute 114
housekeeping 18–20
    allowances 54
    'empty nest' 124
    visits 39–40, 116–17
humour
    joking behaviour and relationships
        91–8
    mother-in-law jokes 98–107
husbands
    household chores 41
    interview interruptions 7
    marital roles 64–5
    research, reactions to 7–8
    wife and mother
        conflicts 74–6
        discussions 89–90
    see also sons
hypothetical interview questions 6

illness
    and babysitting 47, 51
    responsibilities 140–1

Index

incest taboo 164
incontinence 164
independence, mothers-in-law 44–5
  financial 59
  old age 152, 153, 160
India 110–11n.2
indirect financial aid 59–60
industrial societies, joking relationships in 92–3
informal visits 38–9
  geographical distance 114
institutionalized care 152–3, 155, 159–60, 167
insurance policies 55
'interference' 81–5
  geographical distance 117
  and jealousy 77
  in marital break-down 118–19
interruptions to interviews 7
interviews 6–10
intimacy and kin-keeping 70

jealousy 76–81
jokes, mother-in-law 98–107
joking behaviour and relationships 91–8

kin-keeping
  between mothers and sons 62–71, 115
  between mothers-in-law and daughters-in-law 35, 71–6
  divorce 122

labour relationship, marriage as 12
laudatory stereotypes 109–10
legislation, care 138
leisure and 'empty nest' 127–8
letters, contact through 113
life-course, family 112–13, 130
loans, financial 55–60
long-term childcare 48–52
love and marriage 12–13
loyalty 105–6

manipulation by mothers-in-law 83
marital problems 89–90
masculinity 66–7
  and childishness 80
  and joking behaviour 103
material disadvantages of divorce 120–1
meals, formal 20–2
men
  as carers 140, 164–5
  friendship with widows 150

joking behaviour 93–107
see also husbands; sons
middle-class families
  financial aid 52, 53, 56
  geographical distance 113
Mongolia 111n.2
morality, public 155

naming 4, 16–18
National Health Service and Community Care Act (1990) 153, 160
negative imagery 107–10
  in jokes 99
negative stereotypes 107–10
  'empty nest' 127
  'interfering' mothers-in-law 81–2
  and jealousy 78, 79, 80
  jokes 95, 97
  stand-up comedians 99
neglect and interference, boundaries between 81, 82
nicknames as terms of address 17
nurturing skills 63–4
  community care 128

oppressed groups, stereotypes 109–10

parental terms of address 17–18
parents, relationship between 22–5
peace-keeping 62, 71–6
  and jokes 101–2
pejorative stereotypes 109
Poor Law Act (1601) 138
positive regard 85–90
positive stereotypes 109
possessiveness
  and interference 84
  and jealousy 77, 78–80
power relationships
  dependent mothers-in-law 161–2
  financial aid 58
  financial control 54
  food as expression of 22
  joking behaviour 94, 95–6, 97–8
  kin-keeping 69
  mixed-sex conversation 69
pregnancy
  care 141–6
  premarital 134, 135
premarital sexuality 131
prescriptive rules 71
privacy
  and confidence 87–9
  financial aid 54

Index

private residential care 153
proscriptive rules 71
protection and privacy 88–9
public domain and views of families 170–1
public morality 155
put-down humour 105, 106

reciprocity 43–6, 154–5
regulating rules 71
remarriage 120, 121–2
   care 139
residence, choice of 33–4
   dependent mothers-in-law 152
   geographical distance 113–17
   cohabiting couples 133
residential homes 152–3, 155, 159–60, 166–8
respite care 166
retired parents 114
rewarding rules 71
role reversal, dependent elderly 161

sarcasm and banter 94
savings 54–5
self-deprecatory humour 105, 106
self-disclosure 86, 87–90
sentimental model of family 138, 139
separation 117–22
sexual morality, double standards 134
shared care 166, 168
sheltered housing 167
short-term childcare 46–8
single mothers
   interviews 8–9
   problems 121
sleeping arrangements, visiting unmarried couples 132
smiling, social pressures 96
'snowballing' sampling 4
social class
   differences 13, 14–15
   financial aid 52, 53–6
   middle 52, 53, 56, 113
   working 52, 53–6, 99
social control
   joking behaviour 91–8
   mother-in-law jokes 98–107
social disadvantages of divorce 120–1
social policy, care 128, 138
socialization 172
sons
   'empty nest' 122–8
   joking behaviour 92

possessive mothers 79–80
relationship with mothers 65–70
widowed mothers 147–9, 150–1
wife and mother
   conflicts 74–6
   discussions 89–90
   see also husbands
'spoiling' of grandchildren 82–3
stand-up comedians 98–107
stateless societies 110n.1
   joking relationships 91–2, 93, 97
stereotypes 107–10
   'empty nest' 127
   'interfering' mothers-in-law 81–2
   and jealousy 78, 79, 80
   jokes 95, 97
   stand-up comedians 99
Stoke-on-Trent 5
surnames as terms of address 17

talk
   descriptions of women's 100
   mother-son kin-keeping 65–9
   between mothers-in-law and daughters-in-law 86–90
telephone contact 34–5
   geographical distance 113

unmarried couples 131–5

vacations, visits as substitute 114
vignettes 6
visiting 34–43
   geographical distance 113–16
   unmarried couples 132

warmth 85–90
   and caring 162
weddings
   arrangements 25–31
   ceremonies 28
   presents 60
widowed mothers-in-law 26
   care 146–51
   financial aid to children 55
   helping 44
working-class families
   financial aid 52, 53–6
   financial management 55
   proximity, and mother-in-law jokes 99
working mothers
   childcare 48–52
   financial control 54

For Product Safety Concerns and Information please contact our EU
representative GPSR@taylorandfrancis.com
Taylor & Francis Verlag GmbH, Kaufingerstraße 24, 80331 München, Germany

www.ingramcontent.com/pod-product-compliance
Lightning Source LLC
Chambersburg PA
CBHW052117300426
44116CB00010B/1700